AMERICAN FOLK ART CANES

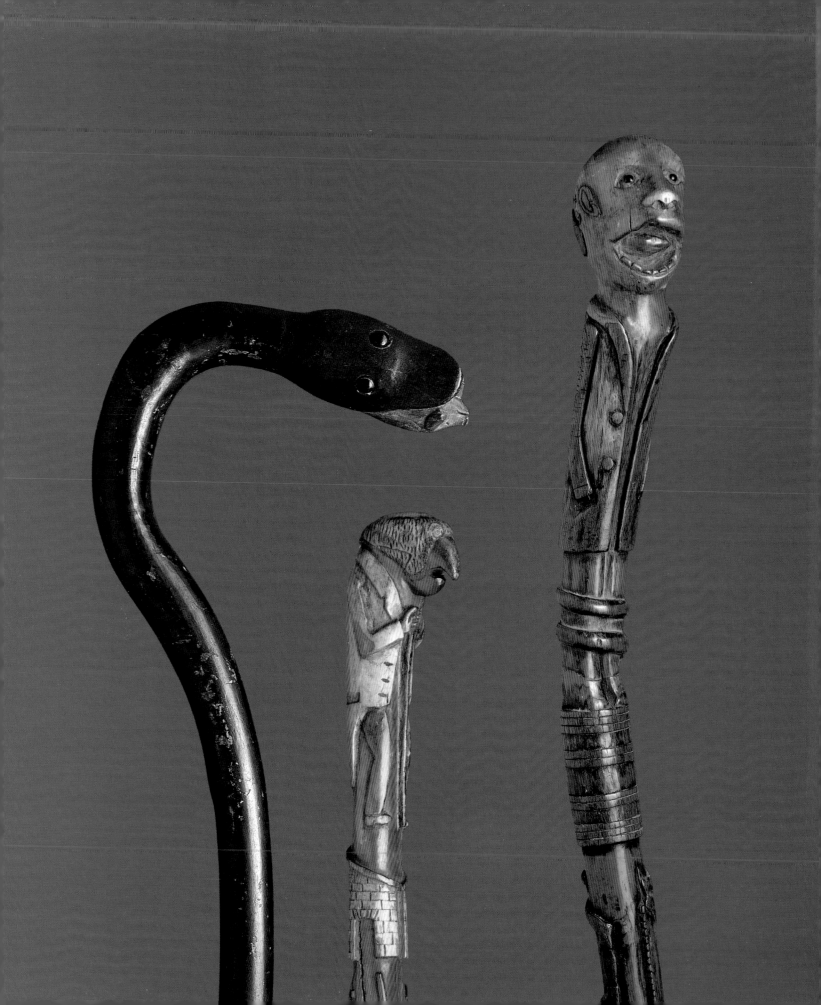

AMERICAN
FOLK ART CANES

Personal Sculpture

George H. Meyer

with Kay White Meyer

Photographs by Charles B. Nairn

Sandringham Press

Bloomfield Hills, Michigan

in association with

Museum of American Folk Art

New York

University of Washington Press

Seattle · London

Published in conjunction with an exhibition of American folk art canes from the collection of George H. Meyer held at the Museum of American Folk Art, New York, June 4–September 14, 1992

Produced by Marquand Books, Inc., Seattle
Designed by Ed Marquand
Edited by Patricia Draher
Text typeset by The Type Gallery, Inc., Seattle; display lines typeset by Solotype, Oakland
Printed and bound by C & C Offset Printing Co., Ltd., Hong Kong

Frontispiece: *Snake Swallowing Pig* (no. 9), *Man with Parrot Head and Cane* (no. 165), *Man Standing on a Barrel* (no. 102)
Title page: *Egg and Rattlesnake* (no. 16)

Library of Congress Cataloging-in-Publication Data

Meyer, George H.
    American folk art canes : personal sculpture / George H. Meyer, with Kay White Meyer ; photographs by Charles B. Nairn.
      p.   cm.
    "Published in conjunction with an exhibition of American folk art canes from the collection of George H. Meyer, held at the Museum of American Folk Art, New York, June 4–September 14, 1992"—T.p. verso.
    Includes bibliographical references and index.
    ISBN 0-295-97200-9
    1. Staffs (Sticks, canes, etc.)—United States—Exhibitions.
2. Wood-carving—United States—Exhibitions. 3. Folk art—United States—Exhibitions. 4. Meyer, George H.—Art collections—Exhibitions. 5. Staffs (Sticks, canes, etc.)—Private collections—United States—Exhibitions. 6. Sculpture, American.   I. Meyer, Kay White.
II. Nairn, Charles B.   III. Museum of American Folk Art.   IV. Title.
NK9712.M49   1992
    736'.4—dc20   92-9714

First edition

The author welcomes corrections, additions, and comments from readers. These may be sent to Sandringham Press, 100 West Long Lake Road, Suite 100, Bloomfield Hills, Michigan 48304.

CONTENTS

FOREWORD

On returning from a trip to Michigan in 1988, Dr. Robert Bishop, then Director of the Museum of American Folk Art, told me that he had discovered a most remarkable collection of American folk canes. That collection—part of which is featured in this book and the related exhibition—is owned by George H. Meyer, a longtime collector and museum trustee. Those who have had the privilege of seeing the collection share Dr. Bishop's enthusiasm. George Meyer was among the first to recognize that the best canes, apart from their historical and cultural importance, are works of art in their own right. By exhibiting this highly significant group of canes, we hope to expand the public's awareness and appreciation of these extraordinary objects.

The reproductions in this book eloquently demonstrate the artistry of folk canes, while the text analyzes and categorizes the diverse carving styles, imagery, and intent of the many gifted and largely unknown American wood-carvers who have fashioned walking sticks over the years. Other books have been published on the general topic of canes, but this is the first to examine the depth and breadth of this American folk art tradition.

As traditional objects that serve as vehicles for both self-expression and group communication, canes embody many of the most important aspects of American folk art. Whether they carry complex cultural meaning, obscure personal references, or lighthearted, humorous social commentary, they speak to the soul of our individuality and national identity.

This book offers the first comprehensive, scholarly look at American folk canes and, by so doing, also presents the opportunity for further research and discussion. The museum is proud to be a part of this endeavor.

Gerard C. Wertkin
Director
Museum of American Folk Art, New York

PREFACE

Curators, collectors, and dealers have been aware of American folk art canes for several years, but surprisingly little has been written about these works. This book is intended to show that many American folk art canes are true sculpture, as well as objects of American material culture, and to explore what led generations of nineteenth- and twentieth-century American carvers to create works of art in the cane form. Equally important, the book is meant to serve as a foundation and catalyst for further research and scholarship on the subject.

After seriously collecting American folk art canes for about fifteen years, I believe I now have one of the largest private collections of this art form. The collection has been designed to be comprehensive in scope rather than concentrating on any particular style, period, region, or maker, with an emphasis on nineteenth- and early twentieth-century wood canes. Not included are scrimshaw and glass whimsy canes, both highly specialized areas in themselves.

I have tried to apply strict standards in selecting canes for the collection and used the same criteria to decide which would be included in this publication. At a minimum, a cane has to satisfy all of the following requirements: it needs to be American folk art; it must be very good sculpture or good sculpture and of historic interest; and it must be utilitarian, for example, functional as support or attire. (Contemporary canes, which are often made solely as works of art, are an exception to this last criterion.) A collector is not infallible, but I believe that all the canes pictured in this book are American and fully satisfy the other criteria. In selecting the 305 canes for this book, representing about one-third of my collection, I restudied every cane, looking at each one in relation to others in the collection and elsewhere. I also consulted scholars and respected collectors and dealers, as well as specialists in wood and metal identification.

Some of the folk art canes in the collection have been displayed informally in our home, and over the years I have been pleasantly surprised by the positive reactions of both the art community and others. Everybody, of course, recognized the canes as utilitarian, but many said that they had not realized the great variety of subjects and possible approaches to this simple object. Most important, others commented that they had not appreciated that a walking stick could be a work of art.

I have long wanted to do a book on the subject, and I welcomed the invitation in July 1990 from the Museum of American Folk Art to curate an exhibition of my canes with an accompanying book. I might add, however, that the one pleasure that cannot be shared through a book is the tactile quality of this form of art: a cane is meant to be held.

George H. Meyer

Acknowledgments

This book simply could not have been done but for the help of many gracious people. The late Dr. Robert Bishop, as Director of the Museum of American Folk Art, was the first to suggest that I curate an exhibition of my collection in New York. He generously offered ideas and advice for the project, as did Gerard Wertkin, Director, Stacey Hollander, Associate Curator, Alice Hoffman, Director of Exhibitions, Ann-Marie Reilly, Registrar, Karen Schuster, Director of the Eva and Morris Feld Gallery, Catherine Fukushima, Assistant Gallery Director, Elizabeth Warren, Consulting Curator, and Ralph Sessions, former Chief Curator.

Over the years it has been my special pleasure to have had many conversations about American folk art with pioneer collectors Herbert Hemphill, Jr., Michael Hall, and Tim Hill. These discussions were particularly helpful in defining the goals for the formation of my collection.

James Rutkowski, a sculptor in his own right and a very knowledgeable collector of folk, American Indian, and photographic art, not only supplied a number of period photographs but also offered many excellent insights on the project and suggestions for the selection of canes for this book.

Charles Nairn went well beyond his photographic assignment with his skill, imagination, and sensitivity to the work. Paul Langmuir, a graphic designer, laid out the creative basic approach to the design of the book, and graphic designer Robert Ketelhut offered sage advice on production. My thanks also go to the staff of Marquand Books: to Ed Marquand for the handsome final design, Patricia Draher for the thorough editing, Suzanne Kotz for her expert editorial guidance, and Marie Weiler for skilled editorial assistance. John Pierce, Maria Lacey, and Tomarra LeRoy all lent valuable support toward the book's production.

David Good, a highly knowledgeable art and antiques dealer, looked at each cane to help identify the period in which it was made and generously offered his wealth of background information on American antiques. Dr. Alan Sliker, Forestry Department, Michigan State University, Lansing, who has taught wood identification for thirty-six years and written extensively on the subject, visually analyzed the wood of each cane. Gary Griffin, M.F.A., Head of the Metalsmithing Department at Cranbrook Academy of Art, Bloomfield Hills, Michigan, likewise identified the metals on the canes.

William Spencer, a dealer and historian of walking sticks and Civil War artifacts, and Roger Heiple, a scholar and collector of G.A.R. material, were both of immeasurable help in providing photographs and sharing information on the Civil War and its aftermath. Lawrence E. Eckert, Jr., Curator of Collections at the Gettysburg National Military Park Museum, Russ A. Pritchard, Director of the Civil War Library and Museum in Philadelphia, and Malinda Collier, Registrar, and Connie Hudgins, Manager of Photographic Services, the Museum of the Confederacy, Richmond, Virginia, kindly supplied additional information.

Also of great help were Barbara Luck, Curator of the Abbey Aldrich Rockefeller Folk Art Center, Williamsburg, Virginia; Edmund Sullivan, Director, Museum of American Political Life, West Hartford, Connecticut; Jean Neff, Executive Director, and Emma Sedore, Researcher, the Tioga County Historical Society, Owego, New York; Stuart Frank, Director, Kendall Whaling Museum, Sharon, Massachusetts; and James Moffet, Carol Thompson, Lynne Garza, Ileane Thal, and Carol Woodward from the Baldwin Public Library, Birmingham, Michigan.

Lee Kogan, Assistant Director/Senior Research Fellow, Folk Art Institute of the Museum of American Folk Art, New York, and Fran Lieu, a graduate student at the institute, exhaustively researched the existing materials on canes in New York libraries and institutions.

Catherine Dike, an international scholar and author on the subject of canes, examined the collection during a visit from Switzerland and provided important information, particularly concerning European counterparts of American canes.

Katherine Henderson, Museum Specialist at the Division of Political History, Smithsonian Institution, showed us the institution's extensive collection of political canes and allowed them to be photographed.

All the writers went well beyond their thought-provoking essays to take an active and helpful interest in the project. Ramona Austin, Larry Hackley, Lynda Roscoe Hartigan, and David Penney spent time at our house, studying the collection and reviewing the information we had assembled about it. Simon Bronner, John Hamilton, and Kurt Stein examined detailed photographs and materials from the collection. I exchanged and explored observations and ideas with each writer, particularly with Lynda Hartigan and Larry Hackley.

John Michael Vlach, Chairman, American Studies Program, George Washington University, Washington, D.C., offered a number of incisive comments and thoughts about canes as objects of material culture.

A number of dealers were particularly helpful in this project. These include but certainly are not limited to Aarne Anton, Greg Berry, Tom Delach, Tom and Nicki Deupree, Carl Hammer, Tim and Pam Hill, Frank Maresca, Louis Picek, Eugene Rappaport, Roger Ricco, Ted Trotta, and Don Walters.

Others who helped with the project include Linda Beeman, Joyce Blake, Annie Brewer, Ralph Esmerian, Ken Fadeley, Julie Hall, Laurie Harris, Joan Johnson, Gene and Linda Kangas, Chris Machmer, Don Moylan, Don Stonestreet, Frederick Ruffner, and George White.

Many fellow cane collectors kindly sent me photographs of their walking sticks, which not only permitted better identification of the canes in my collection (and their own) but also pointed out that the number of American folk art cane collectors was far greater than any of us had imagined.

My daughter Karen and my son George, Jr., not so many years ago had to listen as I talked on and on about a wonderful cane I had just found. Nobody, however, was more helpful than my wife, Kay, who I found has an extraordinary talent for design concepts and organization, and who demonstrated an unflappable patience and good humor as our home for many months turned into a cluttered work area and photographic studio.

George H. Meyer

Fig. 1. Men with carved canes. Top: Ca. 1870; ca. 1880. Courtesy
of James Rutkowski, Birmingham, Michigan. Bottom: Ca. 1890;
ca. 1900. Courtesy of George H. Meyer.

George H. Meyer

INTRODUCTION

Benjamin Franklin wrote in his will: "My fine crab-tree walking stick with a gold head curiously wrought in the form of the cap of Liberty I give to my friend and the friend of mankind, General Washington."[1] Other American presidents carried canes, including James Madison, John Quincy Adams, James Buchanan, Abraham Lincoln, Andrew Johnson, Ulysses Grant, William McKinley, Warren Harding, Franklin Roosevelt, and Harry Truman. Formal decorated walking sticks were carried—"worn" in the terminology of the time—by the fashionable well-to-do, but the less affluent used them as well.

Although some may remember a grandfather with a walking stick, it is hard to realize today how popular canes were. The *New York Times* of November 21, 1877, stated in a humorous editorial about women adopting the fashion of canes that "at least fifteen millions of Americans are carrying . . . canes."[2] The popularity of decorated canes in the United States reached its peak in the late nineteenth century, but walking sticks continued to be used, although less and less frequently, until World War II.

Canes were utilitarian; they aided the infirm and aged. But they also served younger men as articles of fashion and symbols of status. A completely plain cane could ably support an elderly man. If, however, a walking stick were to serve as an apparel accessory or show a man's status (or his vanity), it had to be decorated. A cane might be a walnut stick with a gold- or silver-plated handle bought from a jewelry catalogue, or an ebony shaft with an expensive, custom-made, solid gold handle. A cane also might be the equally handsome handmade work of an American folk artist.

A cane can be considered folk art if, using one commonly accepted definition, it was made by a self-taught or nonacademic artist.[3] If the artist is unidentified, the cane's classification as folk art may be determined from the materials and construction. Clearly identifiable symbols (such as a flag), a proved provenance, a native wood, a distinctive style, or the carving help determine whether a cane is American.

In making a decorative cane, a folk art carver first faces the challenge of the limitations imposed by the form—a piece of wood about thirty-four inches long and about one and one half inches wide with a handle that is probably a different size and shape than the shaft. Most American folk art canes seem to have been made from a single piece of wood with the handle an extension of the shaft.[4] The wood may be a tree limb or a root that the maker simply found, or it may be a certain natural shape for which he had been searching. The stick itself may give the carver an idea for the cane, or he might impose his design on the wood. Although unusual in period folk art canes, the wood can be precut lumber or a piece split from a log, offering the maker more freedom over the carving. The carver might utilize the flat surface of the stick for relief carving, or he might wrap the carving around the shaft or handle. He might also incorporate the natural burls, knots, or crotches in the wood, use an existing entwining vine, or even add a found object. Whatever he does, the test of the maker's ability is whether he can accomplish his design by both utilizing and transcending the limitations of the form.

The masculinity of canes is evident. Walking sticks were almost always carved by men, and except when canes served as an aid in walking or, briefly, as a part of women's fashion, they belonged to the male world. Although the parallel is incomplete, it has been said that the male cane maker is the counterpart of the female quilt maker and that canes may be as symbolically important to men as a gender group as quilts are to women.[5]

To be better studied and understood, American folk art canes, like other art objects, need to be classified, but organizing folk art canes by the common classifications of period, region, or maker is difficult, and sometimes impossible. Most of the canes pictured in this book were probably made between the Civil War and World War I. But in the absence of an inscribed date or proved provenance, establishing precisely when a cane was made is at best a problem. Apart from the subjects on a walking stick, few prevailing stylistic differences were evident during this time.[6] Many period folk art canes as a result cannot be dated with any specificity.

Perhaps even more challenging is determining where a cane was made. Walking sticks were (and are) made in all fifty states. In addition to the type of evidence used to attribute dates, it may be helpful in establishing a place of origin if a cane has unique regional decorations, is by a known carver or from the school of a known regional carver, or is constructed of wood native to only one geographic area. Although studies have indicated some state or regional styles of cane carving and decoration,[7] such characteristics have not yet been identified sufficiently to clearly establish that a cane was made in a particular state or region of the United States.[8] It also seems unlikely that local stylistic identifications will ever be as reliable as they are for more complex handcrafted objects, such as period American furniture, because carved walking sticks, wherever found, tend to be relatively simple in form and construction. In many cases, the only evidence of a cane's origin is the place where it was found, and given the highly portable nature of the object, this is hardly conclusive evidence. It is likely, in fact, that there will be no reliable information about where a particular American folk art cane was made.

Certain woods seem to have been favored for American folk art canes, including maple, walnut, cherry, ash, hickory, willow, elm, birch, pine, poplar, and cedar, but a great many other kinds were used. Determining the particular type of wood from which a shaft or handle is made can be extremely challenging. Varieties and species of American trees alone number nearly eight hundred,[9] and there are over one thousand species of American shrubs. More than forty thousand species of woody plants exist worldwide, and many species found elsewhere are closely related to the woods native to the United States.[10]

Canes can be made from tree limbs, roots, saplings, shrubs, and vines. The bark, grain, or color—if visible—may differ depending on the variety of wood, its distance from the center of the tree, and the part of the tree from which the cutting was taken. At best, many woods are not easy to identify visually. Moreover, many canes are painted or stained and have a ferrule, in which case no wood is exposed. Even spectroanalysis, which requires a cutting or core from the cane, is often inconclusive: reference slides of the specific wood might be unavailable, or the wood could be from a part of the tree other than that covered by the sample.

Determining a cane's maker presents another problem. Many nineteenth- and early twentieth-century American folk artists have not yet been identified. Like much early

folk art, walking sticks were infrequently signed by the maker,[11] although they may have been signed more often than other utilitarian folk art objects, perhaps because of their aspect of personal communication. When a name or initials do appear, they might refer to either the maker or the user, although the latter is more likely. Occasionally the carvers of unsigned canes have been identified by family history or by a distinctive style, technique, or iconography (nos. 270–81).

It has been said that a cane may have sculpture on it or may itself be sculpture. Regardless of whether the decoration is located on the handle, the shaft, or both, a walking stick, like any other sculpture, needs to be viewed as a whole. Even a single carving—and any paint or other surface decoration—should be related to the cane and integrated into its form.

A skilled maker recognizes that a cane must be designed visually as sculpture but also as a tactile object to be held. He also appreciates that a cane is held vertically by the user, waist high and next to the body, which means a viewer ordinarily sees it from a short distance, with the details sometimes requiring even closer examination.

Michael Hall has said, "Folk-made objects as art witness to the dynamic character of the thing we call culture."[12] This is true of folk art canes. The imagery and symbolism on a carved walking stick were often drawn from the popular graphics of the day. By the mid nineteenth century, books, magazines, and newspapers with engravings were readily available to Americans, and these and other images and symbols were freely adopted by folk artists.[13]

Period folk art canes were often personally decorated for a user to identify himself as an individual or as a member of a group. Americans were joiners. Alexis de Tocqueville wrote in *Democracy in America* in 1838: "The Americans of all ages, all conditions and all dispositions constantly form associations. They have not only commercial and manufacturing companies in which all take part but associations of a thousand other kinds, religious, moral, serious, futile, restricted, enormous, or diminutive." As an example of the number of organizations available, the 1895 city directory for Pontiac, Michigan, a city then with a population of around seven thousand, listed in detail in a separate section thirty-five different organizations. Almost all of these were for men, and almost all had unique imagery or symbols to identify membership.

John Vlach has said that the cane functions as "a gesture of communication."[14] A maker designed a stick to say what he wanted about himself or his world. Unlike the words and logos on today's T-shirts, the message was generally not blatant. It might have been intended only for the bearer's friends or peer group or, alternatively, for the general public. The communication could be spiritual, as in examples by Native Americans (no. 90) or by African-

Americans (no. 119). It might celebrate a boxing match (no. 220) or horse race (no. 222); announce a bearer's status as a barber (no. 191), carpenter (no. 190), or veteran (no. 234); proclaim the owner's belief in drinking (no. 214) or in temperance (no. 213); state his concern about death (no. 99) or his taste for comics (no. 215), movies (no. 216), or sex (no. 103). Such communications can be achieved with carved words (no. 264), portraits (no. 131), simple carvings of an animal (no. 84) or snake (no. 1), or complex interrelated references to the Odd Fellows (no. 199) or to professional experiences (no. 200).

The artistic quality of the many canes made in the United States varied greatly. Some remained utilitarian objects, others were craft, and a few became art. The difference lay in the creativity of the maker. Edgar Tolson (1904–84), one of America's preeminent folk carvers, in talking about the difference between whittling and carving (i.e., art), said "When you're carving something, you've got your mind with it. You have your whole being in it. You have to. But just sitting there whittling on a stick, you ain't got nothin' in it but a little time."[15]

A cane can be regarded as artistically successful without understanding either the imagery or symbolism or the maker's intent. Whether an object linked to a particular person, time, and place can be divorced from its background and remain fully aesthetically successful is hardly a new question. But the question is particularly pertinent to decorated period folk art canes, which frequently emphasize the maker's personal communication. That message may be only partly appreciated, even lost, if we do not understand the imagery or symbolism or know the maker's identity. When this happens, the work's richness is lessened.

The best American cane makers transformed a small, relatively simple utilitarian object into something aesthetically beautiful and challenging, an object to be seen and touched. At the same time they made objects that reflected both the culture of the period and their own position in that culture. American cane makers accomplished this using an extraordinary variety of personal styles, forms, and subjects—encompassing them within the narrow confines of a three-foot-long piece of wood. In doing so, they made the American folk art cane a work of art.

Notes

1. Cited in Kurt Stein, *Canes and Walking Sticks* (York, Pa.: Liberty Cap Books, 1974), 41. The walking stick was actually a staff.

2. The editorial was entitled *A New Vice* (p. 4). The number of persons carrying canes was probably exaggerated. The 1880 official census of the United States shows a population of just over fifty million.

3. There are various sometimes conflicting definitions of folk art. See George H. Meyer, ed., *Folk Artists Biographical Index*, introduction (Detroit: Gale Research Company, 1987), ix–xi.

4. Conversely, most formal decorated canes have attached handles, probably because handles, almost always the sole decorated element on the cane, were manufactured separately.

5. Larry Hackley, *Sticks: Historical and Contemporary Kentucky Canes* (Louisville: Kentucky Art and Craft Foundation, 1988), n.p. Canes are, of course, also weapons. In a well-known incident on the U.S. Senate floor in 1856, Congressman Preston S. Brooks of South Carolina caned abolitionist Charles Sumner of Massachusetts until Sumner fell unconscious. Brooks said later "I wore my cane out completely but saved the head—which is gold." Southern sympathizers sent Brooks a number of replacement canes. See Geoffrey C. Ward, with Ric Burns and Ken Burns, *The Civil War: An Illustrated History* (New York: Alfred A. Knopf, 1990), 21.

6. In contrast, formal canes were more likely to reflect the artistic styles and tastes of the day. U.S. patents for designs on canes were issued, for example, in 1909 and as late as 1976.

7. See, for example, Cynthia Elyce Rubin, ed., *Southern Folk Art* (Birmingham, Ala.: Oxmoor House, 1985), 107–8.

8. There are few if any regional characteristics that establish the particular country or area of origin for a European folk art cane. European folk art canes were generally hardwood, rarely painted, and when they were, it was only with browns, blacks, or other dark colors. Conversation on November 24, 1991, with Catherine Dike, an authority on European canes.

9. Forest Service, U.S. Department of Agriculture, *Release 541* (September 1979).

10. Dr. Alan Sliker provided this information and estimate.

11. Some interesting statistics are obtained if we treat the canes pictured (excluding the contemporary pieces and all but one example of a maker) as a limited sample of very good American folk art canes. Approximately 6 percent are signed by the maker, and 1 percent are signed with the maker's initials; another 6 percent are signed by a person who is either the maker or the owner. Approximately 8 percent contain a stated geographic location; 13 percent are dated; and 11 percent have a handle separate from the shaft. Approximately 19 percent have carvings only on the handle; about 36 percent have carvings only on the shaft; and about 45 percent have carvings on both the handle and shaft. About 44 percent of the canes have a ferrule. Some 8 percent of the carvers made more than one cane. (There is some overlap in these percentages since, for example, both a maker's name and the date might appear on the same cane.) Five of the twenty signers identified themselves as "carvers," one called himself the "maker"; none used the word "artist." The vocations of eight of the signers were determined from reliable sources independent of the information on the cane. Those identified were a doctor, a carpenter, a blacksmith, a carver, two farmers, a miller, and the owner of two businesses.

12. Michael D. Hall, *Stereoscopic Perspective: Reflections on American Fine and Folk Art* (Ann Arbor, Mich.: UMI Research Press, 1988), 4.

13. Symbols are of great importance in American culture. "Symbols . . . embody cultural meanings by assuming shapes and configurations dictated by the culture; they are timeless storehouses for anything a culture produces of enduring significance. Folk artifacts then contain endless information rather than bits and pieces—potsherds of the psyche—that must be scrounged out of the dust of the historic past." Richard C. Paulsen, *The Pure Experience of Order, Essays on the Symbolic in the Folk Material Culture of Western America* (Albuquerque, N. Mex.: University of New Mexico Press, 1982), 5. There are many symbols, including the American Indian, the Liberty Cap, the eagle, and George Washington, "that have spoken of our pride and our hopes, our chauvinism and our bona fide love of country." See Louis C. Jones, *Outward Signs of Inner Beliefs: Symbols of American Patriotism* (Cooperstown, N.Y.: New York State Historical Association, 1975), 3.

14. Telephone conversation with John Vlach on June 4, 1991.

15. Hall, *Stereoscopic Perspective*, 163.

CONTRIBUTORS

Ramona M. Austin is Assistant Curator of African, Oceanic, and Americas Art at the Art Institute of Chicago where she specializes in the art of Africa and the African diaspora. She has a Master of Philosophy from Yale University.

Simon J. Bronner, Ph.D., is Distinguished Professor of Folklore and American Studies at the Pennsylvania State University at Harrisburg, Middletown. He is the author of several books, including *Chain Carvers: Old Men Crafting Meaning*, 1985.

Larry Hackley received his M.F.A. from the University of Kentucky and has taught ceramics and design at Kentucky State University. He curated and wrote the catalogue for *Sticks: Historical and Contemporary Kentucky Canes*, a 1988 exhibition at the Kentucky Art and Craft Foundation, Louisville.

John D. Hamilton is Curator of Collections, Museum of Our National Heritage, Lexington, Massachusetts. He received a B.A. from the University of Buffalo and has special expertise in fraternal regalia. He is the author of *The Ames Sword Company, 1829–1935* (1983).

Lynda Roscoe Hartigan, M.A., is Associate Curator of Painting and Sculpture at the National Museum of American Art, Smithsonian Institution, Washington, D.C. She is the author of *Made with Passion: The Hemphill Folk Art Collection*, written for the exhibition she curated in 1990 for the National Museum of American Art.

George H. Meyer, a graduate of the University of Michigan and the Harvard Law School, is the senior partner of a Michigan law firm where one of his specialties is art law. He is the editor of *Folk Artists Biographical Index*, 1987, and is a member of the board of trustees of the Museum of American Folk Art in New York. He is a longtime serious collector of American folk art.

Kay White Meyer has a B.A. in American Literature from Colby College, Maine, and served in the Peace Corps in Panama. She is associate editor of *Folk Artists Biographical Index*, 1987.

Charles B. Nairn began his career as a professional photographer while working his way through Wayne State University, Detroit, from which he received a B.S.E.E. He has taught courses on radio, television, and film at Wayne State and won numerous national and international awards for his photographs.

David W. Penney, Ph.D., Columbia University, New York, is Associate Curator of African, Oceanic, and New World Cultures at the Detroit Institute of Arts. He is the author of many publications, including *Great Lakes Indian Art*, 1989, and *Ancient Art of the American Woodlands Indians*, 1985.

Kurt Stein is the author of *Canes and Walking Sticks*, 1974, and many articles about canes for both scholarly and popular publications. He was consultant on canes to *The Encyclopedia of Collectibles* (Time Life Books, 1978). He is a past president of the Pennsylvania Antique Gun Collectors' Association and edits its monthly journal.

NOTES TO THE READER

The terms "cane," "walking stick," "walking cane," and "stick" are treated in this book as interchangeable, since there is no generally accepted distinction among them. "Staff" means a stick that is generally chest or shoulder high, unlike a cane, which is usually waist high. A staff is sometimes also distinguished from a cane because it is grasped below the handle, while a cane is held by the handle.

The major parts of a cane are the handle (or grip or head), the collar (or band), the shaft, and the ferrule (or tip). The collar covers the area where the handle and shaft are joined. Some canes also have an eyelet that passes through the shaft where a cord or tassel can be threaded, allowing the walking stick to be hung from the user's arm.

The full length of the cane is not always pictured. Canes are particularly difficult to photograph because they are long and narrow and often have many fine details that may not only be carved in low relief but also encircle the shaft.

Unless otherwise noted, plate captions generally indicate objects from left to right. Plate captions provide the object number; a short descriptive title; artist information, including birth and death dates, place where active, and ethnicity; place where the cane was made; date of the work; medium, including the ferrule; and dimensions. "Painted" refers to a single color, "polychromed" to more than one color. Most artists have not been identified. An inscribed name (or initials) is given as "owner/maker" when the person may be either the user or the carver or both. "Owner" and "user" are interchangeable, as are "maker," "carver," and "artist."

The relative certainty of information is indicated by "probably" (more likely) or by a question mark (less likely). If a caption element is missing, the information is not certain enough to justify its inclusion.

For dimensions, height refers to the length of the cane from top to bottom; width refers to the greatest horizontal measurement at a right angle to the height (generally the handle); and diameter indicates the second greatest horizontal dimension (generally the shaft). If width and diameter are the same, diameter is used. Measurements are accurate to the nearest quarter inch.

An asterisk after the title indicates additional information in the documentation, including a full description of the decoration read from top to bottom. Decoration that is evident in the photograph may not be repeated. Inscriptions, which appear in italics, do not precisely reproduce the form of the lettering. Minor spelling errors are transcribed uncorrected. The documentation may include the cane's construction and general condition. It may also include information or comments, even if unverified, that might assist future scholarship. The captions and documentation in general neither discuss nor judge the aesthetics of the canes.

Since information was insufficient to classify the canes by period, region, or maker, they are grouped thematically in broad categories, based on what was perceived as the main subject of the cane.

Snakes and the Natural World

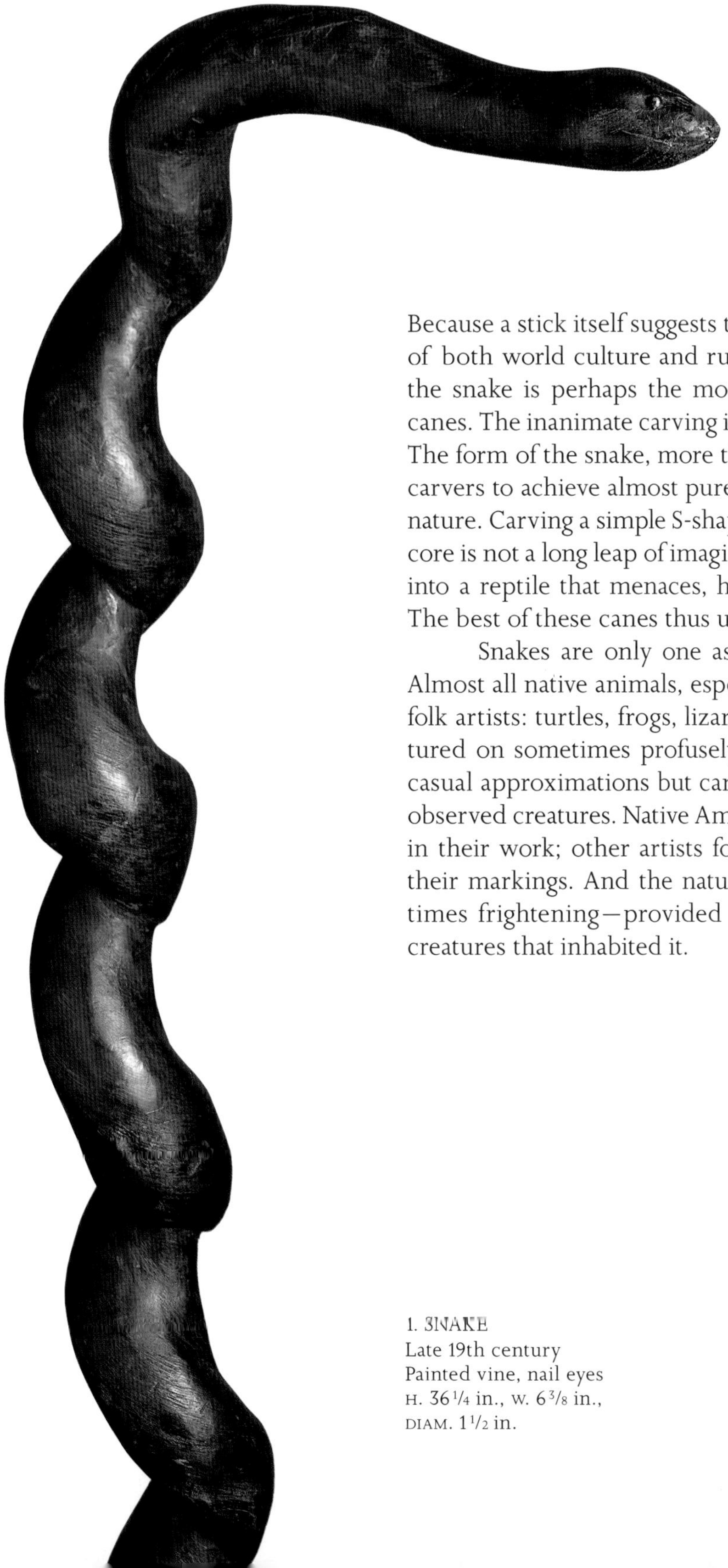

Because a stick itself suggests the image of a snake—a creature that is part of both world culture and rural American life—it is not surprising that the snake is perhaps the most common subject on American folk art canes. The inanimate carving is often as fascinating as its live counterpart. The form of the snake, more than that of any other creature, has allowed carvers to achieve almost pure design rather than merely a semblance of nature. Carving a simple S-shape from a sapling that suggests a snake at its core is not a long leap of imagination. But to find and shape a vine or limb into a reptile that menaces, hunts, or strikes requires uncommon skill. The best of these canes thus uniquely combine natural and artistic form.

Snakes are only one aspect of nature captured by cane makers. Almost all native animals, especially those of the woods, are subjects for folk artists: turtles, frogs, lizards, bees, birds, squirrels, and deer are featured on sometimes profusely populated canes. Many carvings are not casual approximations but carefully worked out depictions of intimately observed creatures. Native Americans put the spiritual essence of animals in their work; other artists found humor in animal forms or beauty in their markings. And the natural world—known, fascinating, and sometimes frightening—provided the wood that was transformed into the creatures that inhabited it.

1. SNAKE
Late 19th century
Painted vine, nail eyes
H. 36 1/4 in., W. 6 3/8 in.,
DIAM. 1 1/2 in.

Right:
2. RATTLESNAKE EATING FROG*
(Reverse: Bust of woman, *above*)
Probably southwestern U.S.
Early 20th century
Polychromed wood
H. 34 in., W. 2¾ in.,
DIAM. 2¼ in.

18

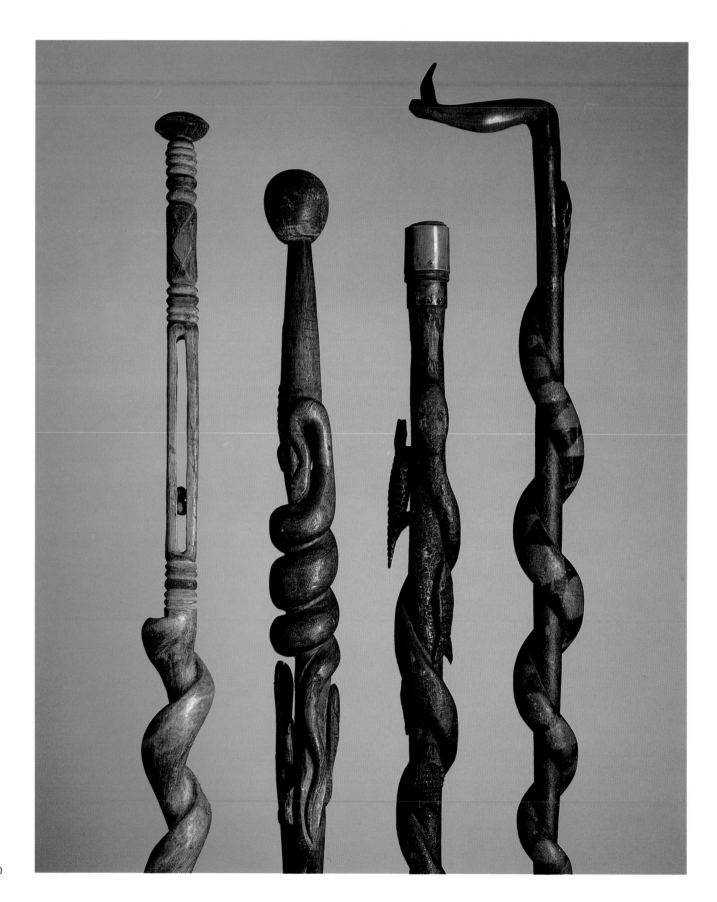

Left:
3. SNAKE AND BALL-IN-CAGE*
Sioux
Standing Rock Reservation,
Sioux County, North Dakota
Ca. 1870
Polychromed wood, leather
knob
H. 44 in., w. 2⁷/₈ in.,
DIAM. 2⁷/₈ in.

4. CRAYFISH, SNAKE,
LIZARD, AND FISH*
J. H.U. (owner/maker?)
Probably African-American
Late 19th–early 20th century
Varnished wood, probably
pine, glass eyes
H. 36¹/₂ in., w. 2³/₈ in.,
DIAM. 2¹/₂ in.

5. RATTLESNAKE, LIZARD,
AND FISH*
African-American(?)
Louisiana(?)
Early 20th century
Painted wood, probably
cypress, metal,
1¹/₄ in. brass ferrule
H. 34 in., w. 2³/₄ in.,
DIAM. 2 in.

6. WOMAN'S LEG AND SNAKE*
D. H. Hixson
Ohio
Dated January 23, 1903(8?)
Varnished polychromed
wood, 1¹/₂ in. copper ferrule
with steel tip
H. 39¹/₄ in., w. 3 in.,
DIAM. 2¹/₂ in.

7. LARGE SNAKE*
(Two details)
Luke
Probably African American
Probably western Pennsylvania
Dated 1816
Painted root
H. 35¹/₂ in., w. 3³/₄ in.,
DIAM. 3¹/₄ in.

21

8. ROOT SNAKE*
Probably Maryland
Late 19th–early 20th century
Painted root, nail eyes,
1 3/8 in. lead ferrule
H. 43 1/2 in., w. 13 3/4 in.,
DIAM. 7 1/2 in.

9. SNAKE SWALLOWING PIG*
Last quarter 19th century
Polychromed wood,
probably maple, glass eyes,
wire teeth
H. 35 1/4 in., w. 6 1/2 in.,
DIAM. 1 1/4 in.

Left:

10. SNAKE ON BRANCH*
Late 19th–early 20th century
Varnished painted vine,
1 1/4 in. metal ferrule
H. 35 1/2 in., DIAM. 1 3/8 in.

11. HEAD AND THREE SNAKES*
(Detail right)
19th century
Polychromed wood (oak or
ash?), nail and glass eyes,
7/8 in. brass ferrule
H. 38 1/2 in., DIAM. 1 3/4 in.

12. TWO SNAKES ON
KNOBBY SHAFT
Probably last quarter 19th
century
Partly varnished painted
wood (maple or a shrub?)
H. 36 3/8 in., DIAM. 1 1/2 in.

13. SNAKE WITH SEVEN HEADS*
African-American
New England
Last quarter 19th century
Varnished painted hickory
(or pecan?), 1 3/8 in. brass
ferrule
H. 36 in., DIAM. 1 3/8 in.

25

14. WOODPECKER AND SNAKE
Probably early 20th century
Varnished polychromed
wood, probably maple
H. 36 1/2 in., W. 7 3/8 in.,
DIAM. 3 in.

16. EGG AND RATTLESNAKE*
Second half 20th century
Polychromed redwood, nail
eyes, metal tongue
H. 35 3/4 in., W. 3 in.,
DIAM. 2 1/2 in.

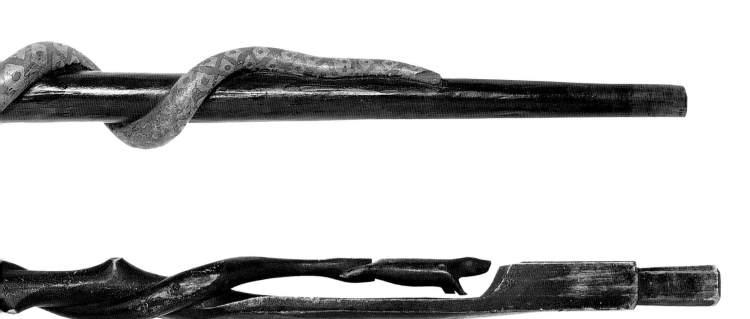

15. SNAKE EATING RAT*
Probably late 19th century
Polychromed wood,
probably yellow poplar
H. 34 in., W. 1 3/8 in.,
DIAM. 1 1/4 in.

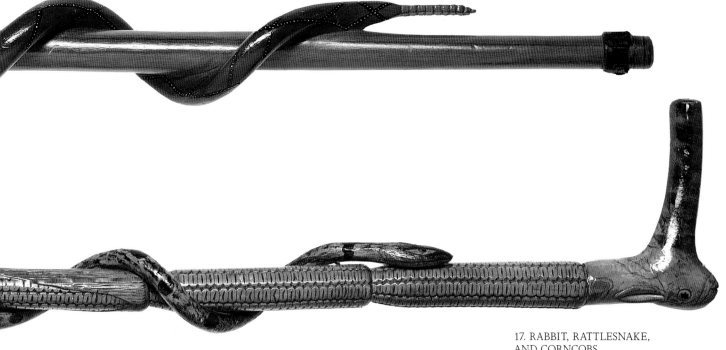

17. RABBIT, RATTLESNAKE,
AND CORNCOBS
Early to mid 20th century
Varnished polychromed
hardwood (maple?),
nail eyes
H. 37 in., W. 5 3/8 in.,
DIAM. 2 1/4 in.

27

Left:
18. ALLIGATOR, BEETLE,
AND SNAKE*
Ca. 1890
Varnished walnut, 1³/₈ in.
metal ferrule
H. 35¹/₂ in., DIAM. 1¹/₂ in.

19. BIRD HEAD AND SNAKES
EATING FROGS*
Probably last quarter 19th century
Varnished painted maple,
1¹/₈ in. brass ferrule
H. 33³/₄ in., W. 2¹/₂ in.,
DIAM. 1³/₄ in.

20. EAGLE AND SEVEN SNAKES*
Iroquois
Eastern U.S.
Probably 19th century
Varnished stained wood,
³/₄ in. metal ferrule
H. 36 in., W. 3 in., DIAM. 1¹/₄ in.

21. TWO GREEN SNAKES*
Probably last quarter 19th century
Varnished polychromed maple,
1¹/₂ in. cartridge case ferrule
H. 35¹/₂ in., W. 3 in., DIAM. 1 in.

22. SIX FROGS AND SNAKE*
Southern Indiana
Ca. 1870–80
Varnished painted wood,
1³/₈ in. metal ferrule
H. 36⁷/₈ in., DIAM. 1¹/₈ in.

Right:
23. DEER HEADS, TURTLES,
AND SNAKES*
Iroquois
Probably northeastern U.S.
Probably 20th century
Varnished stained wood, nail eyes,
6¹/₈ in. tin ferrule with steel tip
H. 36 in., DIAM. 1¹/₂ in.

24. TWO SNAKES ON RED SHAFT
Late 19th–early 20th century
Polychromed wood (maple?)
H. 33 in., DIAM. 1³/₄ in.

25. SNAKE WITH GOLD HEAD*
H.K.M. (owner/maker?)
Probably West Virginia
Probably late 19th–early 20th century
Polychromed wood, probably cedar,
bead eyes, ³/₄ in. metal ferrule
H. 34 in., DIAM. 1¹/₂ in.

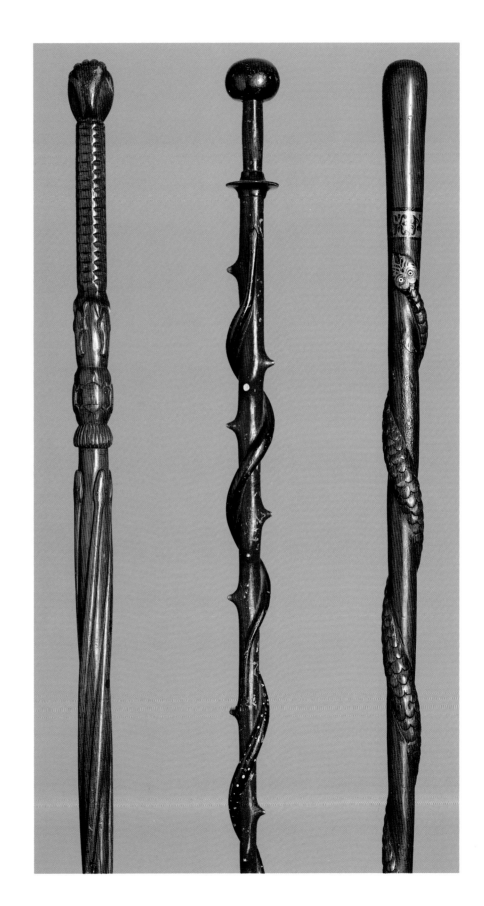

29

26. SNAKE BETWEEN SWIRLS*
Southern Indiana
Ca. 1865–75
Painted wood, probably
maple
H. 32 1/4 in., DIAM. 1 3/8 in.

27. SNAKES EATING FROGS*
Late 19th century
Painted tiger maple
H. 35 1/2 in., W. 1 3/8 in.,
DIAM. 1 1/4 in.

28. TWO SNAKES AND
CIVIL WAR INSCRIPTION*
T. Reierson (owner/maker?)
Probably Illinois
Ca. 1863
Painted white pine, nail
eyes, 1/2 in. metal ferrule
H. 36 1/2 in., DIAM. 1 1/2 in.

29. TWO ENTWINED SNAKES*
Probably Pennsylvania
Late 19th–early 20th century
Varnished hardwood (maple?),
nail eyes, leather, metal
H. 38 3/4 in., W. 7 1/2 in.,
DIAM. 2 1/8 in.

30. TWO SWIRLED SNAKES*
Probably Central Algonkian,
Great Lakes region
Probably late 19th–early 20th
century
Painted wood, 3/8 in. metal
ferrule
H. 35 in., DIAM. 2 3/8 in.

Right:
31. SNAKE CANE WITH STICK SUPPORT*
Last quarter 19th century
Painted root or sapling, nail eyes, nails, 1 1/4 in. brass cartridge case ferrule
H. 35 in., DIAM. 2 7/8 in.

32. TWISTED SNAKE*
(Detail above)
Ca. 1900
Polychromed hardwood, nail eyes
H. 33 1/4 in., W. 4 1/2 in., DIAM. 4 in.

33. SNAKE WITH SCALES
Probably southern Ohio
Ca. 1900
Painted wood, bead eyes
H. 31 in., W. 4 in., DIAM. 1 1/2 in.

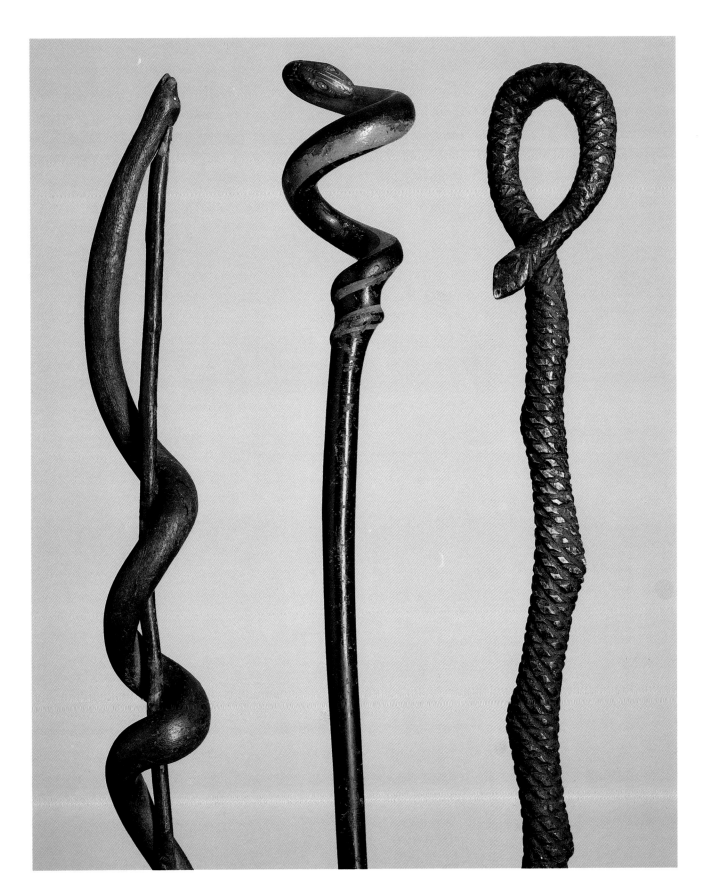

34. RATTLESNAKE ON STICK*
Indiana
Early 20th century
Varnished, stained, and
painted pine with smoke
markings
H. 34 1/2 in., DIAM. 1 3/4 in.

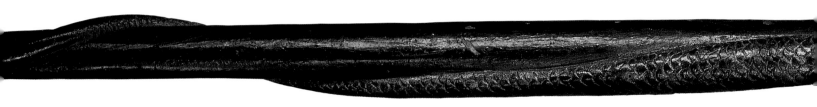

**35. RATTLESNAKE WITH
MECHANICAL TONGUE***
Midwestern U.S.
20th century
Polychromed wood, metal,
nail eyes, wooden button,
1 in. metal ferrule
H. 34 1/2 in., W. 2 1/4 in.,
DIAM. 1 7/8 in.

36. SNAKE ON "BAMBOO" SHAFT
Late 19th–early 20th century
Varnished, stained, and
burned wood, probably
maple, nail eyes, 1 1/4 in.
metal ferrule
H. 36 in., W. 2 1/2 in.,
DIAM. 1 1/4 in.

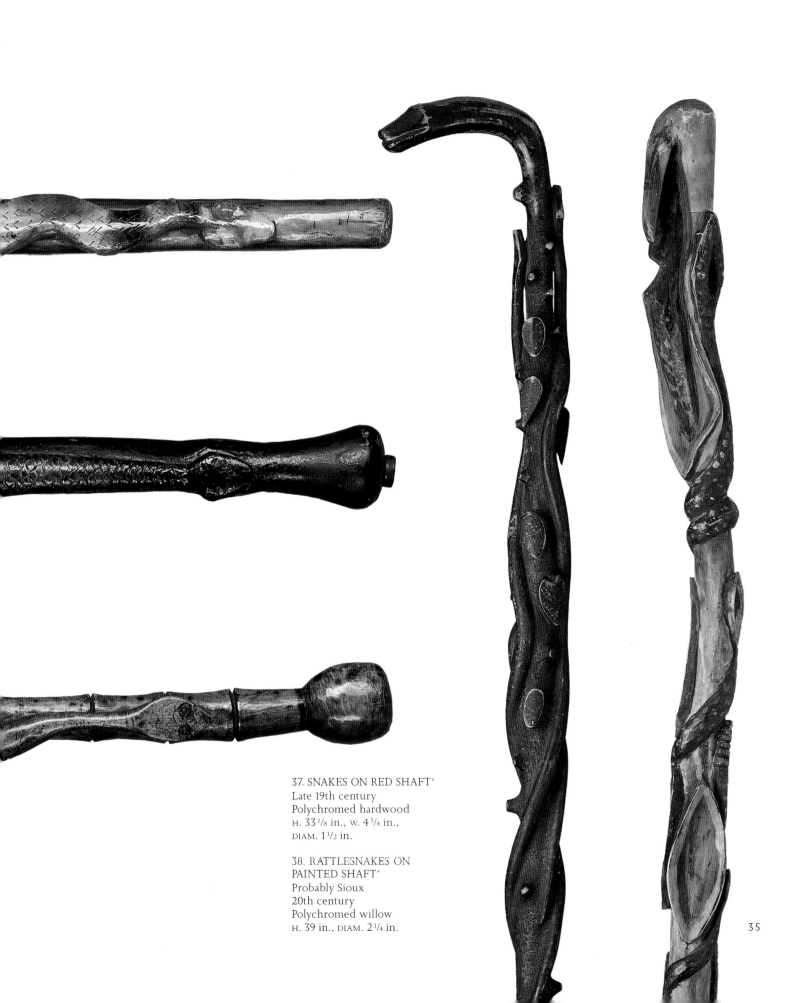

37. SNAKES ON RED SHAFT*
Late 19th century
Polychromed hardwood
H. 33 1/8 in., W. 4 3/4 in.,
DIAM. 1 1/2 in.

38. RATTLESNAKES ON
PAINTED SHAFT*
Probably Sioux
20th century
Polychromed willow
H. 39 in., DIAM. 2 1/4 in.

35

39. LIZARD WITH LEAVES
AND BALL*
(Detail right)
Early 20th century
Varnished wood,
probably maple
H. 30 1/4 in., DIAM. 2 1/2 in.

40. RATTLESNAKE AND
ANIMALS*
(Detail far right)
Frederick Allen
Southern Michigan
Last quarter 19th century
Varnished polychromed
hardwood, nail eyes
H. 33 1/2 in., DIAM. 2 1/2 in.

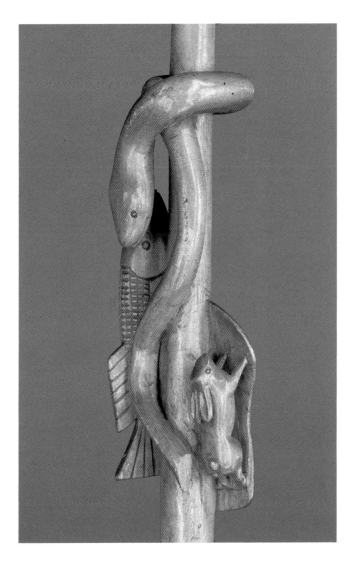

41. CUPOLA, ALLIGATOR, FROG, AND SNAKE*
Probably African-American
Probably Michigan
Probably last quarter 19th century
Polychromed wood
H. 36 1/2 in., DIAM. 2 in.

Right:
42. LIZARD, TURTLE, CRAYFISH, AND SNAKES*
African-American(?)
Probably southern U.S.
Late 19th–early 20th century
Varnished stained hickory
H. 35 1/2 in., W. 2 in.,
DIAM. 1 5/8 in.

43. BALL-IN-CAGE, TWO LIZARDS, AND SNAKE
Probably African-American
New England(?)
Last quarter 19th century
Painted maple
H. 35 in., DIAM. 1 5/8 in.

44. PAIRED RATTLESNAKES, LIZARDS, AND FROGS*
J. Pearcy (owner/maker?)
Probably Ohio
Dated 1886
Polychromed ash
H. 34 1/2 in., DIAM. 1 1/4 in.

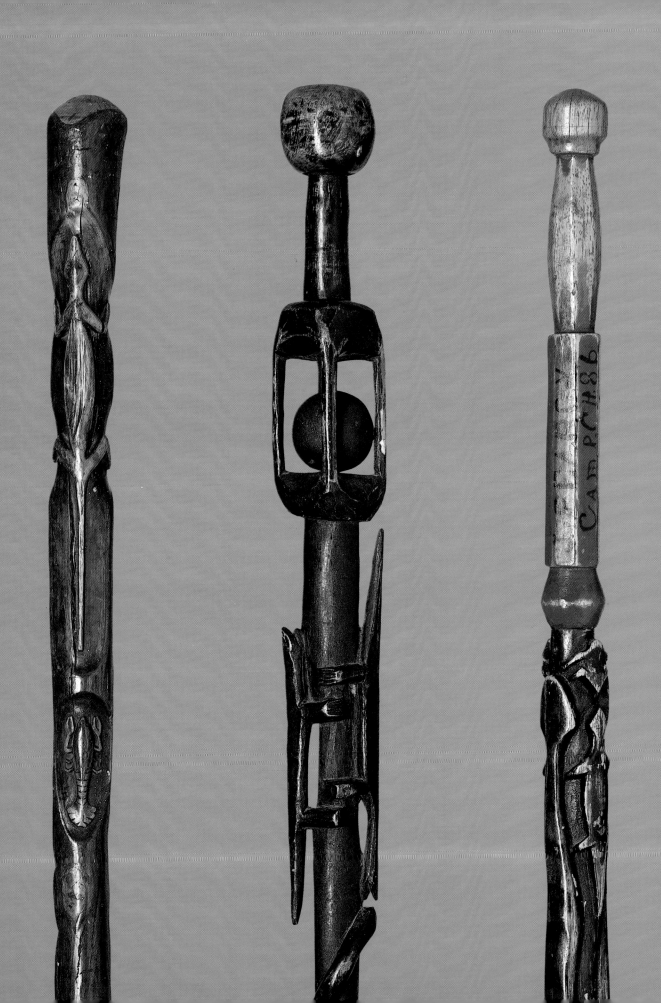

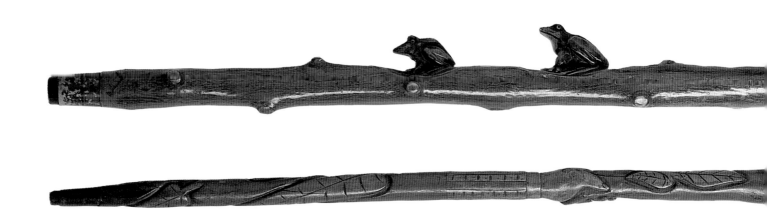

Top to bottom:
45. ALLIGATOR AND
TWO FROGS*
Probably Florida or
Kentucky
Dated 1891–92
Varnished, stained, and
polychromed ash, glass eyes,
1¼ in. brass ferrule
H. 35½ in., w. 2 in.,
DIAM. 1¼ in.

46. ALLIGATOR AND FROG*
Late 19th century
Stained maple, 1¼ in. brass
ferrule
H. 35¾ in., w. 2⅛ in.,
DIAM. 1¼ in.

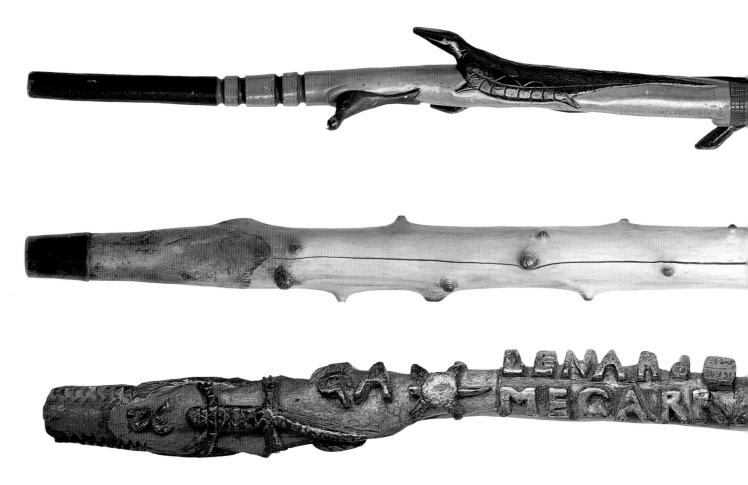

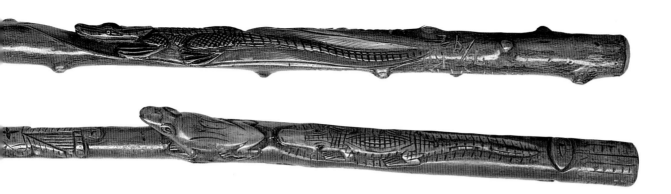

47. BIRDS, SNAKES, AND
LIZARDS*
Ca. 1920
Polychromed hardwood,
glass, mica, metal
H. 39 in., W. 3¹/₂ in.,
DIAM. 2³/₄ in.

48. FROG AND ALLIGATOR*
Indiana
Early 20th century
Partly varnished
polychromed wood,
probably maple, nail eyes,
1⁵/₈ in. heavy brass ferrule
H. 38 in., W. 4¹/₂ in.,
DIAM. 2 in.

49. RATTLESNAKE EATING FROG*
Lenard Megarr
African-American
Georgia
Dated 1932
Polychromed softwood, nail
and glass eyes, metal button
H. 38 in., W. 2⁵/₈ in.,
DIAM. 2¹/₄ in.

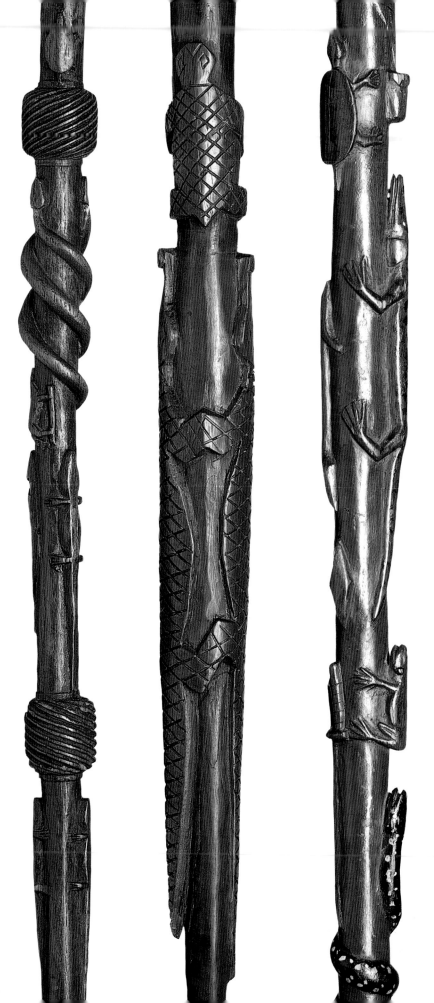

50. SNAKES, LIZARDS,
AND ANIMALS*
Probably African-American
Late 19th century
Stained ash
H. 35 in., DIAM. 1¼ in.

51. PAIRED TURTLES
AND ALLIGATORS*
Georgia(?)
Ca. 1900
Varnished stained walnut
H. 28½ in., DIAM. 1⅞ in.

52. EAGLE, LIZARD,
AND REPTILES*
Probably Georgia
Ca. 1905
Varnished, stained, and
polychromed wood,
probably cherry, metal
collar, nail eyes, 1 in. steel
ferrule
H. 35½ in., w. 5½ in.,
DIAM. 1¼ in.

53. ALLIGATOR WITH TEETH*
Probably coastal Florida or
South Carolina
Early 20th century
Polychromed wood,
probably cypress with bark,
gar teeth, nail eyes, nails
H. 36 in., W. 9 in., DIAM. 1 in.

54. ALLIGATOR ON HANDLE*
L. B. S. (owner/maker?)
North or South Carolina
Early 20th century
Varnished stained wood,
probably maple
H. 32 1/4 in., W. 4 1/2 in.,
DIAM. 1 5/8 in.

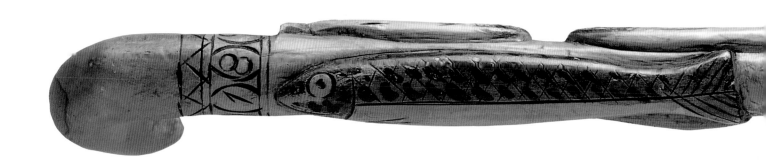

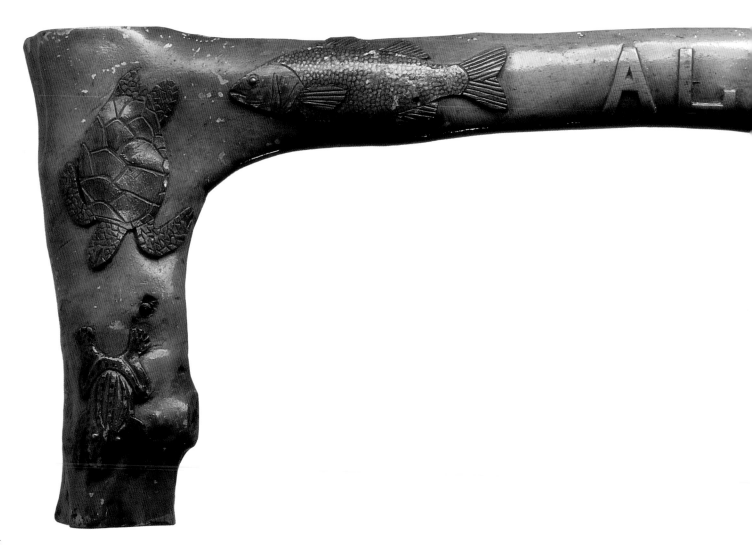

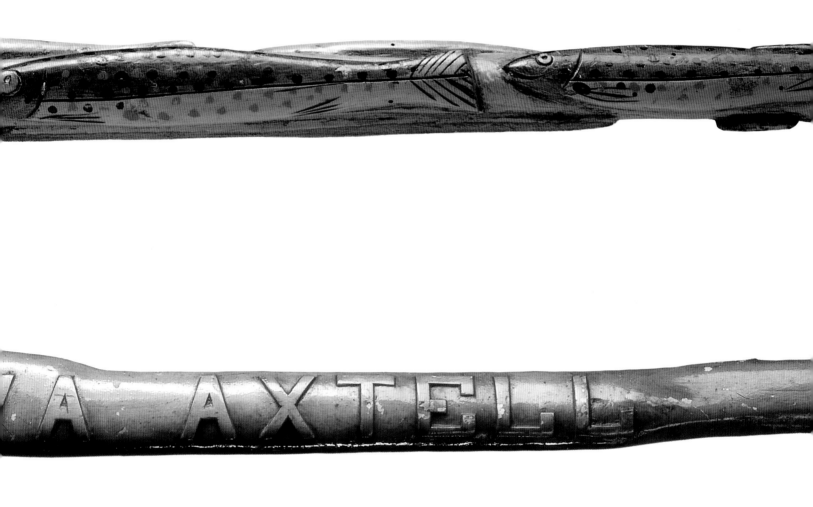

55. TROUT*
Michigan
Dated 1896
Varnished polychromed
wood, probably maple,
metal
H. 34 1/2 in., W. 4 in.,
DIAM. 1 3/8 in.

56. FROG, TURTLE, AND FISH*
Alva Axtell (owner/maker?)
Dated 1925
Polychromed maple
H. 39 3/4 in., W. 8 1/2 in.,
DIAM. 1 3/4 in.

45

57. DOG WITH LONG EARS
Late 19th–early 20th century
Painted wood, 1 in. metal
ferrule with metal tip
H. 36 3/4 in., W. 3 in.,
DIAM. 2 1/4 in.

Right:
58. DOG WITH COLLAR*
Probably the "Bally carver"
Pennsylvania German
Berks County, Pennsylvania
Late 19th–early 20th century
Varnished maple
H. 38 1/2 in., W. 5 in.,
DIAM. 1 in.

59. DOG'S HEAD WITH
NAIL DECORATION*
"Schtockschnitzler"
Simmons (act. 1870–1910)
Pennsylvania German
Berks County, Pennsylvania
Late 19th–early 20th century
Shellacked wood (maple?), nails
H. 34 1/2 in., W. 4 3/4 in.,
DIAM. 1 in.

60. DOG WITH HEART-
SHAPED EARS*
"Schtockschnitzler"
Simmons (act. 1870–1910)
Pennsylvania German
Berks County, Pennsylvania
Late 19th–early 20th century
Shellacked wood (dogwood?)
H. 37 in., W. 3 1/4 in., DIAM. 1 1/4 in.

61. BLACK DOG*
Ohio(?)
Probably late 19th–early 20th
century
Painted vine (or maple
sapling?), 3/4 in. brass ferrule
H. 34 in., W. 5 1/2 in.,
DIAM. 1 1/2 in.

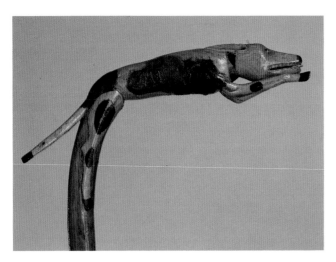

62. SPOTTED RUNNING DOG*
Probably 20th century
Varnished polychromed maple
H. 36 1/4 in., W. 7 1/8 in.,
DIAM. 3/4 in.

63. RUNNING DOG*
Probably 20th century
Varnished polychromed
wood, leather, nails
H. 37 1/4 in., W. 6 in.,
DIAM. 1 1/2 in.

Right:
64. DOG WITH LONG SNOUT*
Probably 20th century
Polychromed wood, glass,
abalone shell, probably
oilcloth, nail eyes
H. 32 3/4 in., W. 5 in.,
DIAM. 1 5/8 in.

65. DOG WITH EYEBROWS*
Λ. K. (owner/maker?)
20th century
Varnished maple or gum,
1 1/8 in. metal ferrule
H. 36 in., W. 5 in.,
DIAM. 1 3/8 in.

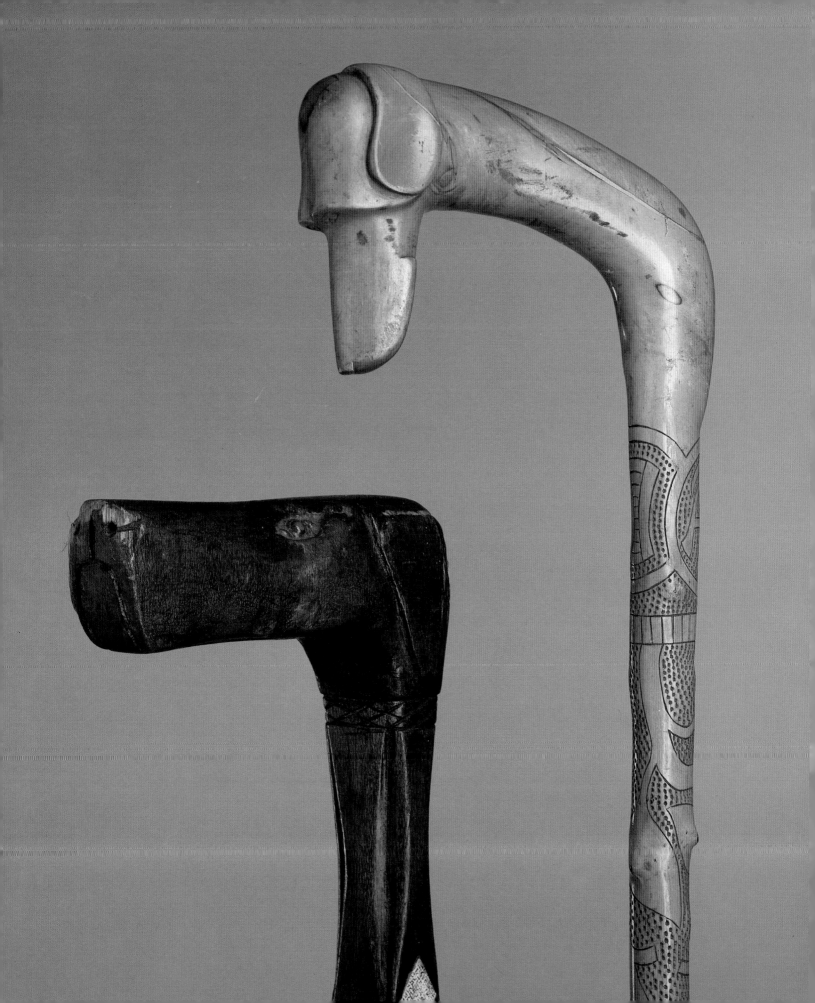

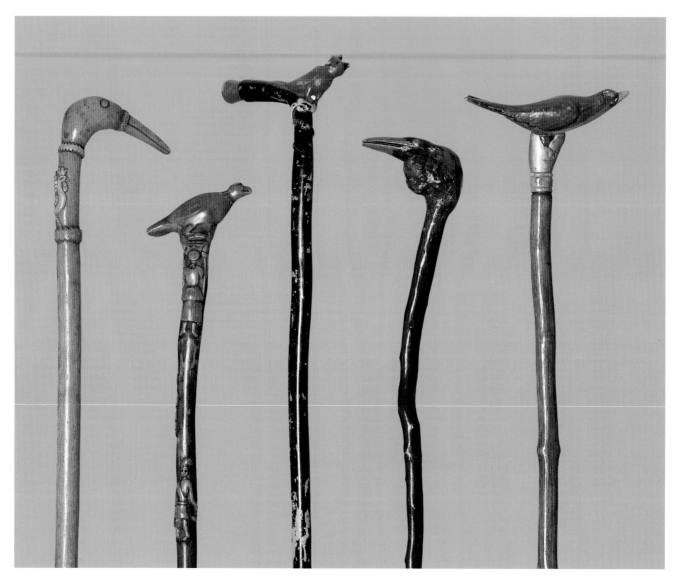

66. DUCK HEAD*
Probably "Schtockschnitzler"
Simmons (act. 1870–1910)
Pennsylvania German
Berks County, Pennsylvania
Late 19th–early 20th century
Varnished wood, 1¼ in.
brass ferrule with steel tip
H. 36½ in., w. 4⅞ in.,
DIAM. 1 in.

67. EAGLE AND WOMAN*
19th century
Varnished stained maple,
⅞ in. brass ferrule
H. 35 in., w. 4½ in.,
DIAM. 1⅛ in.

68. RED OWL HOLDING PREY*
J. L. (owner/maker?)
Probably Pennsylvania
Dated 1884
Polychromed wood, ¾ in.
steel thimble ferrule
H. 36 in., w. 6 in.,
DIAM. ¾ in.

69. BIRD HEAD*
Probably Michigan
Last quarter 19th century
Varnished painted wood,
metal eyes, ⅜ in. steel
plumbing bushing ferrule
H. 31 in., w. 4¼ in.,
DIAM. ⅞ in.

70. ROBIN
Pennsylvania(?)
Late 19th–early 20th century
Polychromed wood, 1¼ in.
brass ferrule with steel tip
H. 35 in., w. 6½ in.,
DIAM. ⅞ in.

71. BIRD IN HAND
Probably North Carolina
Ca. 1900
Varnished painted white
pine, glass eyes, ⁷/₈ in. brass
ferrule with steel tip
H. 31¼ in., W. 4 in.,
DIAM. 3 in.

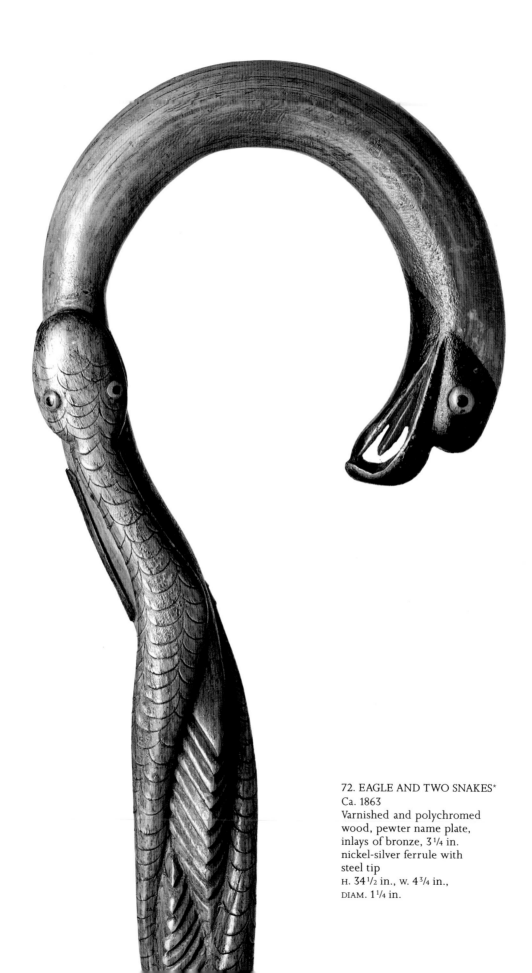

72. EAGLE AND TWO SNAKES*
Ca. 1863
Varnished and polychromed
wood, pewter name plate,
inlays of bronze, 3¼ in.
nickel-silver ferrule with
steel tip
H. 34½ in., W. 4¾ in.,
DIAM. 1¼ in.

73. EAGLE HEAD
Probably Lancaster County,
Pennsylvania
Probably second half 19th
century
Varnished polychromed
wood, nail(?) eyes, 1 5/8 in.
nickel-silver ferrule with
steel tip
H. 35 3/4 in., W. 3 1/4 in.,
DIAM. 1 1/4 in.

74. EAGLE EATING SNAKE*
(Child's cane)
Probably Berks County,
Pennsylvania
Varnished wood, probably
beech
H. 19 1/2 in., W. 1 1/4 in.,
DIAM. 7/8 in.

75. EAGLE*
John Bellamy(?) (1836–1914)
Active in Kittery, New
Hampshire
Probably New Hampshire or
Maine
Late 19th–early 20th century
Varnished wood (shrub?)
H. 36 in., W. 5 3/4 in.,
DIAM. 7/8 in.

Above:
76. RESTING LION*
Probably Berks County,
Pennsylvania
Probably second half 19th
century
Maple
H. 36½ in., w. 3⅞ in.,
DIAM. 1¼ in.

Right:
77. MONKEY HOLDING A STICK*
African-American(?)
Third quarter 19th century
Polychromed wood,
probably maple
H. 37¼ in., DIAM. 1⅜ in.

78. MONKEY WITH GLASS EYES*
Probably Pennsylvania
Ca. 1890
Polychromed maple, glass eyes
H. 33½ in., DIAM. 2 in.

79. LONG-TAILED BIRD
AND ANIMALS*
Probably late 19th–early 20th
century
Varnished polychromed
wood, nail eyes, 2 in. copper
ferrule with steel tip
H. 34½ in., w. 6 in.,
DIAM. 1 in.

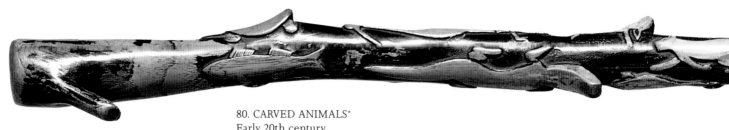

80. CARVED ANIMALS*
Early 20th century
Varnished painted wood,
1/2 in. metal ferrule
H. 34 1/2 in., w. 1 3/4 in.,
DIAM. 1 1/4 in.

81. NOAH'S ARK*
Probably third quarter 19th century
Varnished, stained, and polychromed
wood, probably honey locust, metal
plate, 1 3/8 in. brass ferrule
H. 35 3/4 in., DIAM. 1 1/2 in.

82. DINOSAURS*
H. C.
Hampton, Iowa
Ca. 1920–30
Varnished basswood
H. 37 in., DIAM. 1 3/4 in.

83. ANIMAL BLOCKS*
Samuel Nicholson (1832–ca. 1890)
Brunswick County, Virginia
Dated 1856
Varnished stained maple,
5 in. brass ferrule with steel tip
H. 38 in., DIAM. 1 in.

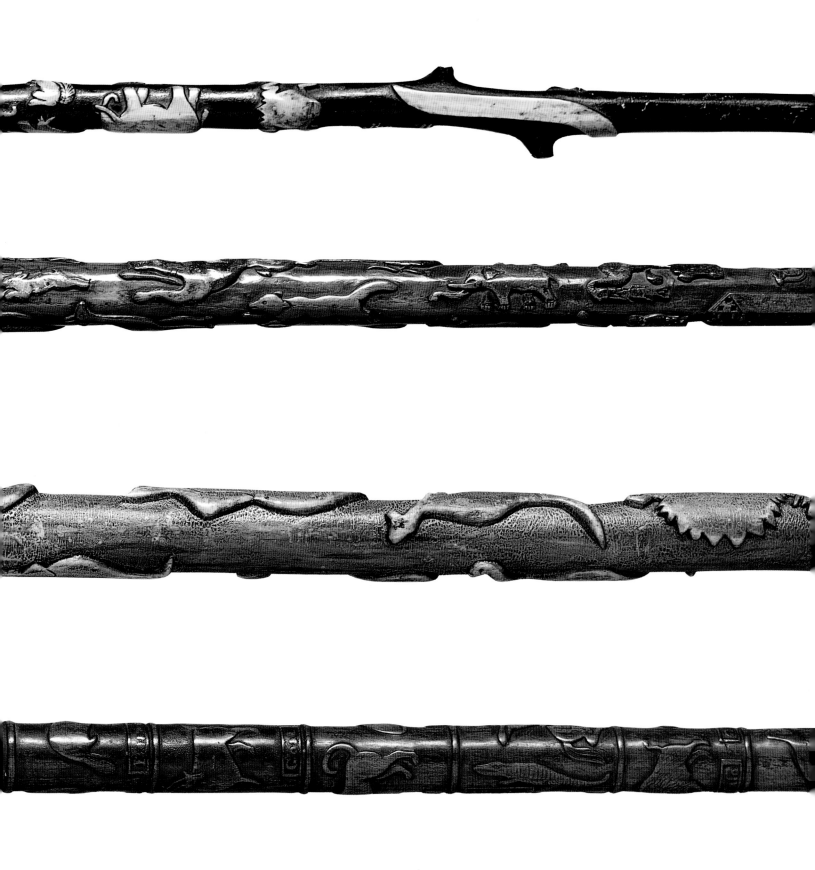

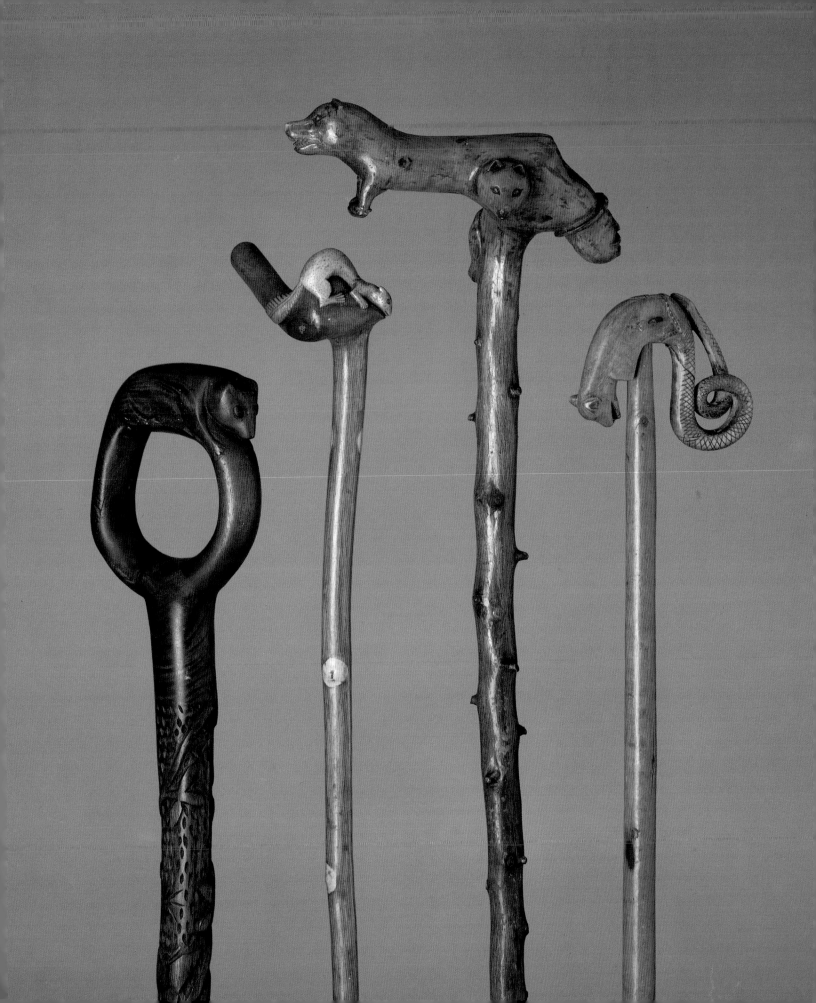

Left:

84. SQUIRREL ON OPEN HANDLE*
Last quarter 19th century
Stained wood, probably walnut
H. 36 1/2 in., W. 4 1/2 in.,
DIAM. 1 1/4 in.

85. SQUIRREL WITH FEATHERLIKE TAIL
Probably mid 20th century
Stained wood, probably maple
H. 38 in., W. 4 5/8 in.,
DIAM. 3 in.

86. FOUR-HEADED CANE*
Late 19th–early 20th century
Varnished stained fruitwood
H. 35 in., W. 8 3/4 in.,
DIAM. 4 7/8 in.

87. TWO-HEADED SNAKE SWALLOWING OPOSSUM*
Last quarter 19th century
Varnished wood, probably cherry (handle) and maple (shaft)
H. 40 3/4 in., W. 5 in.,
DIAM. 3/4 in.

88. DEER WITH LARGE EARS*
Probably Algonkian or Eastern Woodland Indian
Probably Maine
Last quarter 19th century
Polychromed hardwood, metal eyes, glass beads, 1/4 in. brass ferrule
H. 42 3/4 in., W. 5 1/4 in.,
DIAM. 1 1/4 in.

89. BURL OTTER OR MINK
Probably Native American
Probably 19th century
Stained wood, probably
maple burl, 4 1/2 in. brass
ferrule with lead tip
H. 34 in., W. 2 1/2 in.,
DIAM. 1 in.

90. OTTER
Probably Iroquois
18th century(?)
Painted maple
H. 39 in., W. 3 in.,
DIAM. 2 3/8 in.

60

91. PARROT AND ANIMALS*
Early 20th century
Hardwood with polychromed
galls, nail eyes
H. 40½ in., w. 2½ in.,
DIAM. 2¼ in.

92. RAVEN, BEAR,
THUNDERBIRD, AND
EAGLE*
Probably Kwakiutl or Haida
Probably early 20th century
Polychromed wood,
probably cedar
H. 36½ in., w. 1¾ in.,
DIAM. 1¼ in.

93. OCTOPUS SPIRIT IMAGE*
Probably Haida
Probably early 20th century
Stained wood, probably
cedar, inlays of shell, 1½ in.
metal cartridge case and
bullet ferrule
H. 34 in., DIAM. 2 in.

61

94. LION AND CATS*
New Jersey(?)
Late 19th–early 20th century
Varnished painted wood,
probably cherry, 1½ in.
metal ferrule
H. 36 in., DIAM. 2¾ in.

95. SPANIEL, BIRD,
AND DEER*
Pennsylvania
Second half 19th century
Painted wood
H. 36 1/2 in., W. 5 1/2 in.,
DIAM. 2 3/8 in.

Right:
96. SQUIRREL AND
GARDEN*
Late 19th century
Varnished stained cherry
H. 33 in., DIAM. 1 1/2 in.

97. VINE AND LEAVES*
Probably Pennsylvania or
New York
Probably third quarter 19th
century
Painted wood (walnut?)
H. 37 in., DIAM. 1 3/8 in.

98. ACORNS AND
OAK BRANCH*
Probably Pennsylvania
Probably third quarter 19th
century
Stained polychromed wood,
7/8 in. brass ferrule
H. 36 1/2 in., DIAM. 1 1/2 in.

99. SKULL, SCORPION,
MAGPIE, AND ALLIGATOR*
Kentucky(?)
Ca. 1900
Varnished polychromed wood,
probably cedar
H. 37 in., W. 2 in.,
DIAM. 1 5/8 in.

100. INSECTS AND
RATTLESNAKE*
Ca. 1890
Varnished polychromed
yellow poplar, 1 3/8 in. brass
ferrule with steel tip
H. 32 1/2 in., DIAM. 1 1/2 in.

101. SNAKES AND
BUTTERFLY MOTIFS*
(Child's cane)
Pennsylvania
Second half 19th century
Varnished polychromed
hickory
H. 27 in., W. 4 1/2 in.,
DIAM. 1 in.

65

THE HUMAN FORM

The human form has long been a favorite subject of sculptors, and American folk art cane carvers are no exception. Carved on walking sticks are full-length figures, busts, torsos, and heads, even hands and feet. Using a hand as a grip is relatively common, perhaps because a cane is grasped by the hand. Feet on the handle may gently mock the cane's function as an aid to walking.

Folk artists often carved heads on canes that were not only decorative but imaginative portraits—sometimes of the cane's owner. Cane carvers, in the same way as other good sculptors, captured the essence of the subject in the telling details of a rakish hat, a laughing mouth, or a melancholy expression.

With very rare exceptions, folk art canes were carved by men and consequently present a masculine point of view. Few female heads are carved as handles, and full-length figures of women are often portrayed in unflattering or uncomfortable poses. In scenes of Eve and the snake, for instance, the female form is depicted as a sex symbol, while a Chinese woman carved below a pickax handle seems almost a slave, possibly a prostitute. When fully clothed women are carved, they are often associated with farm chores or some other work.

Many pre–World War I canes reflect the attitudes of their time, expressing Victorian ideas about the nature of men and women and different races. Depictions of American Indians and African-Americans display the stereotypes of the era, just as portrayals of vintage bathing beauties and movie stars represent the ideal of glamour in the 1920s and 1930s. Similarly, contemporary canes celebrate such stars of today as Dolly Parton. Regardless of the period, a cane maker occasionally moves beyond stereotypes and shows the human form as beautiful in itself.

102. MAN STANDING
ON A BARREL*
19th century
Varnished stained hickory,
nail eyes, 3/4 in. brass ferrule
with lead tip
H. 36 1/2 in., DIAM. 1 1/8 in.

103. RECLINING NUDE*
Ca. 1930
Varnished polychromed
wood
H. 37 1/4 in., W. 9 3/4 in.,
DIAM. 3/4 in.

104. SUPINE MAN*
Late 19th century
Stained wood
H. 35 in., W. 8 in., DIAM. 1 in.

105. NUDE BENT
BACKWARD*
New York(?)
Late 19th–early 20th century
Varnished painted wood
H. 34½ in., W. 4¼ in.,
DIAM. 1⅜ in.

69

Left:
106. WOMAN AND MAN
ON FARM*
Probably North Carolina
First quarter 20th century
Stained, painted wood
H. 36 1/4 in., w. 1 5/8 in.,
DIAM. 1 1/4 in.

107. WOMAN WITH
SMALL FEET*
Early 20th century
Varnished wood, probably
birch, glass eyes
H. 33 1/2 in., DIAM. 1 3/8 in.

108. BATHING BEAUTIES*
Probably Pennsylvania
Ca. 1930–50
Polychromed wood,
probably birch
H. 32 in., w. 5 1/4 in.,
DIAM. 7/8 in.

109. HUMAN FIGURES
AND ANIMALS*
Early 20th century
Varnished painted maple,
ink
H. 35 in., DIAM. 1 5/8 in.

Right:
110. KNEELING MAN
AND BUTTON*
African-American
Probably California
20th century
Varnished, stained, and
polychromed sequoia, metal
button, coral bead eyes, 1 1/8 in.
metal ferrule, 3/4 in. nut and bolt
H. 33 in., w. 2 1/8 in., DIAM. 2 in.

111. WOMAN AND SNAKE*
Probably African-American
New York
Dated 1903
Varnished stained wood,
probably birch, abalone
shell(?) button, nail eyes,
1/2 in. brass ferrule with
steel screw tip
H. 33 1/2 in., DIAM. 2 in.

112. FIGURE OF A MAN*
Loganton, Pennsylvania
Dated May 1922
Varnished stained wood,
probably walnut
H. 35 1/2 in., DIAM. 1 1/8 in.

113. WOMAN AND PICKAX*
F. T. (owner/maker?)
Third quarter 19th century
Polychromed wood,
probably hickory (handle)
and cherry (shaft), nails, wire
H. 34 1/2 in., W. 9 1/4 in.,
DIAM. 1 1/2 in.

114. SAILOR*
Early 20th century
Varnished stained wood,
probably maple, 1/8 in. metal
ferrule
H. 31 1/2 in., DIAM. 1 in.

116. BANJO PLAYER*
Probably African-American
Probably southern U.S.
Probably second half 19th
century
Varnished polychromed
wood, probably maple, nail
eyes and buttons
H. 33 1/4 in., W. 3 1/2 in.,
DIAM. 7/8 in.

115. MAN WITH BOWLER HAT*
Early 20th century
Polychromed wood, 1 in.
steel ferrule with brass
washer
H. 34 1/8 in., DIAM. 3/4 in.

Left:
117. MAN BRAIDING
WOMAN'S HAIR*
E. M. (owner/maker?)
Pennsylvania(?)
Late 19th–early 20th century
Varnished wood, probably
maple
H. 36 in., W. 3 1/4 in.,
DIAM. 2 1/8 in.

118. WOMAN IN COFFIN*
Probably late 19th–early 20th
century
Varnished stained wood
H. 34 1/4 in., W. 3 in.,
DIAM. 3/4 in.

Right:
119. MAN AND WOMAN*
(Two views)
African-American
Georgia
First half 19th century
Polychromed hickory
H. 35 in., DIAM. 1 3/8 in.

120. CONTORTED MAN*
Late 19th century
Varnished polychromed
wood, glass eyes, 1 in.
copper alloy ferrule
H. 35 in., W. 5 1/4 in.,
DIAM. 3/4 in.

121. FOUR WRESTLERS*
Probably Buffalo, New York
Early 20th century
Varnished, stained, and
painted hardwood burl,
³/₄ in. steel ferrule
H. 43 in., w. 12¹/₂ in.,
DIAM. 1¹/₂ in.

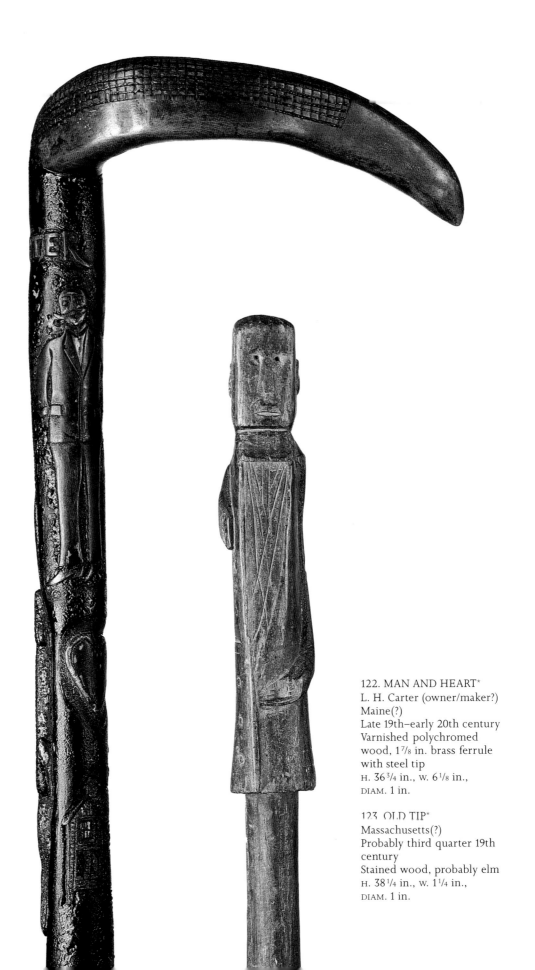

122. MAN AND HEART*
L. H. Carter (owner/maker?)
Maine(?)
Late 19th–early 20th century
Varnished polychromed
wood, 1⁷/₈ in. brass ferrule
with steel tip
H. 36³/₄ in., W. 6¹/₈ in.,
DIAM. 1 in.

123. OLD TIP*
Massachusetts(?)
Probably third quarter 19th
century
Stained wood, probably elm
H. 38¹/₄ in., W. 1¹/₄ in.,
DIAM. 1 in.

124. FIGUREHEAD AND
DRAGON*
Second or third quarter
19th century
Painted wood, probably
cherry (handle) and
varnished maple (shaft)
H. 32 in., W. 3 5/8 in.,
DIAM. 1 in.

125. SERPENT AND EVE*
Probably northern Indiana
Late 19th–early 20th century
Varnished polychromed
wood, probably maple,
1 3/8 in. copper ferrule
H. 37 1/2 in., DIAM. 1 3/4 in.

126. EVE AND THE SNAKE
20th century
Varnished polychromed
hardwood
H. 36 1/2 in., DIAM. 1 3/8 in.

Facing page:
127. UPSIDE-DOWN MAN*
19th century
Varnished stained willow(?),
nail eye
H. 51 in., W. 3 in., DIAM. 2¾ in.

128. SEVEN NUDES*
Ca. 1920–50
Stained hickory
H. 34¾ in., DIAM. 2 in.

Near left:
129. PENSIVE MAN
Late 19th–early 20th century
Varnished stained wood
H. 38½ in., DIAM. 2⅛ in.

130. HEAD WITH SIDEBURNS
AND GOATEE*
Ohio
Last quarter 19th century
Varnished polychromed
wood
H. 35 in., W. 3 in., DIAM. 1 in.

131. OVERSIZED HEAD
WITH SIDEBURNS AND
GOATEE*
Ohio
Last quarter 19th century
Varnished polychromed
willow
H. 38½ in., W. 4 in.,
DIAM. 3¼ in.

82

132. MAN WITH LONG BEARD*
Probably California
Late 19th–early 20th century
Varnished painted wood,
ink, bead eyes, nail teeth,
metal collar, ¹/₂ in. metal
ferrule
H. 39¹/₄ in., w. 3¹/₂ in.,
DIAM. 1 in.

133. MAN WITH LACE COLLAR*
Pennsylvania(?)
Probably late 19th–early 20th century
Varnished wood, ³/₄ in. thimble ferrule
H. 28 ¹/₂ in., w. 2 in., DIAM. 1¹/₂ in.

134. MAN WITH PARTED HAIR*
Probably New York
Ca. 1900
Varnished stained cherry
H. 36 in., w. 2 in., DIAM. 1³/₄ in.

135. MAN WITH FLAT NOSE*
First half(?) 19th century
Varnished stained wood, silver collar,
1 in. nickel-silver ferrule
H. 32³/₄ in., w. 2 in., DIAM. 1³/₄ in.

136. MAN'S HEAD*
Probably 19th century
Varnished wood, white
composition repair
H. 36¹/₂ in., w. 2¹/₂ in., DIAM. 1⁵/₈ in.

137. HEAD OF INDIAN WOMAN*
Colorado(?)
Late 19th–early 20th century
Varnished painted walnut
H. 34¹/₄ in., w. 3 in., DIAM. 1³/₄ in.

138. MAN WITH HOOKED NOSE*
Connecticut(?)
Ca. 1850
Varnished maple, 1³/₄ in. iron ferrule
H. 35¹/₂ in., w. 2 in., DIAM. 1⁵/₈ in.

139. MAN WITH BLACK EYES*
Probably African-American
Southern U.S.(?)
Late 19th–early 20th century
Polychromed wood, bead eyes
H. 33¹/₂ in., w. 2¹/₂ in., DIAM. 2 in.

140. MAN WITH SHELL TEETH*
Pennsylvania(?)
Probably late 19th–early 20th century
Varnished painted wood, shell, ³/₄ in.
metal ferrule
H. 33 in., w. 2¹/₈ in., DIAM. 1³/₄ in.

**141. MAN WITH NAIL AND
LEATHER EYES***
S. S. Coleman
Fayette County, Kentucky
Ca. 1860–80
Painted hickory, nail and leather eyes
H. 41¹/₂ in., w. 3¹/₈ in., DIAM. 1¹/₈ in.

142. ABSTRACT HEAD*
Fred Wilson
African-American
Florida
Late 19th–early 20th century
Painted hickory
H. 36 1/2 in., DIAM. 1 1/2 in.

143. MAN WITH RED
MOUTH*
Virginia(?)
Probably second half 19th
century
Polychromed wood, 3/4 in.
metal ferrule
H. 40 in., W. 2 in.,
DIAM. 1 5/8 in.

144. PRIMITIVE HEAD*
African-American
Probably southern U.S.
Late 19th–early 20th century
Polychromed wood, metal
H. 37 in., DIAM. 1 3/4 in.

145. HEAD OF A
BLACK MAN
African-American(?)
Probably mid 19th century
Painted wood (cherry?)
H. 45 in., W. 2 3/4 in.,
DIAM. 1 3/4 in.

146. SKULL, SNAKE,
AND ANIMALS*
Probably mid 19th century
Varnished painted wood
H. 35³/₄ in., W. 2¹/₄ in.,
DIAM. 1¹/₂ in.

147. SKULL*
Oley Valley, Pennsylvania
Probably late 18th–early
19th century
Varnished painted wood
H. 35¹/₂ in., W. 2¹/₄ in.,
DIAM. 1¹/₄ in.

148. COMPASS AND
MANY HEADS*
Colorado(?)
Late 19th century
Varnished painted wood,
glass eyes, metal compass
H. 38 1/4 in., DIAM. 3 in.

149. CARNIVAL HEADS*
O. E. C. (owner/maker?)
Portland, Oregon
Ca. 1920–35
Varnished polychromed
birch, 1 1/2 in. rubber ferrule
H. 32 1/4 in., DIAM. 1 3/4 in.

150. TATTOOED MAN*
C. E. Smith (owner/maker?)
Probably Ohio
Late 19th–early 20th century
Varnished polychromed ash,
glass eyes, brass tacks,
plastic tag, rubber ferrule
H. 34 in., W. 2 3/4 in., DIAM. 2 in.

151. LARGE HEAD*
New York(?)
Late 19th–early 20th century
Polychromed wood (cherry?)
H. 39 1/4 in., DIAM. 7/8 in.

152. HEAD AND HEART
IN HAND*
Probably early 20th century
Varnished wood, pebble eyes
H. 36 in., W. 7 1/2 in.,
DIAM. 2 5/8 in.

153. MOUNTAIN MAN
WITH CIGAR
Probably North Carolina
Late 19th–early 20th century
Painted wood, nail eyes,
metal rods, 1 1/2 in. iron
ferrule
H. 36 1/2 in., W. 8 in.,
DIAM. 4 in.

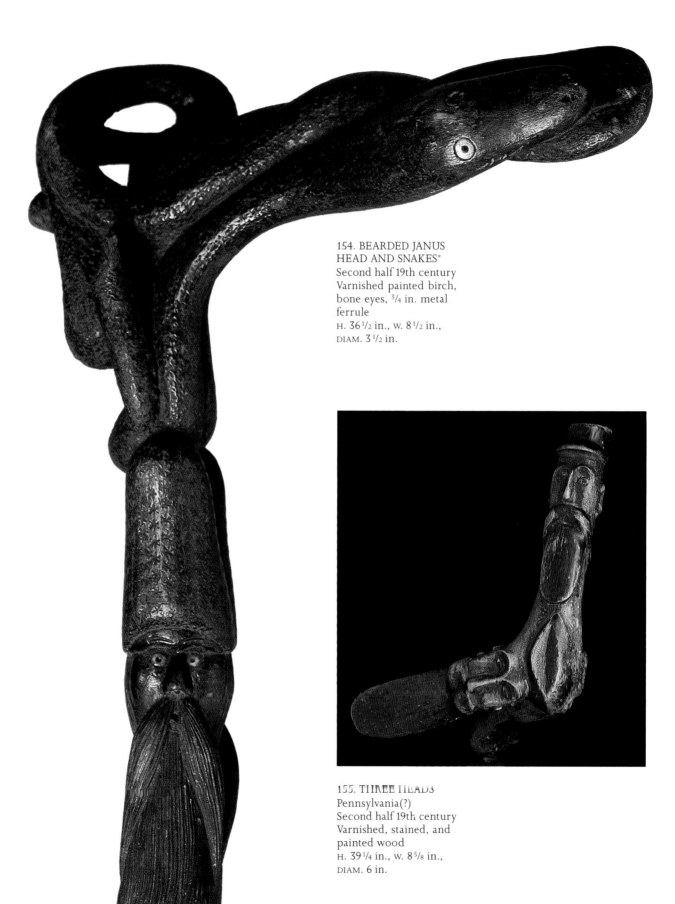

154. BEARDED JANUS
HEAD AND SNAKES*
Second half 19th century
Varnished painted birch,
bone eyes, ¾ in. metal
ferrule
H. 36½ in., W. 8½ in.,
DIAM. 3½ in.

155. THREE HEADS
Pennsylvania(?)
Second half 19th century
Varnished, stained, and
painted wood
H. 39¼ in., W. 8⅝ in.,
DIAM. 6 in.

Left:
156. BALD MAN
Probably Iroquois
Probably early to mid 19th
century
Painted maple, nail eyes
H. 36½ in., w. 6¾ in.,
DIAM. 3 in.

157. EAGLE AND TWO
GNOMES*
African-American(?)
Tennessee(?)
Probably late 19th century
Varnished painted wood,
tack eyes
H. 27 in., w. 6 in., DIAM. 3 in.

Right:
158. HEADS ON KNOBBY
SHAFT*
Probably Penobscot
Probably late 19th–
early 20th century
Varnished painted hickory,
glass eye
H. 39 in., w. 3⅞ in.,
DIAM. 3 in.

159. HEAD WITH
MIRRORED EYES
Western U.S.(?)
Probably 20th century
Burned redwood, mirrors
H. 35¼ in., w. 2½ in.,
DIAM. 2 in

160. MAN'S HEAD AND
MONKEYS*
Probably 20th century
Varnished basswood
H. 34 in., DIAM. 2 in.

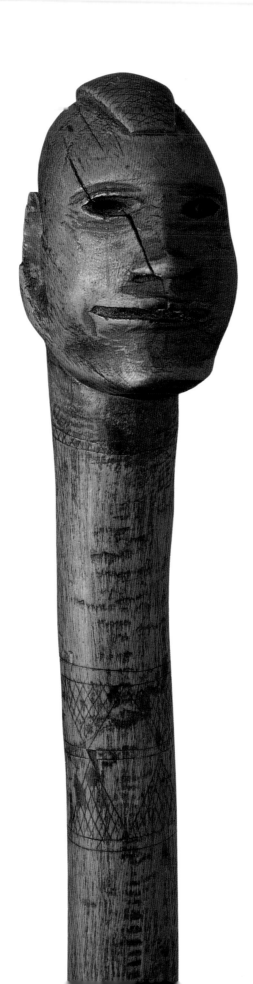

94

161. HEAD OF IROQUOIS MAN*
Probably Iroquois
Northeastern U.S.
19th century(?)
Varnished wood, ink, bead eye
H. 42 in., W. 1¼ in.,
DIAM. 1 in.

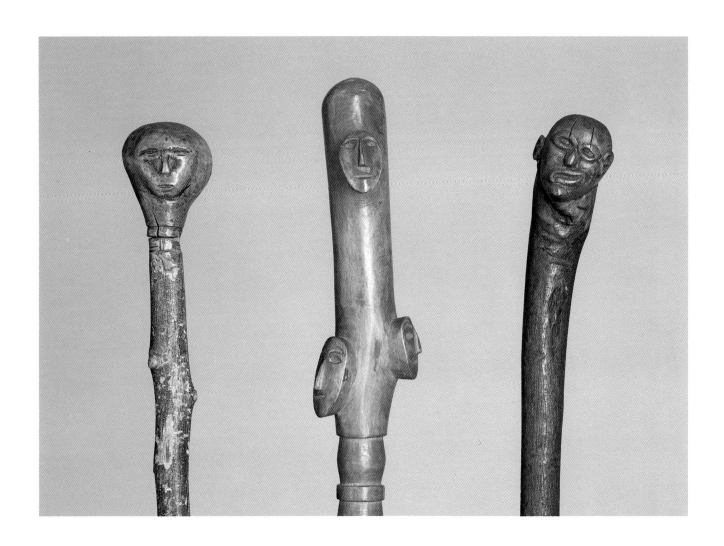

162. FACE IN BURL*
Iroquois
Northeastern U.S.
Probably 18th or 19th
century
Varnished hardwood with
burl handle
H. 30 1/4 in., DIAM. 1 7/8 in.

163. IROQUOIS FALSE FACES*
Probably Iroquois
Northeastern U.S.
(New York?)
Probably 20th century
Varnished stained wood
H. 36 in., DIAM. 2 1/4 in.

164. MAN WITH
TWISTED MOUTH
Probably Iroquois
Probably late 19th century
Varnished stained hickory
H. 34 1/4 in., w. 2 in.,
DIAM. 1 5/8 in.

Left:
165. MAN WITH PARROT
HEAD AND CANE*
Probably Iowa or Missouri
Dated 1881
Varnished, stained, and
painted wood
H. 35 3/4 in., W. 3 in.,
DIAM. 1 1/4 in.

Right:
166. MAN WITH CAP*
Late 19th century
Polychromed wood, 1/2 in.
iron ferrule
H. 36 1/2 in., DIAM. 2 in.

167. BUST OF MAN*
Illinois
Second half 19th century
Varnished painted willow,
copper collar, 2 in. metal
ferrule with small nails
H. 35 3/4 in., W. 2 1/4 in.,
DIAM. 2 in.

168. MAN AND RINGS*
Probably Pennsylvania
German
Probably Lancaster County,
Pennsylvania
Probably mid 19th century
Varnished polychromed
wood
H. 34 1/2 in., DIAM. 1 1/2 in.

169. MAN WITH HAT*
Kentucky
Ca. 1890–1900
Varnished stained hickory
H. 34 1/2 in., W. 2 in.,
DIAM. 1 1/2 in.

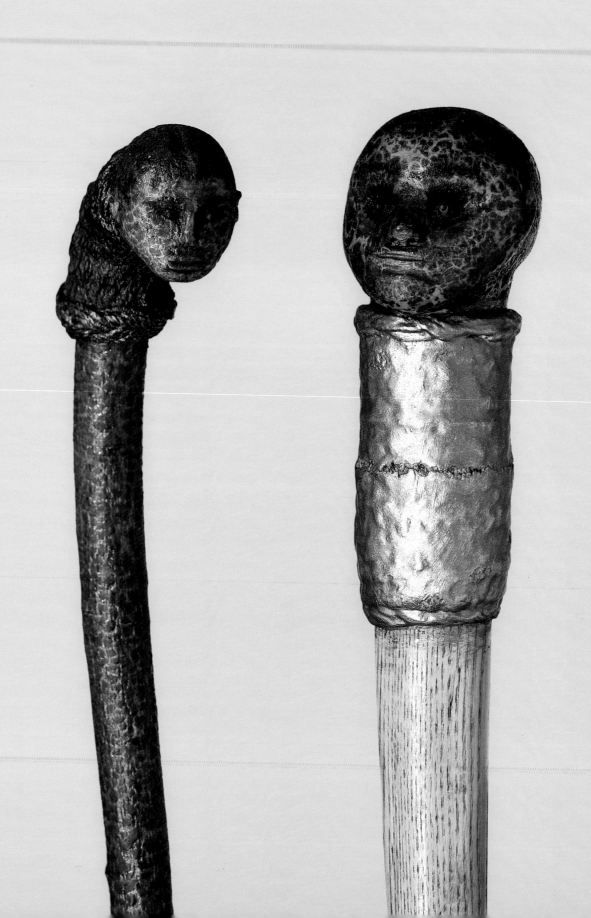

Left:
170. MAN'S HEAD WITH
ROPE COLLAR*
Maine
19th century
Varnished polychromed
wood, nail eyes, rope, 2 in.
brass tubing ferrule
H. 34¼ in., DIAM. ¾ in.

171. MAN'S HEAD WITH
GOLD ROPE COLLAR*
Maine
19th century
Varnished polychromed ash,
nail eyes, rope, 1¼ in. metal
ferrule
H. 37 in., W. 3 in., DIAM. 2 in.

Right:
172. CAPTAIN A. E. RAWLEY*
C. K. Willer(?)
Camden, Maine
19th century(?)
Varnished polychromed wood
H. 36¾ in., W. 2¾ in.,
DIAM. 2¼ in.

99

Left:
173. HAND HOLDING BALL*
Late 19th century
Varnished stained wood,
probably cherry
H. 36½ in., w. 2½ in.,
DIAM. 2¼ in.

Right:
174. HAND WITH BALL IN
CAGE MOTIFS*
Late 19th–early 20th century
Varnished stained yellow
poplar, ink
H. 36½ in., DIAM. 1⅞ in.

175. CUFFED HAND
HOLDING SNAKE
Late 19th–early 20th century
Varnished stained
hardwood, nail eyes
H. 35 in., DIAM. 1½ in.

101

176. CATLINITE HAND HOLDING BALL*
Sioux
Flandreau area, South Dakota
Last quarter 19th century
Varnished stained ash, catlinite,
bone collar
H. 34 in., DIAM. 1 1/2 in.

177. HAND GRASPING STICK*
Late 19th–early 20th century
Varnished stained maple, 1 3/8 in. brass
ferrule with steel tip
H. 35 in., W. 2 5/8 in., DIAM. 1 3/8 in.

178. HAND HOLDING OVAL BALL*
Iroquois
Probably late 19th century
Varnished, stained, and painted
white pine
H. 35 in., W. 2 1/8 in., DIAM. 1 1/4 in.

179. CUFFED HAND HOLDING BALL*
W. B. (owner/maker?)
Dated 1888
Varnished stained wood (ash?), 2 3/8 in.
steel ferrule
H. 35 1/4 in., W. 1 1/2 in., DIAM. 1 in.

180. HAND HOLDING LIBERTY TORCH*
Last quarter 19th century
Stained wood, probably maple, 1 1/4 in.
brass ferrule with steel tip
H. 43 in., W. 1 5/8 in., DIAM. 1 1/8 in.

181. CLOSED HAND*
Late 19th–early 20th century
Varnished stained mahogany and maple,
inlays of bone, mother-of-pearl, mica,
abalone shell, 1 1/4 in. nickel-silver ferrule
with steel tip
H. 34 in., W. 1 3/4 in., DIAM. 1 1/8 in.

182. VICTORIAN LADY'S
SHOE AND STOCKING
(Three views)
Late 19th century
Varnished wood, probably
maple, ink
H. 36¼ in., W. 5½ in.,
DIAM. 1½ in.

103

DAILY LIFE

The nineteenth-century Masonic gauge divided a day into three eight-hour parts for "work, sleep, and refreshment." This typical pattern of daily life is reflected in numerous folk art canes expressing fraternal membership, religious sentiment, vocational affiliation, recreational interest, and artistic appreciation. Walking sticks proudly proclaimed a man's allegiance to the Odd Fellows, his favorite Bible verse, his trade as a carpenter, or his enthusiasm for boxer "Gentleman Jim" Corbett. An owner could thus communicate and reaffirm his position in a community by displaying such widely recognized symbols on his cane. Moreover, in addition to parading his public persona, a cane owner often recorded unique, personal details on his walking stick, transforming it into a carved autobiography or diary. By commemorating episodes of a man's life—friendship, achievement, military service, retirement, domestic comfort—folk art canes act as three-dimensional documents of personal history.

183. FRATERNAL EMBLEMS*
Iowa(?)
Late 19th–early 20th century
Varnished painted wood,
1 1/2 in. copper alloy ferrule
H. 32 3/4 in., W. 1 7/8 in.,
DIAM. 1 3/4 in.

184. RAILROAD MAN*
Probably Iowa or Missouri
Ca. 1880
Varnished painted wood,
⁵/₈ in. copper ferrule
H. 36¹/₂ in., DIAM. 1¹/₂ in.

Right:
185. SHOEMAKER*
J. B. (owner/maker?)
Dated 1888
Varnished elm, leather,
steel screw
H. 35³/₄ in., W. 2¹/₂ in.,
DIAM. 1¹/₄ in.

186. FIREMEN*
New York City(?)
Late 19th century
Varnished painted wood,
ink, 2 in. copper alloy
ferrule with steel tip
H. 33³/₄ in., DIAM. 1¹/₂ in.

187. COAL MINER'S CANE*
African-American(?)
Probably Virginia or
West Virginia
Ca. 1900
Polychromed wood, glass
H. 34³/₄ in., DIAM. 2 in.

188. TINSMITH OR
CARPENTER'S CANE*
James Newhall
Iowa
Late 19th century
Varnished hickory or ash,
lead, tin, ¹/₂ in. lead ferrule
H. 36 in., DIAM. 1¹/₄ in.

189. FARM SCENE*
Michigan(?)
Late 19th century
Varnished, stained, and
polychromed wood,
probably hickory
H. 33 in., DIAM. 1 in.

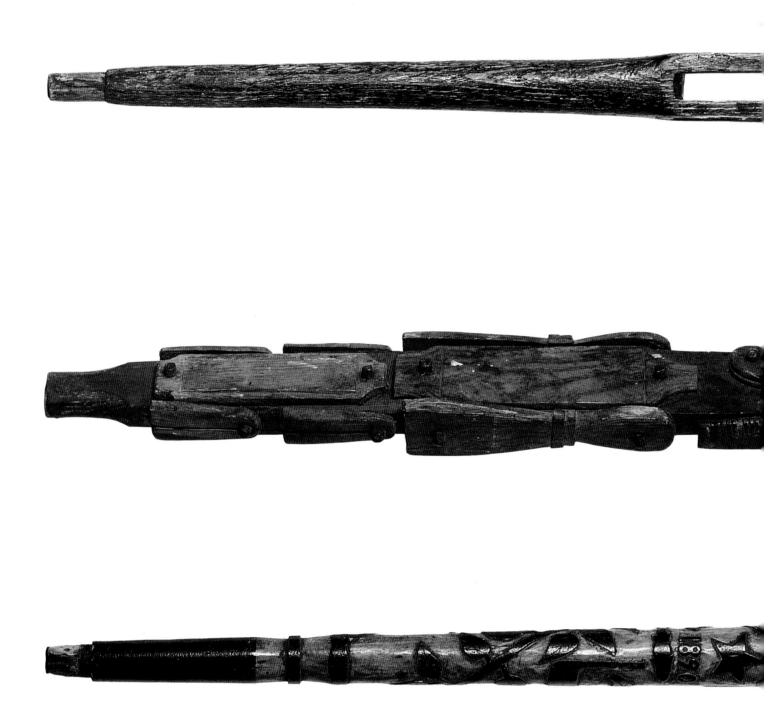

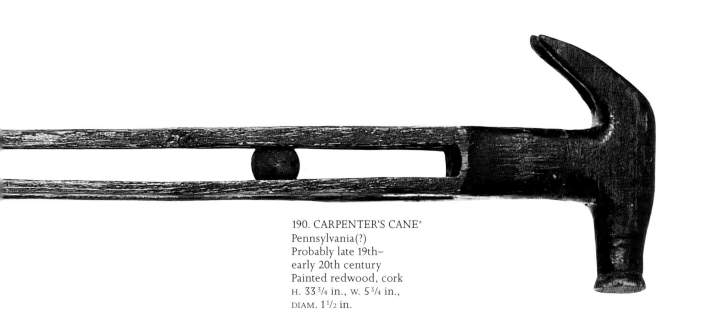

190. CARPENTER'S CANE*
Pennsylvania(?)
Probably late 19th–
early 20th century
Painted redwood, cork
H. 33 3/4 in., w. 5 3/4 in.,
DIAM. 1 1/2 in.

191. BARBER'S TOOLS*
Probably Nebraska
Early 20th century
Painted ash and pine,
wooden pegs
H. 34 1/4 in., w. 2 1/2 in.,
DIAM. 3/4 in.

192. RAILROAD TRAIN*
Minnesota or Ohio(?)
Dated 1890
Varnished painted wood
H. 36 3/4 in., DIAM. 1 3/4 in.

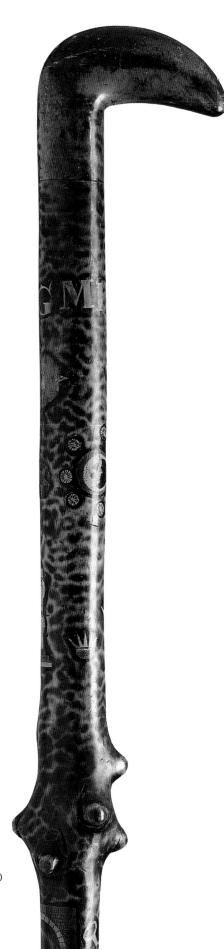

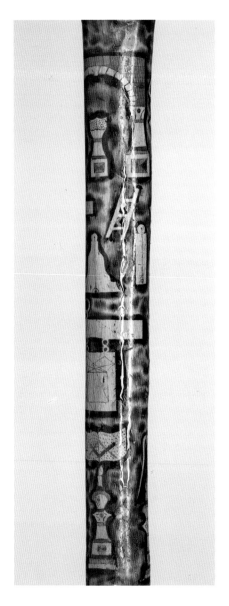

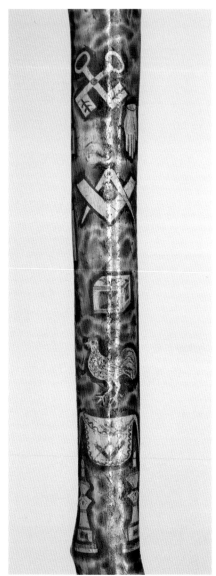

193. MASONIC CANE*
(Three views)
Probably early 19th century
Varnished polychromed
wood, ink, 1 3/8 in. steel
ferrule
H. 37 5/8 in., W. 3 1/2 in.,
DIAM. 1 1/8 in.

194. FRATERNAL MAN
WITH BEARD*
James A. Meli (b. 1854)
Moline, Michigan
Dated 1899
Varnished painted wood
H. 38 1/8 in., W. 2 1/8 in.,
DIAM. 1 3/8 in.

195. CANE OF
GOVERNOR CONE*
Florida
Ca. 1945
Varnished stained wood,
probably beech, 1 7/8 in.
copper alloy ferrule with
steel tip
H. 35 in., DIAM. 1 in.

196. BOXER/FRATERNAL
CANE*
African-American(?)
Probably Louisiana
Probably 20th century
Painted wood, 7/8 in. brass
ferrule
H. 35 in., W. 3 in., DIAM. 1 in.

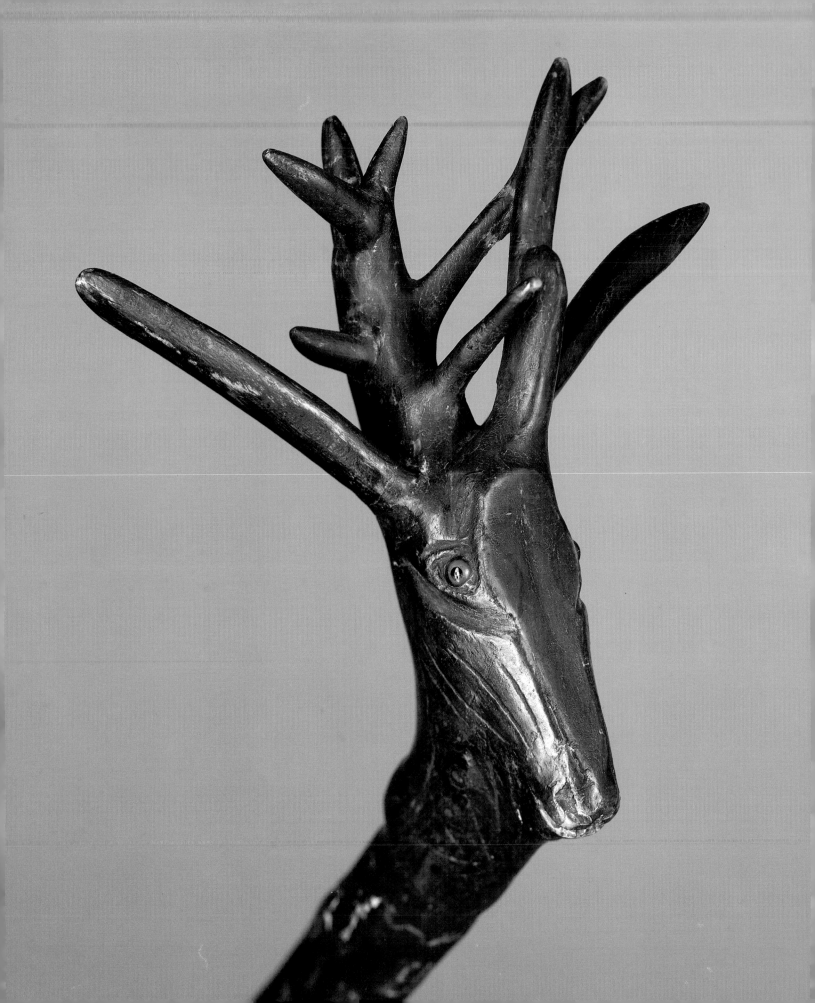

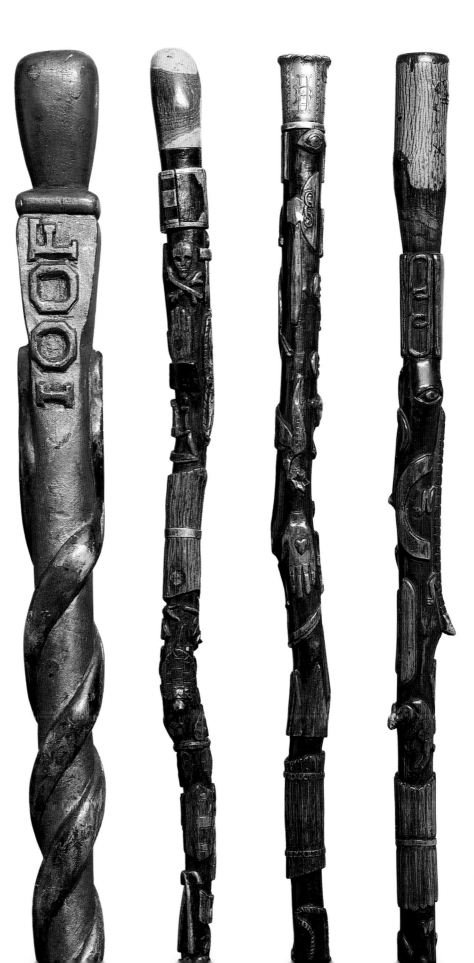

Left:

197. ELKS FRATERNAL CANE*
Philadelphia
Dated 1907
Varnished painted wood,
nails, glass taxidermic eyes
H. 35 1/2 in., DIAM. 6 in.

Right:

198. THREE INTERLOCKING
RINGS*
Probably first half 20th
century
Polychromed wood
H. 34 in., DIAM. 1 3/4 in.

199. ODD FELLOWS CANE*
Robert M. Foster (1830–after
1900)
Sparta, Missouri
Probably late 19th century
Varnished polychromed
wood, 5/8 in. lead ferrule
H. 35 1/2 in., w. 2 1/2 in.,
DIAM. 1 in.

200. DICK'S BREWING
COMPANY*
Quincy, Illinois
1880s
Varnished polychromed
wood, silver, 3/4 in. steel
ferrule
H. 34 1/2 in., DIAM. 1 1/4 in.

201. ODD FELLOWS PLAIN
HANDLE CANE*
Probably late 19th century
Varnished painted wood,
4 in. brass ferrule with
steel tip
H. 33 1/2 in., DIAM. 1 1/4 in.

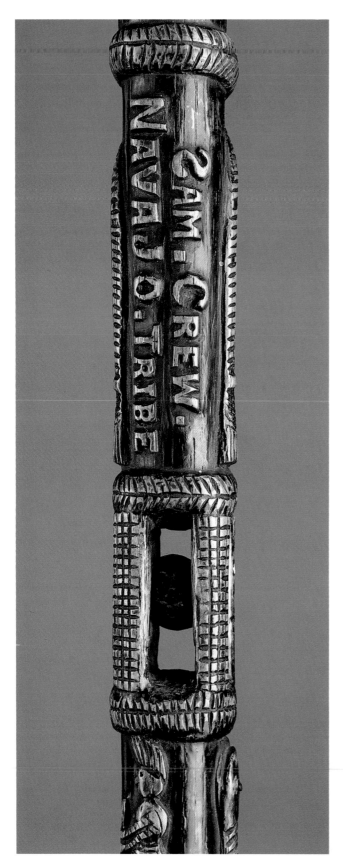

Left:
202. IMPROVED ORDER OF
RED MEN*
(Two views)
Sam Crew (owner/maker?)
Probably last quarter 19th
century
Varnished polychromed
wood, metal handle, 1³/₈ in.
steel ferrule
H. 37¹/₂ in., DIAM. 1³/₄ in.

Above:
203. WOMAN'S LEG AND
T.O.T.E. ANAGRAM*
Late 19th–early 20th century
Stained maple and mixed
woods, inlays of mother-of-
pearl, 2⁷/₈ in. brass ferrule
H. 34¹/₂ in., W. 4¹/₈ in.,
DIAM. 1 in.

Right:
204. INDIAN-HEAD CANE*
Late 19th century
Varnished wood, inlays of
mother-of-pearl
H. 35¹/₄ in., W. 1⁷/₈ in.,
DIAM. ⁷/₈ in.

115

205. MILL EXPERT*
(Three views)
George W. B. McKnight
(1839–1906)
Columbus, Georgia
Ca. 1890
Varnished wood
H. 37 in., W. 1 1/2 in.,
DIAM. 1 1/4 in.

116

Above:
206. UNITED AMERICAN
MECHANICS*
C. F. Snyder (owner/maker?)
Alburtis, Pennsylvania
Dated 1900
Wood
H. 39 1/2 in., DIAM. 1 3/8 in.

207. ODD FELLOWS
CEREMONIES*
(Three views)
W. A. Spotts (owner/maker?)
Harrisburg, Pennsylvania
Dated 1882
Varnished polychromed red
cedar, 5/8 in. steel ferrule
H. 37 in., W. 6 in., DIAM. 1 in.

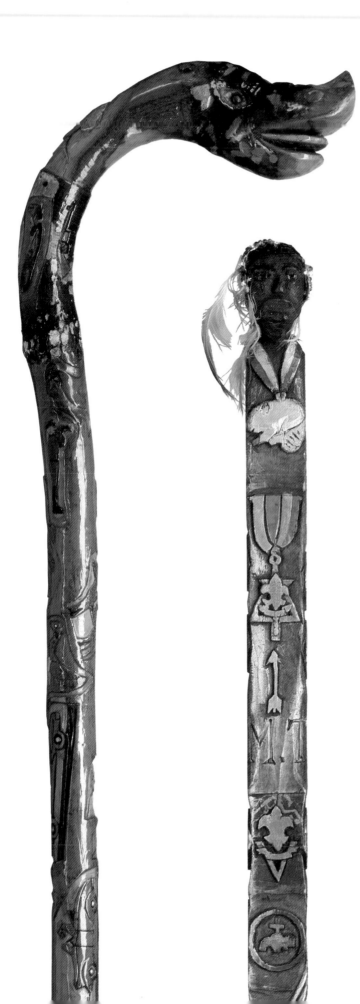

Overall views left:
208. FARM LIFE MEETS
MODERN LIFE*
Ca. 1940
Varnished polychromed
wood, nails, ⁷⁄₈ in. 12-gauge
shotgun shell ferrule
H. 36 in., W. 6¼ in.,
DIAM. 1¼ in.

209. BOY SCOUT CANE*
Edward M. Zopff
Detroit area
1934–61
Polychromed white pine,
feathers, beads
H. 36 in., DIAM. 1⅛ in.

210. LIFE IN A TOWN*
J. Y. K. (owner/maker?)
Ca. 1890
Varnished painted wood,
silver-plated brass, ⅝ in.
steel ferrule
H. 33¼ in., DIAM. 1⅛ in.

211. BIBLE STORIES*
(*Details left to right:* wicked children and bears, Daniel in the lions' den, Jonathan, David, and Moses in the wilderness)
Minnesota(?)
Late 19th century
Varnished maple, ink
H. 34 3/4 in., W. 3 3/4 in.,
DIAM. 1 in.

212. BIBLICAL ANIMALS*
(Two views)
Alanson Porter Dean
(1812–88)
New York
Dated 1884
Varnished American
boxwood(?), 3 in. nickel-
silver ferrule with steel
washer with screw
H. 35¼ in., w. 6 in.,
DIAM. 2 in.

213. THE EVILS OF DRINK*
(Details right)
Robert M. Foster (1830–
after 1900)
Sparta, Missouri
Late 19th century
Varnished polychromed
wood, ink, nails
H. 34 3/4 in., W. 3 1/2 in.,
DIAM. 1 in.

214. THE JOYS OF DRINK*
(*Details right*)
Probably Nantucket or
Martha's Vineyard,
Massachusetts
20th century
Varnished wood, 1³/₈ in.
brass ferrule
H. 37¹/₈ in., W. 4³/₈ in.,
DIAM. 2 in.

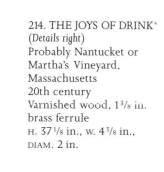

Left:
215. COMIC STRIP
CHARACTERS*
Ca. 1910
Varnished painted hickory,
ink, 1³/₈ in. brass ferrule
H. 36³/₄ in., W. 5¹/₈ in.,
DIAM. 1¹/₈ in.

216. FOUR FAMOUS
ACTRESSES*
E. P. Mares (owner/maker?)
Ca. 1925
Varnished polychromed elm
(handle stained), ink, ³/₄ in.
brass ferrule
H. 34¹/₄ in   DIAM. 1⁷/₈ in.

217. BATHING BEAUTIES*
Ca. 1940
Varnished polychromed
wood, photographs, ⁵/₈ in.
steel ferrule
H. 34 in., W. 5¹/₂ in.,
DIAM. 1 in.

Right:
218. KING KONG*
Leonard Taylor
Ca. 1940
Varnished painted wood,
glass eyes, 1⁷/₁₆ in. steel
ferrule
H. 36¹/₂ in., DIAM. 2¹/₄ in.

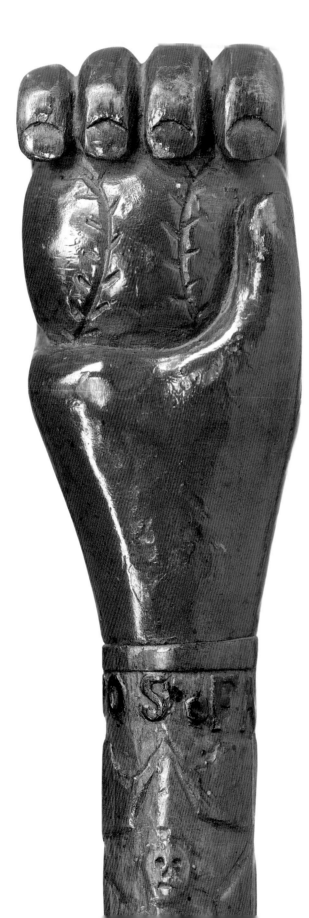

219. HAND HOLDING
BASEBALL*
C. Kocher (owner/maker?)
Probably last quarter 19th
century
Varnished polychromed
wood, probably cherry
(handle) and maple (shaft),
7/8 in. metal ferrule
H. 36 in., DIAM. 1 5/8 in.

220. TIGER AND BOXERS*
(*Detail above*)
Ca. 1897
Varnished stained maple
H. 30 1/2 in., w. 1 7/8 in.,
DIAM. 1 1/2 in.

**221. CORBETT-MITCHELL
FIGHT***
Ca. 1894
Varnished painted maple,
ink, 1 in. horn ferrule
H. 36 3/4 in., DIAM. 1 5/8 in

222. PACERS*
Ca. 1890–1900
Varnished stained wood,
ink, bone, 1 1/8 in. copper
ferrule
H. 35 in., DIAM 1 1/4 in

223. BIRD HEAD AND BOXER*
20th century
Varnished painted wood,
1 in. steel ferrule
H. 33 1/2 in., w. 3 1/2 in., DIAM. 2 1/4 in.

129

224. INTERLOCKING
PIECES*
Georgia(?)
Probably 20th century
Stained walnut
H. 35³/4 in., DIAM. 1¹/4 in.

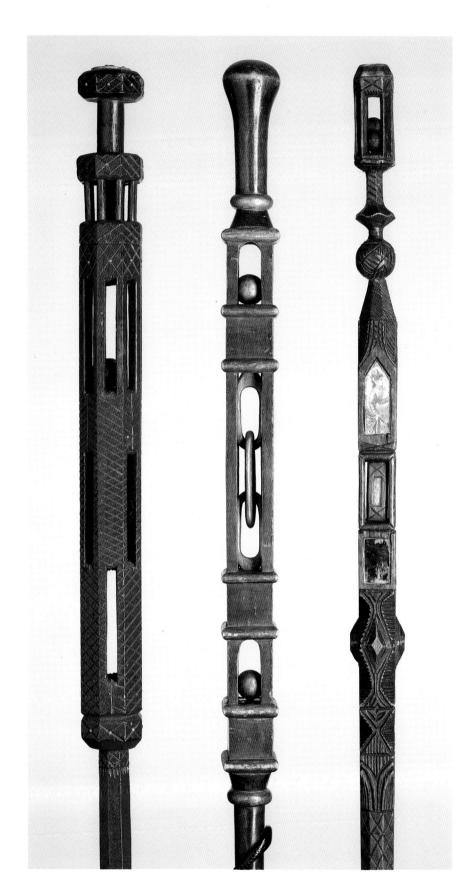

225. ELABORATE CAGES*
Amos Fisher (1857–1934)
Lancaster County,
Pennsylvania
Late 19th century
Painted softwood, button,
brass tacks, 2¾ in. steel
ferrule
H. 36½ in., DIAM. 2 in.

226. ELEGANT CAGES*
(?) Zaunheiser
Mercer, Pennsylvania
Last quarter 19th century
Varnished polychromed
pine, ⅝ in. brass ferrule
H. 36¾ in., DIAM. 1½ in.

227. VICTORIAN CANE*
Late 19th century
Varnished stained walnut,
lithographs, glass, mirrors,
hair or straw(?), 1⅜ in.
brass ferrule
H. 34½ in., DIAM. 1¾ in.

Top to bottom:
228. TENNESSEE CANE*
Beersheba Springs,
Tennessee
Probably early 20th century
Varnished stained walnut
or hickory
H. 35 3/4 in., DIAM. 1 1/8 in.

229. SIOUX CANE*
Sioux
Ca. 1870
Stained painted wood
(aspen or willow?), buffalo
horn, nails
H. 38 1/2 in., W. 5 1/2 in.,
DIAM. 1 5/8 in.

230. CANE WITH BASKET-
WEAVE DESIGN*
N. C. Woolley
Dated 1895
Stained painted maple
H. 37 in., W. 4 3/8 in.,
DIAM. 1 1/8 in.

231. CRAZY-QUILT CANE*
Probably Oklahoma
Ca. 1920–30
Wood, Bakelite, 1/2 in.
rubber tip
H. 36 3/4 in., DIAM. 1 1/2 in.

232. RED AND BROWN
SIOUX CANE*
Sioux
Pine Ridge, North Dakota
Dated 1885
Painted wood, probably
elm, ink
H. 40 3/4 in., W. 1 7/8 in.,
DIAM. 1 1/4 in.

233. ROPE TRIMMED CANE*
Probably last quarter 19th
century
Painted wood, hemp,
braided canvas, flat metal tip
H. 33 1/2 in., DIAM. 1 3/4 in.

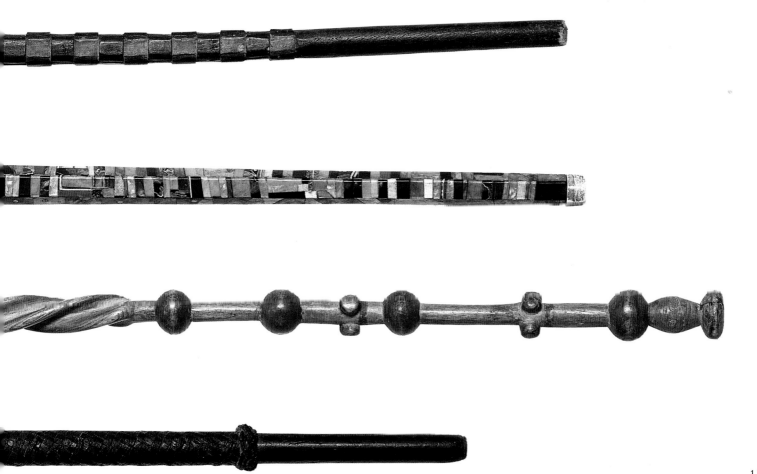

Politics, Patriotism, and the Military

Canes with political, patriotic, and military themes were especially popular during the late nineteenth and early twentieth centuries—a time of pronounced nationalism. Particularly in the 1880s and 1890s, men displayed their political beliefs on commercially made canes that they carried in campaign parades and rallies. Such canes were manufactured by the same companies that made campaign buttons and other political paraphernalia. A common presidential campaign cane featured a small white metal bust of the candidate on the handle. Folk art counterparts include elaborately carved canes for the 1896 campaign of the populist William Jennings Bryan against Republican William McKinley.

The flag, the Statue of Liberty, centennial exhibitions, and the Spanish-American War emerged in the late nineteenth century as themes celebrating America's national pride that were readily embraced by makers of folk art walking sticks. Canes that relate to the military, particularly those made during the post–Civil War years and the Spanish-American War, often combine political and patriotic motifs with symbols of the owner's membership in a veterans organization such as the Grand Army of the Republic.

The turn of the century also saw the worship of war heroes—Lincoln, Grant, Lee, Dewey, and Roosevelt—and cane makers often unabashedly idolized such champions on walking sticks. With later wars military subjects continued to appear on canes, but in the 1960s jingoism gave way to antiwar protest.

234. CIVIL WAR SOLDIER*
Probably J. B.
Probably New York
Last quarter 19th century
Varnished stained wood,
probably mahogany, metal,
³/₄ in. metal ferrule
H. 34 in., w. 3 ¹/₈ in.,
DIAM. 1 ³/₄ in.

235. SERPENT OF
REBELLION
(Three views)
Ca. 1861–62
Polychromed wood, 1⁷/₈ in.
metal ferrule
H. 38¹/₂ in., w. 3⁷/₈ in.,
DIAM. 1⁷/₈ in.

Left:
236. EAGLE, CANNON, AND
CORPS BADGES*
Probably third quarter 19th
century
Varnished, stained, and
polychromed maple, 1 1/8 in.
brass ferrule
H. 33 1/4 in., W. 1 5/8 in.,
DIAM. 1 in.

237. SOLDIER WITH FLAG*
H. Keller
Ohio
Probably last quarter 19th
century
Varnished wood, pewter,
2 3/4 in. metal ferrule
H. 33 in., DIAM. 1 5/8 in.

238. MAN WITH
SNAKE AT THROAT*
Massachusetts(?)
Last quarter 19th century
Varnished polychromed
wood, 3/4 in. iron ferrule
II. 33 in., W. 2 3/4 in.,
DIAM. 1 in.

Right:
239. HERO OF HATCHER'S RUN*
Probably Michigan or
New York
Probably 1864
Varnished wood, bone
H. 33 in., DIAM. 1 3/8 in.

240. WAR SCENE ON
EAGLE HEAD*
Probably last quarter 19th
century
Varnished painted maple,
3 1/2 in. brass sleeve ferrule
H. 34 3/4 in., W. 3 3/4 in.,
DIAM. 1 1/8 in.

139

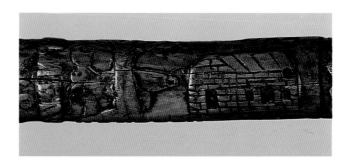

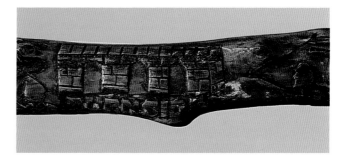

241. THE BATTLE OF
ANTIETAM*
(*Overall view above, details
top to bottom: Siege, Burnside
Bridge, Wounded*)
Probably Pennsylvania
Probably third quarter 19th
century
Varnished painted wood
H. 31 3/4 in., DIAM. 7/8 in.

242. HEAD OF A CIVIL WAR
SOLDIER*
1861–70
Varnished wood, metal,
7/8 in. brass ferrule
H. 38 in., W. 2 in.,
DIAM. 1 3/4 in.

141

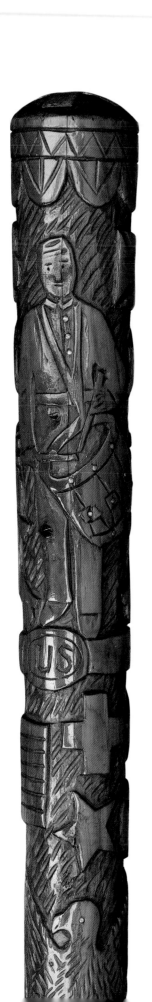

243. DRUMMER BOY*
(Two views)
Probably Pennsylvania
Late 19th–early 20th century
Varnished stained wood
(pine?), brass nails, 1¼ in.
brass ferrule
H. 36 in., DIAM. 1½ in.

142

244. LINCOLN AND GRANT*
(Two views)
Late 19th century
Varnished stained hickory,
ink, 1 in. brass ferrule
H. 33 1/4 in., W. 4 1/8 in.,
DIAM. 3/4 in.

Left:
245. ABRAHAM LINCOLN
AND SCHOOLHOUSE*
African-American(?)
Kentucky(?)
20th century
Walnut
H. 40 in., w. 2 1/2 in.,
DIAM. 2 in.

246. ABRAHAM LINCOLN*
(?) Maynard
Clarksville, Kentucky
Ca. 1920
Varnished stained wood, 1 1/8 in.
metal and plastic ferrule
H. 36 1/2 in., w. 2 1/2 in.,
DIAM. 2 in.

Right:
247. EAGLE HEAD AND
CARVINGS*
Late 19th–early 20th century
Varnished maple
H. 34 1/2 in., w. 4 3/4 in.,
DIAM. 1 in.

248. ALLIGATOR, EAGLE,
SOLDIER, AND SAILOR*
Late 19th–early 20th century
Varnished maple, 5/8 in. brass
ferrule
H. 35 in., w. 5 1/2 in.,
DIAM. 1 in.

249. ANTLER HANDLE,
EAGLE, SOLDIER, AND
SAILOR*
Late 19th–early 20th century
Varnished maple, bone,
5/8 in. metal ferrule
H. 34 in., w. 5 1/4 in.,
DIAM. 1 in.

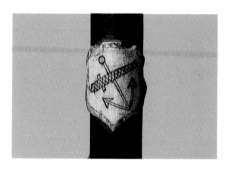
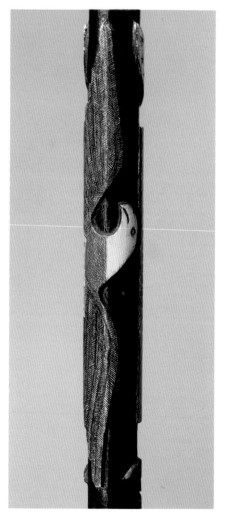
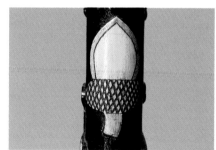

Left:

250. BIRD AND FLAG*
Late 19th century
Polychromed beech, brass
tack, 2¼ in. metal ferrule
H. 34½ in., w. 5⅝ in.,
DIAM. 1 in.

251. FLAG AND CORPS
BADGES*
New York(?)
Dated 1888
Varnished polychromed
basswood, brass button
H. 36½ in., DIAM. 1⅛ in.

252. EAGLE WITH
SPREAD WINGS*
(With three details)
Charles W. Teale (1817–95)
Bath, New York
Ca. 1870–95
Polychromed wood,
probably maple, ivory, stones
H. 34¼ in., DIAM. 1½ in.

Right:
253. FAVORITES OF
OUR NAVY*
(Two views and concealed knife)
Ca. 1900
Varnished maple, ink, 1¾ in.
metal shell ferrule
H. 35 in., DIAM. 1⅜ in.

254. WORLD WAR I CANE*
B. B. Wilmoth
West Virginia
Ca. 1917
Varnished wood, probably
maple
H. 37⅞ in., DIAM. 1⅞ in.

Top to bottom:
255. OUR HEROES*
Ca. 1900
Maple
H. 40 in., W. 1 3/8 in.,
DIAM. 1 1/8 in.

256. WILLIAM JENNINGS
BRYAN*
J. M.
Pennsylvania(?)
Dated 1896
Wood, probably maple
H. 37 1/2 in., W. 5 1/2 in.,
DIAM. 1 1/4 in.

257. WIFE OF WILLIAM
JENNINGS BRYAN*
J. M.
Pennsylvania(?)
1896
Wood, probably maple
H. 40 3/4 in., DIAM. 1 1/4 in.

Right:
261. ALPHABET CANE*
(Child's cane)
New York
Probably second half 19th
century
Polychromed wood
H. 19 3/4 in., W. 3 in.,
DIAM. 1 in.

258. WE TRUST*
Pennsylvania(?)
Dated 1896
Varnished painted wood
H. 37 in., W. 5 in., DIAM. 1¼ in.

259. HERO FOR FREE SILVER*
Pennsylvania(?)
Ca. 1896
Maple
H. 37 in., W. 6¼ in.,
DIAM. 1⅜ in.

260. CLAYTON C. ADAMS*
Lenhartsville, Pennsylvania
Probably second half 19th
century
Varnished stained wood
H. 40 in., W. 1¾ in.,
DIAM. 1½ in.

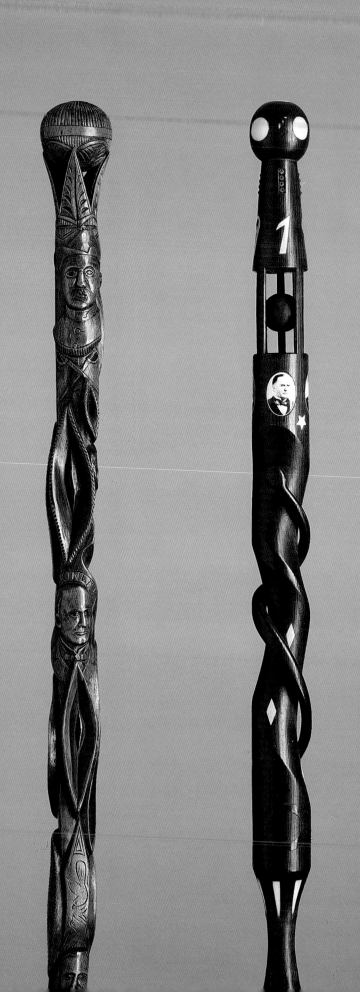

Left:
262. SPANISH-AMERICAN
WAR HEROES*
Ca. 1901
Varnished stained willow
H. 35 1/2 in., DIAM. 1 3/4 in.

263. TAFT CANE*
Dated 1909
Varnished stained wood,
inlays of wood, ivory,
mother-of-pearl, obsidian,
silver, and pewter,
lithographs, 1/8 in. steel tip
H. 36 in., DIAM. 1 1/2 in.

Above:
264. EQUALITY AND
COLUMBIA*
New Hampshire
Dated 1817
Varnished stained wood,
1 in. metal shell ferrule
H. 35 in., DIAM. 1 in.

265. CANE FROM NEAR
JEFFERSON'S TOMB*
Virginia
Late 19th–early 20th century
Varnished wood, 1 1/4 in.
metal ferrule
H. 36 1/2 in., DIAM. 1 3/8 in.

151

266. STATUE OF LIBERTY
AND EIFFEL TOWER*
(*Three views*)
E. Dasse
Dated 1890
Varnished polychromed
wood, probably maple, ink,
³/₈ in. metal ferrule
H. 32¹/₂ in., DIAM. 1¹/₄ in.

152

267. CONFUCIUS AND
WORLD'S FAIR*
(Two views)
Joel Peffley (1829–1917)
Colburn, Indiana
Dated 1893
Varnished painted cedar,
ink, metal, ³/₈ in. metal
ferrule
H. 37 in., W. 5 in.,
DIAM. 1⅞ in.

153

268. SNAKE, STARS,
AND RIFLES*
Probably midwestern U.S.
Late 19th–early 20th century
Varnished polychromed
wood, 4³/₄ in. metal ferrule
H. 34 in., W. 5³/₈ in.,
DIAM. 3³/₄ in.

269. BLEEDING SKULL*
Probably Indiana
Ca. 1964–81
Polychromed wood
H. 35³/₄ in., W. 6⁵/₈ in.,
DIAM. 3¹/₄ in.

Mike/Orion Canes

The twelve canes pictured here are by a carver who inscribed most of his works with the words "Mike" and "Orion." The two names, however, are never positioned clearly enough to determine their relationship or even whether they together form a man's name. Perhaps twenty Mike/Orion canes are known; also made by him are two carved wood axes with decorations similar to the symbols and words on the canes.

Canes appear to have been made by Mike/Orion from around the Civil War to at least 1902, the latest date on a cane. Most relate to specific locations in southern Michigan, several near the village of Orion. Beyond the likelihood that Mike/Orion lived and carved in this area, little is known about the artist. Nevertheless, his canes compose a known body of work.

Mike/Orion canes are made from the wood of diamond willow trees which has many openings and unusual shapes. Knobs, branches, and natural diamond-shaped formations are incorporated inventively, producing both negative space and forms that emphasize the twist and flow of the wood. Backgrounds are articulated with concentrated fine punch marks. Nearly all the canes have names, places, and dates, often pertaining to military service in the Civil War, carved in high relief and painted gold.

Handles are usually plain elongated knobs painted black and often have gold decorations—either stars or dabs of paint that seem to represent stars, perhaps the constellation Orion. (The same type of star appears on the two axes.) The canes' handcrafted lead ferrules generally have dentate edges.

In addition to the high-relief letters, common carved decorations are fish (often bass), herons, black horses, and rifles with bayonets. Turtles, lizards, and snakes sometimes appear. These carved animals usually face down the shaft and are painted black. Several canes contain a black trefoil corps badge.

Most of these walking sticks bear inscriptions stating that they were presented by Mike/Orion to a named person. A few have a blank diamond area in the wood where the name of the owner would generally be inscribed. This fact, along with the high degree of skill demonstrated in the carvings, points to the possibility that Mike/Orion may have been a professional carver. The supposition is reinforced by cane no. 270, which was carved by "Mike" for someone else to give to a third person.

Eventually the discovery of a cane, other carving, or document will identify this highly imaginative artist.

270. FROM D. YOUNG*
Mike/Orion
Michigan
Dated 1900
Varnished polychromed
willow, 1 in. lead ferrule
H. 34³/4 in., W. 2¹/8 in.,
DIAM. 1¹/2 in.

271. MAN'S FACE AND ANIMALS*
Mike/Orion
Michigan
Last quarter 19th century
Varnished, stained, and
polychromed willow, bead
eyes, 1 in. lead ferrule
attached with steel screw
and washer
H. 34³/4 in., DIAM. 3¹/8 in.

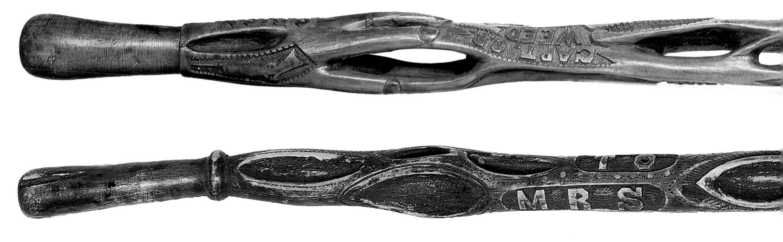

Top to bottom:
272. CAPTAIN O. B. WEED*
Mike/Orion
Michigan
Dated 1902
Polychromed willow, 2¼ in.
lead ferrule
H. 35 in., DIAM. 1¾ in.

273. MRS. S. A. WALTON*
Mike/Orion
Pontiac, Michigan
Last quarter 19th century
Varnished polychromed
willow, 1 in. lead ferrule
attached with metal screw
H. 33½ in., W. 1⅝ in.,
DIAM. 1¼ in.

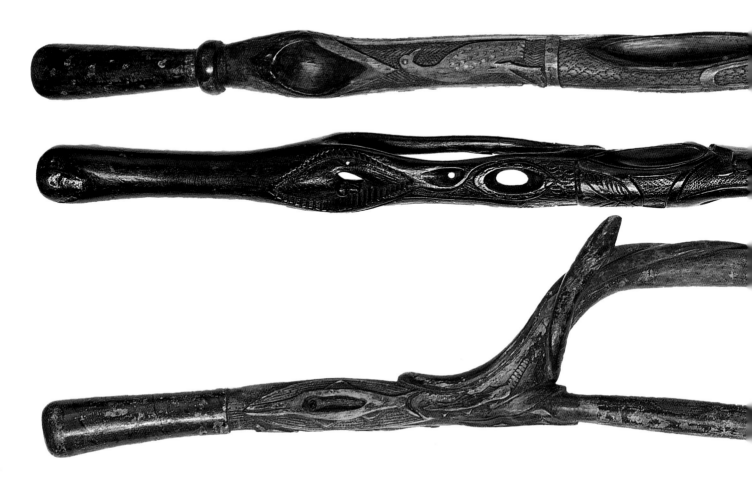

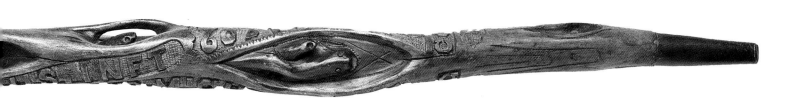

274. ADELBERT C. KELLEY*
Mike/Orion
Michigan
Last quarter 19th century
Varnished polychromed
willow, 1¼ in. lead ferrule
attached with screw
H. 35 in., W. 1⅞ in.,
DIAM. 1⅝ in.

**275. ANIMAL, SHIELD,
AND HORSE***
Mike/Orion
Michigan
Last quarter 19th century
Varnished polychromed
willow, 2 in. lead ferrule
with steel tip
H. 34½ in., W. 2 in.,
DIAM. 1¾ in.

276. FISH AND SNAKES*
Mike/Orion
Michigan
Last quarter 19th century
Polychromed willow, 1⅞ in.
lead ferrule
H. 34½ in., W. 5 in.,
DIAM. 1¼ in.

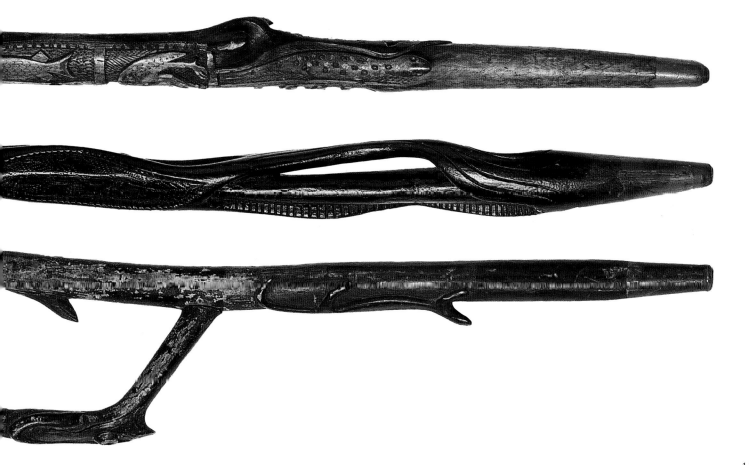

277. ELDRED MONTROSE*
Mike/Orion
Michigan
Last quarter 19th century
Polychromed willow, 1 in.
lead ferrule with steel tip
H. 34 in., W. 3 5/8 in.,
DIAM. 2 1/2 in.

278. HAND AND PIG*
Mike/Orion
Michigan
Last quarter 19th century
Varnished polychromed
willow, 1 1/2 in. lead ferrule
H. 34 1/2 in., W. 2 5/8 in.,
DIAM. 1 7/8 in.

279. ALVIN N. HALL*
(Overall view left, first two
details right)
Mike/Orion
Michigan
Last quarter 19th century
Varnished polychromed
willow, 1 1/2 in. lead ferrule
H. 35 in., W. 3 1/8 in.,
DIAM. 2 1/2 in.

280. TO MY FRIEND*
(Third detail right)
Mike/Orion
Michigan
Last quarter 19th century
Polychromed willow, 1 in.
lead ferrule with steel tip
H. 33 1/2 in., DIAM. 1 1/2 in.

281. MIKE*
(Fourth detail right)
Mike/Orion
Michigan
Ca. 1860–80
Varnished stained willow,
1/2 in. steel ferrule
H. 33 in., W. 4 1/2 in.,
DIAM. 1 1/2 in.

CONTEMPORARY CANES

Because the days of carrying a cane as part of one's attire are gone, contemporary canes are often made primarily as works of art rather than utilitarian objects. Contrary to earlier practice, many are created for—and sold to—the general art market rather than a specific person.

Contemporary canes, considered here, with two exceptions, to be those made after 1970, reflect the popular culture and interests of the day, just as their counterparts did in the past. (Elvis Presley has replaced William Jennings Bryan as the figure on the handle.) Stylistically, recent walking sticks tend to be larger, bolder, and more brightly colored, with fewer details than period examples. Today's carvers play with form more freely and use modern materials imaginatively. Nevertheless, the same sensibilities and aesthetics used to judge a period walking stick as art should be used to decide the artistic value of a contemporary cane: in each case the essential question is whether the cane challenges the viewer to respond. Contemporary canes do have one distinct advantage. Because we often know the carver's identity and recognize modern symbolism more readily than historic images, we are more likely to understand the artist's intent.

282. WOMEN IN BIKINIS
Denzil Goodpaster (b. 1908)
Deniston, Kentucky
1982
Polychromed wood
H. 38 in., w. 7 1/8 in.,
DIAM. 2 1/8 in.

283. MAN ON HORSEBACK*
Henry York (b. 1913)
Kentucky
1983
Clear-finished red cedar,
bead eyes, copper wire,
string, marbles, shell
H. 41 in., W. 10 in., DIAM. 2½ in.

284. DOG WITH MOVABLE
TONGUE*
Procton Cathart
Massachusetts
Ca. 1970
Polychromed wood, glass
eyes, metal spring
H. 33 in., W. 5¾ in.,
DIAM. 1¾ in.

165

285. MAN WITH TURBAN*
Luster Willis (1913–90)
African-American
Crystal Springs, Mississippi
Ca. 1983
Cedar
H. 41 1/2 in., DIAM. 2 1/4 in.

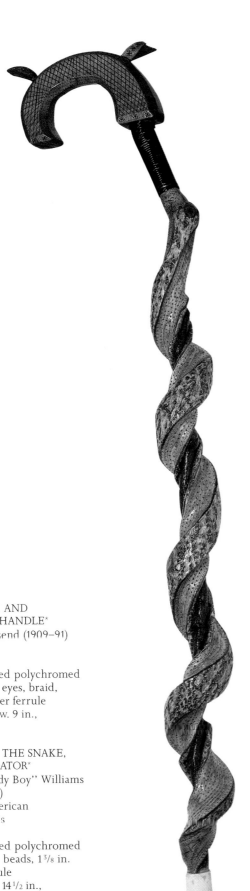

286. SNAKE AND
ABSTRACT HANDLE*
Parks Townsend (1909–91)
Tennessee
Ca. 1985
Clear-finished polychromed
wood, glass eyes, braid,
1 1/4 in. rubber ferrule
H. 37 1/2 in., w. 9 in.,
DIAM. 3 1/4 in.

287. "EVE," THE SNAKE,
AND ALLIGATOR*
Hugh "Daddy Boy" Williams
(ca. 1919–88)
African-American
New Orleans
1982
Clear-finished polychromed
wood, glass beads, 1 3/8 in.
rubber ferrule
H. 42 in., w. 14 1/2 in.,
DIAM. 2 1/2 in.

167

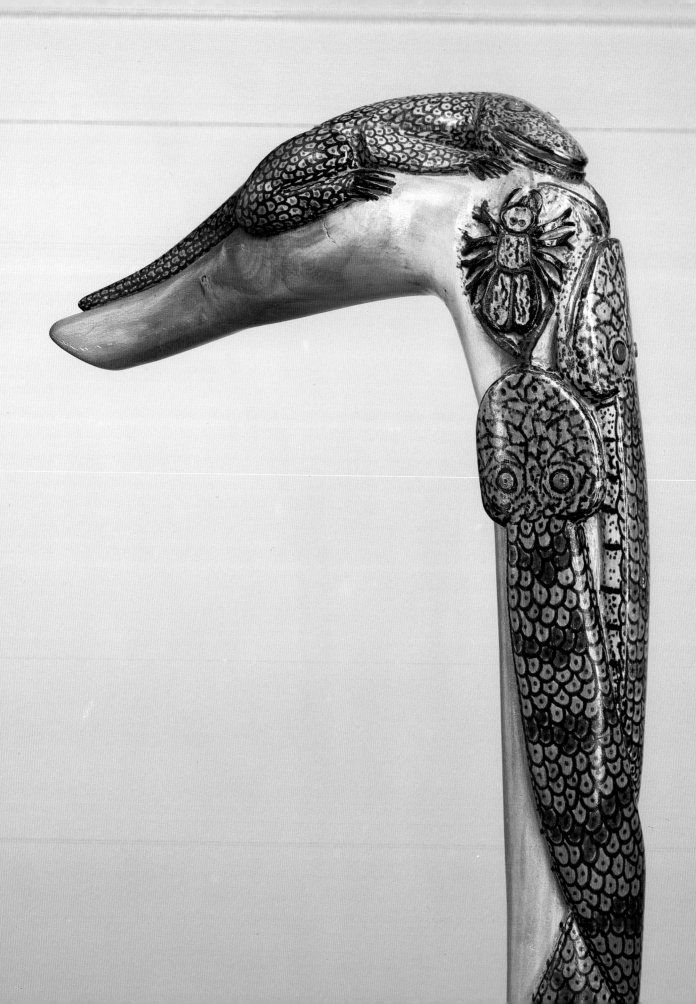

288. ALLIGATOR, TWO
RATTLESNAKES, AND
SPIDER*
Ben Miller (b. 1917)
Breathitt County, Kentucky
1982
Clear-finished polychromed
wood, marker, bead eyes,
1 in. rubber ferrule
H. 37 in., W. 9 1/4 in.,
DIAM. 1 7/8 in.

289. THREE RATTLESNAKES
AND WORM
Ben Miller (b. 1917)
Breathitt County, Kentucky
1989
Clear-finished wood,
marker, bead eyes
H. 37 1/2 in., W. 12 in.,
DIAM. 6 in.

169

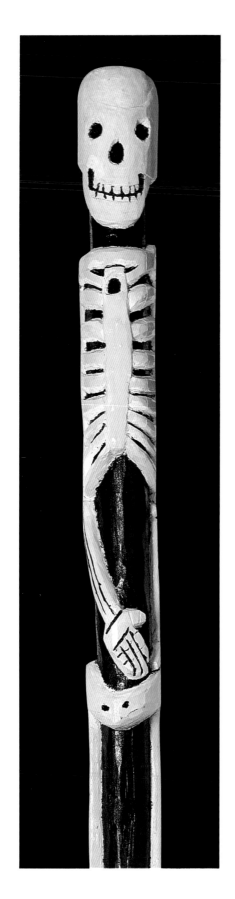

170

Left:
290. SKELETON*
Larry McKee (b. 1941)
Kentucky
1988
Polychromed wood
H. 40³/₄ in., DIAM. 2¹/₂ in.

291. STACKED SKULLS*
Duane Spencer (b. 1946)
Allentown, Pennsylvania
1985
Painted wood
H. 36 in., DIAM. 2¹/₂ in.

292. LAMP POLE CANE WITH HEAD*
"Stick Dog Bob"
African-American
Chicago
Ca. 1960–70
Polychromed composite material,
lamp pole, imitation gems, cork
H. 36½ in., W. 2¼ in., DIAM. 2 in.

171

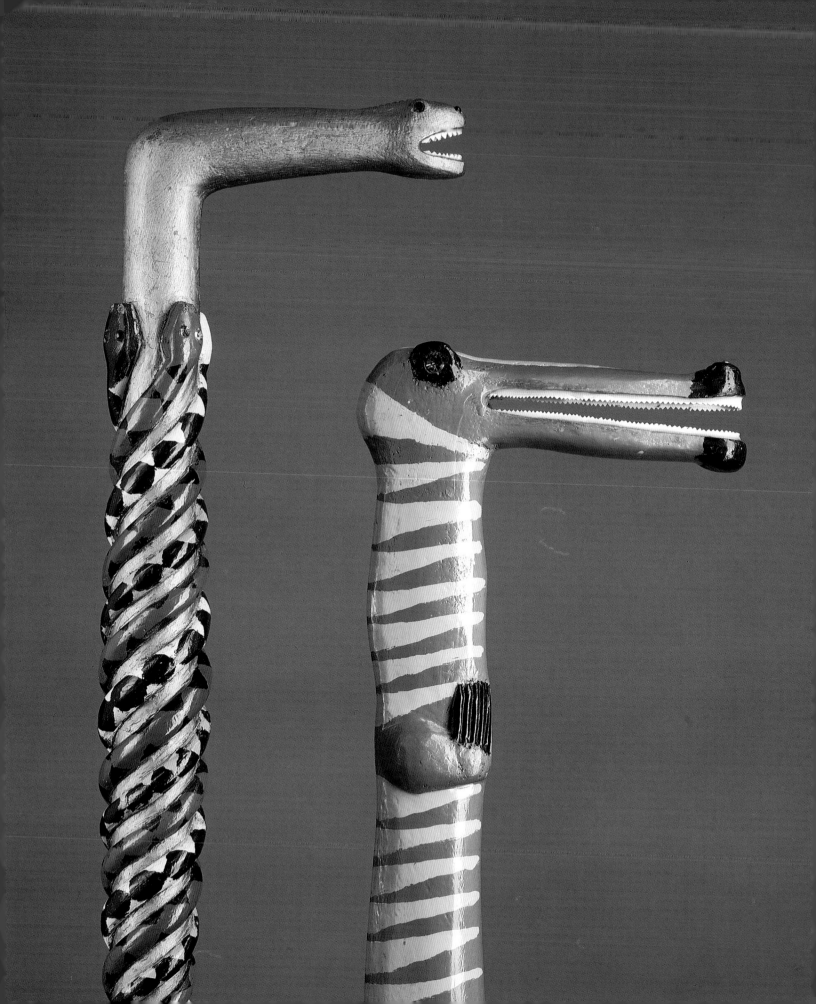

Left:
293. EIGHT SNAKES
CLIMBING ONE SNAKE*
Denzil Goodpaster (b. 1908)
Deniston, Kentucky
1981
Polychromed wood, glass
jewels, beads, plastic
H. 36 1/2 in., W. 7 in.,
DIAM. 2 in.

294. ALLIGATOR WITH
BLUE EYES
Denzil Goodpaster (b. 1908)
Deniston, Kentucky
1981
Polychromed wood, glass
jewels, beads, plastic
H. 34 in., W. 7 in., DIAM. 2 in.

Right:
295. MAN AND SADDLE*
African-American(?)
Second half 20th century
Maple, basswood, and
mixed woods, glass eyes
H. 35 1/4 in., W. 8 3/4 in.,
DIAM. 2 1/4 in.

173

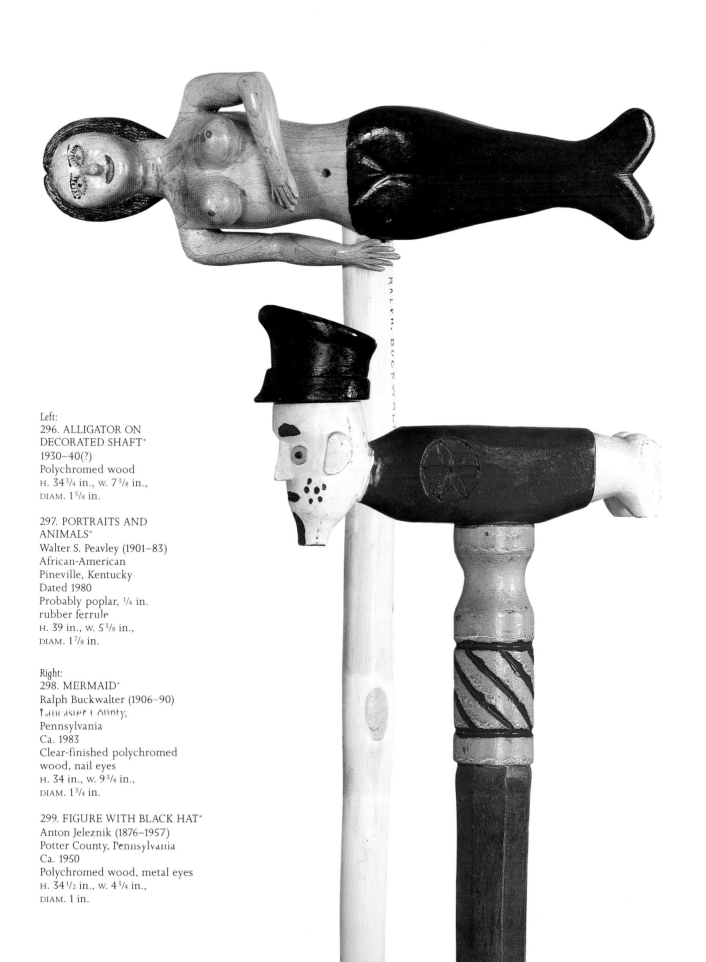

Left:
296. ALLIGATOR ON
DECORATED SHAFT*
1930–40(?)
Polychromed wood
H. 34 3/4 in., w. 7 3/8 in.,
DIAM. 1 5/8 in.

297. PORTRAITS AND
ANIMALS*
Walter S. Peavley (1901–83)
African-American
Pineville, Kentucky
Dated 1980
Probably poplar, 1/4 in.
rubber ferrule
H. 39 in., w. 5 3/8 in.,
DIAM. 1 7/8 in.

Right:
298. MERMAID*
Ralph Buckwalter (1906–90)
Lancaster County,
Pennsylvania
Ca. 1983
Clear-finished polychromed
wood, nail eyes
H. 34 in., w. 9 3/4 in.,
DIAM. 1 3/4 in.

299. FIGURE WITH BLACK HAT*
Anton Jeleznik (1876–1957)
Potter County, Pennsylvania
Ca. 1950
Polychromed wood, metal eyes
H. 34 1/2 in., w. 4 3/4 in.,
DIAM. 1 in.

175

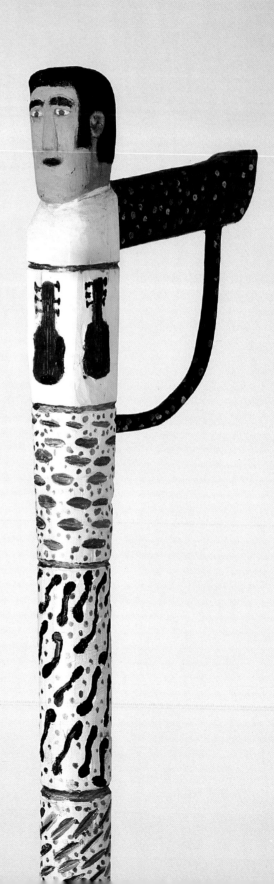

Left:
300. DOLLY PARTON*
Carl McKenzie (b. 1905)
Campton, Kentucky
1985
Polychromed pine
H. 32 in., W. 3 3/8 in.,
DIAM. 1 1/2 in.

301. ELVIS PRESLEY*
Elisha Baker (b. 1922)
Kentucky
1989
Polychromed wood
H. 38 1/4 in., W. 7 1/4 in.,
DIAM. 1 5/8 in.

Right:
302. CACTUS CANE*
Reverend St. Patrick Clay
(b. 1918)
African-American
Columbus, Ohio
Ca. 1988
Polychromed wood, painted
foam, hemp bristles, digital
clock, cigarette lighter, flashlight, plastic bottle, plastic,
egg carton foam
H. 38 in., W. 9 1/2 in., DIAM. 1 1/2 in.

303. TINFOIL SNAKE*
Willie Massey (1910–90)
Brown, Kentucky
1989
Polychromed wood, poly-
chromed plastic tape,
tinfoil, plastic shoes, plastic
key holder, keys, button,
safety pins, rubber band,
walnut, metal spring, beads
H. 34 1/4 in., DIAM. 1 3/8 in.

304. CHINESE MAN
AND TRAIN*
Tim Lewis (b. 1952)
Kentucky
Dated 1990
Polychromed wood
H. 36 1/4 in., W. 6 1/2 in.,
DIAM. 1 1/2 in.

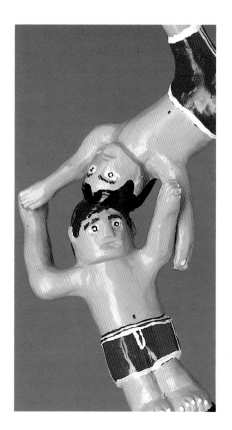

305. TWO SWIMMERS
AT A BEACH*
Tim Lewis (b. 1952)
Kentucky
Dated 1990
Polychromed wood
H. 38 in., W. 10 3/4 in.,
DIAM. 5 1/2 in.

Other American Folk Art Canes and Related Carvings

Scrimshaw and glass whimsy canes are also recognized categories of American folk art canes. Carvings similar in form and content to those on American folk art canes appear on other handcrafted objects. These include staffs, which are longer than canes, other stick forms, and pipes. Some makers carved objects like these in addition to canes. (Unless otherwise noted, all objects are in the Meyer collection.)

Top:
MERMAID SCRIMSHAW CANE
Ca. 1870; painted maple, whalebone, ebony, and whale ivory spacers; L. 40 in., W. 4$^{1/8}$ in., DIAM. $^{7/8}$ in.

Right:
SCRIMSHAW WALKING STICK
Nantucket, Massachusetts; ca. 1845; inlaid whalebone and whale ivory; L. 32$^{1/4}$ in. Private collection.

THREE GLASS WHIMSY CANES
Probably northeastern U.S. probably before 1920; colored glass; varying lengths. Made by glassblowers in production houses during off-hours. Collection of Joyce E. Blake, Elma, New York; photo by Image Makers, Gordon James, courtesy of Joyce E. Blake.

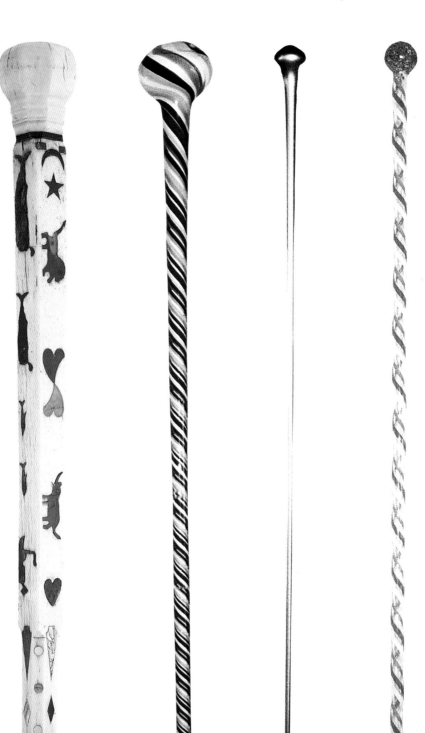

182

HORNED HEAD STAFF
Probably early 20th century; varnished
stained wood and root, flattened glass
button eyes; L. 48 in., DIAM. 6 in.

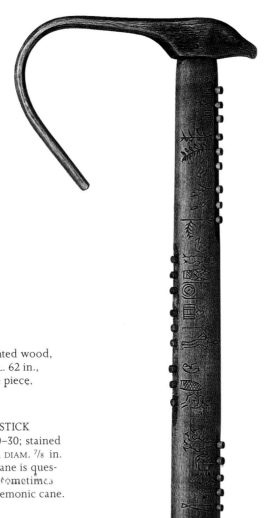

Above:
DOUBLE SNAKE STAFF
New York(?); ca. 1880; painted wood,
brass tack eyes and teeth; L. 62 in.,
DIAM. 3 in. Possibly a lodge piece.

Right:
PICTOGRAPHIC RECORD STICK
Northeastern U.S.; ca. 1920–30; stained
wood; L. 38 in., W. 7³/4 in., DIAM. ⁷/8 in.
Classifying this form as a cane is ques-
tionable, even though it is sometimes
called a condolence or mnemonic cane.

WOMAN ACROBAT
Probably Chippewa; probably Saginaw
area, Michigan; 1930s; polychromed
wood, probably pine; L. 29¹/2 in., DIAM.
2³/4 in. The function of this carving is
unclear. It was apparently not designed
to rest on the ground or bear weight.
There are other examples (including one
in the Meyer collection) in the same
style and with similar subjects.

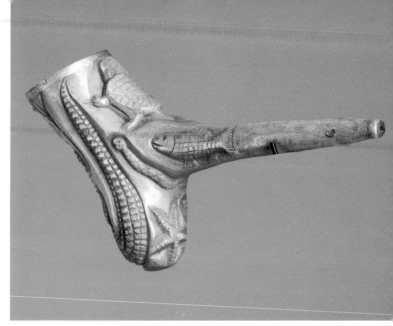

Left:
GUITAR
W.S. McCleary (1817–98); Van Wert,
Ohio; 1894; wood, metal, wire, ivory;
L. 38¾ in., W. (neck) 2¾ in. McCleary
was a barber.

PIPE FORM WITH ALLIGATORS,
TURTLES, FISH, AND SNAKE
Probably Ohio; early 20th century;
varnished painted wood, probably
maple; L. 8½ in.

VICTORIAN PIPE
Probably E. P. Squire; ca. 1873; varnished
stained wood, mother-of-pearl; L. 14 in.
One of a pair of pipes by the same maker
referring to Oliver Hazard Perry's Lake
Erie victory over the British in 1813.

Right:
NEWEL-POST
Hamilton County, Ohio; ca. 1870;
painted wood, probably walnut;
L. 41 in., DIAM. 5¾ in.

LAMP STAND
Probably Michigan; early 20th century;
polychromed wood; L. 48 in., DIAM. 3 in.

POLE WITH AFFIXED CARVINGS
Probably Wisconsin; 1930s; polychromed
wood, wire, nails, metal rod; L. 84 in.,
DIAM. 6 in. Possibly used in a lodge hall.

185

Alvin N. Hall, ca. 1864, whose name, military organization, and enlistment date are carved on cane no. 279. Courtesy of George H. Meyer.

George H. Meyer

Kay White Meyer

Documentation

SNAKES AND THE NATURAL WORLD

No. 2.
Found in Texas.

No. 3.
Collected from the Sioux on Standing Rock Reservation about 1870. For a Sioux pipestem with a similar form, see John C. Ewers, *Plains Indian Sculpture: A Traditional Art from America's Heartland* (Washington, D.C.: Smithsonian Institution Press, 1986), 114–15.

No. 4.
JHU is shallowly incised in the top of the shaft.

No. 5.
The handle has a metal screw top with a replaced metal cap. Found in Louisiana.

No. 6.
Painted on the shaft is *D. H. Hixson/maker/Jan the/23rd/1903[8?]/ HMS 10 Co/Ohio.* The handle is a separate piece of wood. There was a Grand Army of the Republic (G.A.R.) encampment in Marietta, Ohio, in 1903, for which this cane may have been made.

No. 7.
The heavy coils of the snake/root have shallow reliefs of a deer head, cow, spider, man, dogs, bird, man, child(?), woman, three men(?), and bust of a man. Carved on the snake are the date 1816 and *This snake was cut by/an carved Luke.*

No. 8.
Found in northern Maryland.

No. 9.
The snake is swallowing a realistically depicted pig. Found in Connecticut.

No. 10
A snake with incised scales twists around a branch on which are carved a bird, frog, star, snake, fish, heron, and two alligators.

No. 11.
A 9 3/4 inch lizard is carved at the bottom of the shaft.

No. 13.
A carved Turk's head knot forms the handle. A small lizard is also carved on the shaft.

No. 15.
The handle contains a rectangular, hollowed-out box with a sliding cover.

No. 16.
The snake was carved separately from the shaft and glued to it. There are other similar canes by this maker.

No. 18.
On the shaft beside the alligator is a lightly carved empty rectangle, presumably for the name of the cane's owner.

No. 19.
The handle, shaped like a stylized bird head, has an animal on one side and a lizard on the other. Just below, on opposing sides of the shaft, are two carved human heads. Two snakes, each with a frog in its mouth, encircle the remainder of the shaft.

No. 20.
Carved on the shaft are seven snakes with incised scales, their heads equidistant from one another. The cane may be a Seneca chief's staff.

No. 21.
The removable handle has a carved and painted black rifle and two powder horns. Below the joint are a shallowly incised swirl and a carved heart painted red. Between the snakes are a duck, knife, green leaf, fish, frog, acorn on a branch, sole of a shoe and a shoe, another acorn and branch, and a dog's head. Continuing down the shaft are a red star and an ax with a red head, an acorn, and three acorns on a branch. Unless indicated otherwise, all the carvings are painted brown. Several shallowly drilled holes are around the shaft below the longer snake. Part of the last 3 1/4 inches of the shaft is missing.

No. 22.
At least three other canes by this maker are known.

No. 23.
Chip carvings are below the handle, which is a hand holding a ball. Arranged around the shaft are bands of four deer heads, four turtles, and four snakes. The ferrule was handcrafted.

187

No. 25.
A painted gold band at the top of the shaft has the black-painted initials HKM.

No. 26.
A snake eating a frog curves within carved swirls of wood with sawtooth borders. The frog at the top clings to a shallowly cut leaf. There are other known canes by this maker.

No. 27.
Both ends of the handle are broken. The two flat sides of the shaft are similarly carved. Three female legs with painted black boots are carved down one side of the shaft. A black X separates one leg from the next, and a painted black heart separates the second and third legs. On the other side of the shaft are two similar vertical legs with a painted black cross separating them. Found in upstate New York.

No. 28.
Carved on the top of the shaft: *T. Reierson/Gall. Tenn./Feb. 8th 1863/104. R. Ill. Vol.* "Gall." is probably Gallatin, Tennessee.

No. 29.
A leather band over a metal band covers the juncture of the handle and the shaft. Found in Harmony, Pennsylvania.

No. 30.
The handle appears to be a separate piece. The heads of the two snakes have long carved forked tongues. The round center pieces resemble effigy turtles, and the double spirals are similar to those found on the twisted pipestems of the Great Lakes region Algonkians.

No. 31.
The ferrule cartridge case, which appears to be original to the cane, is marked *W.R.A. Co. 38 W.C.F.*

No. 32.
Found in southern New Jersey.

No. 34.
The snake's scales are formed by V-shaped punches.

No. 35.
Depressing a wooden lever at the top of the handle activates a metal tongue. The cane was found near Eaton, Ohio. A similar cane by the same maker was found in Michigan.

No. 37.
Natural protuberances on the shaft have been shaped into flattened hearts, ovals, and spurs and painted black.

No. 38.
The shaft has a large carved rattlesnake and a smaller one below. A horse head, lizard, turtle, and dog are carved on the lower part of the shaft between the natural diamond-shaped forms in the wood (see no. 270).

No. 39.
The large carved lizard has raised scales, and the fish has small square scales on the upper half of its body. Two of the lizard's legs are missing, and the shaft seems to have been shortened

several inches. A cane by the same maker was sold at Sotheby's, New York, on June 26, 1987 (lot 3).

No. 40.
Below the carved rattlesnake are a carved lock, plow, black turtle, ax with a silver head, bull's head with black paint, drill, sheaf of wheat, horse, saw with a silver blade, sheep, yoke, black-spotted cow, duck, black fish, rabbit, horseshoe, squirrel sitting on a black tree, the heads of a roe and a buck with antlers, a spotted dog, and a banner with the black carved initials *F. A.*

This cane was purchased from an elderly descendant of the maker, who said all the symbols were connected with some family history or sentiment. She has a childhood recollection of Allen pounding the cane on the floor at a Coldwater hardware store when making a point. Allen was born in Scotland.

No. 41.
The handle is a carved black onion-shaped cupola above a cage containing a carved miniature locomotive. The shaft is flanked by an alligator and a frog being eaten by a snake that encircles most of the shaft. The shaft also has carvings of a dog chasing a bird and a rabbit. Reportedly made by an African-American cook in a northern Michigan lumber camp. Found in Michigan.

No. 42.
All the creatures are deeply carved and incised, including two snakes at the bottom of the cane, one facing up the shaft and the other down it.

No. 44.
In black paint on a carved $4^{3}/_{8}$ inch red-painted section below the handle is *J. Pearcy/Camp Ch. 86/Oct.-8-1862.* Camp Chase, located near Columbus, Ohio, was a Union prisoner-of-war camp, a Union training camp, and later a place where veterans reunions were held. It is possible that Pearcy was a Union veteran who had fought in the battle of Perryville, Kentucky, on October 8, 1862, and that he attended a G.A.R. reunion at Camp Chase in 1886. Several other known Confederate prisoner-of-war canes are from Camp Chase, including one in the Meyer collection (not illustrated) that is inscribed *Camp. Chase. Prison. Ohio.*

No. 45.
The carved and incised frogs and alligator rest on incised elongated lilypads. Carved on the handle, probably by a different hand, is *Mineral/Spp/St. Augustine/Fla./2/91/Atlanta/Glen Spr's./Ky./7/92.*

No. 46.
On the opposite side of the shaft are a carved and incised heart, a plant with two leaves, and a carved diamond with a cross in the middle. Below the frog are a carved harp and another plant with two leaves. A hand emerging from a sleeve holds the top two-thirds of the shaft, while below the hand three more incised leaves encircle it.

No. 47.
The handle has a metal sleeve. The top of the shaft contains a small piece of mica covered with glass. Bands of color around the shaft are incised with small squares. Found in Crown Pointe, Indiana.

No. 48.
The alligator's back is incised with tiny squares and cross-

hatching. Scratched on the cane in crude lettering is *Cut/Heil/ Dudley*. Found in a German settlement near Oldenburg, Indiana.

No. 49.
Carved on one side of the shaft is *32 Ga/Lenard Megarr/Keep Me*. There may have been a separate handle. A wooden pad is on the bottom of the ferrule. This unusually bold cane was reportedly carved by Megarr while he was an inmate in a Georgia prison. Ex-collection Herbert Waide Hemphill, Jr.

No. 50.
Below the plain handle is a carved swirl followed by three carved frogs. Next are a dog chasing a rabbit, a rifle, snake, and duck. Below are two turtles, a swirl, and two snakes followed by a horse, a lizard, fish, and another carved swirl. The shaft ends with carvings of two lizards.

No. 51.
Two carved turtles with cross-hatching join feet around the shaft, followed by two alligators also with joined feet. Another similar cane by the same maker is known.

No. 52.
Below the black crook handle and metal collar are a carved sawtooth band and then a carved bird next to a twig with three leaves. A 5 inch black carved and incised eagle spreads down the shaft. The eagle is followed by carvings of a heart, an acorn on a twig with a leaf, a potted plant, an apple, and a turtle with traces of black paint on its shell. Following a carved diamond shape are a lizard with spots of black paint, arrow, flower, frog, object with a heart on it, sword, and black snake with yellow dots. Three other canes in the Meyer collection (not illustrated), all with metal collars, are by the same carver. One has an engraved date of 1905 on its collar. Another example is pictured in *Southern Folk Art*, Cynthia Elyce Rubin, ed. (Birmingham, Ala.: Oxmoor House, 1985), 107. Each cane contains many of the same carvings.

No. 53.
The alligator's back is relief carved in squares to represent scales. The natural small knobs on the shaft are decorated with nail heads.

No. 54.
The handle is a separate piece of wood. Climbing the top half of the cane is a carved snake with crosshatched skin. Below the snake are a carved bird, a banner with the carved initials *LBS*, and a small hand pointing toward the bottom of the shaft.

No. 55.
Incised in a decorative band around the top of the cane is ( )(1)(8)(9)(6)( ). Nine trout carved along the shaft are incised and painted in a style very similar to that of Michigan fish carver Oscar Peterson (1887–1951). There are also carvings of four worms and an eel. The bottom of the shaft has distress marks and a carved aquatic plant with two green leaves. There is a metal plate on the end of the handle. Found in Michigan.

No. 56.
Alva Axtell is carved on one side of the oversized shaft. A camel with a black saddle blanket, the initials *CBL*, and *1925* are carved on the other side. The camel (without its trappings) is almost identical to the camel on Camel cigarette packages of this period. A narrow carved decorative band and three circles are at the bottom of the shaft.

No. 58.
Carved below the handle, three five-pointed flower designs circle the shaft, followed by a carved heart, a buck with a full rack of antlers, and a rearing horse.

No. 59.
The head of a dog has incised eyebrows, nail eyes, collar, slightly open mouth, oval ears, and small diamond-shaped cap. At the top of the shaft are the initials JM. Below is a "Pennsylvania Dutch"–type bird and a heart pierced by an arrow. This is followed by a serrated band crossed by random lines. A cross-hatched snake coils around approximately 6 inches of the cane. Between the coils are a bird, a four-pointed star, another bird, and a turkey(?). All the carvings are decorated with nail heads. Numerous other examples of Simmons's canes and carvings are known. See also nos. 60 and 66.

    Richard S. Machmer says of Simmons that he was "a late German immigrant who wandered on foot from farm to farm and tavern to tavern, a pack of canes on his back. Although his given name remains unknown, he had two nicknames, 'der Alt' ('the old one') and 'der Schtockschnitzler' ('the cane carver')." Richard S. Machmer and Rosemarie B. Machmer, *Just for Nice* (Reading, Pa.: Historical Society of Berks County, 1991), 76.

No. 60.
A stylized dog's head with heart-shaped leaves for ears and round incised eyes has a double sawtooth collar. At the top of the back of the shaft a rooster with plumed tail struts on a wood band with serrated edges. A similar cane is pictured in Machmer, *Just for Nice*, 20, fig. 19 (full citation at no. 59).

No. 61.
Found in Springfield, Ohio.

No. 62.
This dog is a more refined version of no. 63 and is probably by the same hand. Part of one leg is missing. There are several other known examples of canes with running dogs carved by this maker.

No. 63.
The handle is a running dog with attached twigs forming the front paws. One leg may be a replacement. The dog's hind legs are carved from the shaft. The eyes are deeply incised, and the mouth is slightly open. The collar is painted with yellow dots. A piece of leather passes through the dog, forming a tail and a penis. The dog was probably originally painted.

No. 64.
The back of the dog's head is crosshatched. On the four-sided section of the shaft are two diamonds and a circle, covered with oilcloth or similar material. Below are a rectangular mirror and a rectangle of cobalt blue glass with two rectangles of abalone shell on either side. On the same side of the shaft as the mirror and glass, the paint has been scratched away in an apparent attempt to remove the carved, gold-painted initials JL. Halfway down the shaft, a narrow carved band divides the square section from the remaining round section.

No. 65.
The initials *AK* are at the top of the shaft, which is covered with a punch-mark design. On the remaining length of the shaft, vines and leaves emerge from the empty spaces not covered by punch marks, and the natural protuberances of the wood become centers of leaves. Found in Kalamazoo, Michigan.

No. 66.
The carved rooster on the back of the shaft is very similar to that of no. 60; see also no. 59.

No. 67.
Below the eagle, which has feathers drawn in ink on its wings and tail, is a relief carving of a pioneer woman wearing a dress and carrying what are apparently a shovel and a hoe. Below her is a soldier with a rifle and bayonet, followed by a carved Indian with a spear and a tomahawk.

No. 68.
On the round end of the handle are the initials *JL* and *1884*. The red owl holds a small yellow animal, while a snake reaches toward the owl's tail.

No. 69.
This cane and a second very similar cane carved by the same hand (not illustrated), which is also in the Meyer collection, were owned by Frederick P. Currier (1812–1900), Almont, Michigan.

No. 72.
Between the lower coils of the two snakes, two painted elongated rectangular bronze inlays are fastened to the shaft. Inscribed on a metal plate at the top of the shaft between the snakes is *Jas. W. Strong/Northfield Minn./HPS Feb 1871.*

The cane is accompanied by a hand-written note: "Cane carved with a pocketknife by a soldier of the Union in the Army of the Southwest, during the Vicksburg campaign. Brought home by surgeon Henry R. Strong, and presented to his brother, who now gives it to his eldest son Wm. B. Strong Northfield Minn. June 28th 1905."

No. 74.
The eagle has incised wings with individual feathers indicated by U-shaped punch marks. The same punch marks form scales on a snake grasped near its middle in the eagle's mouth. The snake twists around itself and then around the length of the shaft, its head hanging one-third of the way down. A pine tree, a lion, and two doves near a branch are also carved on the shaft, as is a decorative band with incised diamond shapes. Folk art canes for children, which are unusual, are often miniatures of canes for adults (see also no. 101). For another approach to a child's cane, see no. 261.

No. 75.
The cane was found in a house in York, Maine, where several carvings by Bellamy were also found. A strip of bark from the shaft is missing.

No. 76.
Found near Kutztown, Pennsylvania.

No. 77.
Below the monkey, which has a very long tail, are a crocodile, turtle, bug, fish, second crocodile, snake, lizard, and turtle. All are painted gold, and all but the fish have additional red paint markings. The shaft is painted red and the tip painted gold.

No. 78.
The 1½ inch ferrule is missing. Found in Pennsylvania.

No. 79.
The reverse side of the bird is an elephant. A small carved bird and a human figure are attached to the inside of the bird's curved tail, which ends in the mouth of a snake coiled halfway down the cane. Facing the bottom of the shaft are two large and four smaller alligators, individually carved and affixed to the shaft, along with two large sluglike creatures. The shaft ends with two carved leaves.

No. 80.
Carved on the shaft below the handle are a headless turtle, fish, kangaroo, snake, heron, alligator, deer with antlers, mountain lion, goose, horse, eagle, squirrel, giraffe eating the leaves on a branch, elephant, dog, frog, rooster, and cow. The final decoration is a curling banner.

No. 81.
An unmarked metal plate is next to a man nailing a flag on a flagpole. Below is an owl sitting on a vine with green leaves and grapes. Facing the top of the shaft are a tiger, lion, buffalo, kangaroo, two rabbits being chased by a dog with white spots, monkey, giraffe with spots, fish, fox, and mountain lion. Next are a pelican, rhinoceros, elephant, hippopotamus, heron standing on a stump with a fish in its mouth, and upright squirrel on another stump. A woodpecker pecks the second stump. At the end of the carvings are a horizontal ark and three Wise Men on camels. The cane was probably painted at one time.

No. 82.
A carved circle containing the initials *H.C.* is followed by eight carved dinosaurs. The carver was a man from Hampton, Iowa, who reportedly worked for Sinclair Oil, which had a dinosaur as a trademark.

No. 83.
Inscribed on the handle is *Carved/by/S. Nicholson M.D./Brunswick County, Virginia 1856/know thyself.* The shaft is divided into approximately 2 inch sections, each of which contains finely carved animals or figures. Under each animal or object is a carefully carved name. Descending the shaft by section: lion; *elephant and ship*; jaguar; *bear and beaver*; *goat and deer*; *cat and dog*; *alligator and boa* (swallowing an archer); *buffalo and ostrich*; *boar and turkey*; *cow and eagle*; *crab*; *duck*; and last, *hare and Shanghais* (pair of chickens). Below is an elaborate carved still-life of fruit and flowers in a vase. The sections of the cane resemble children's blocks. This cane may have been inspired by the fact that Nicholson taught in a one-room school in Stoney Mountain, Virginia, from 1853 to 1856, and had two young children, one born in 1854 and the other in 1856. Nicholson was commissioned as a lieutenant in the Confederate army in 1862, resigning in 1863 for health reasons.

No. 84.
Below the squirrel with an incised tail is a vine with three leaves. Within the spaces between the twisting vine are a beetle, moth, and flowers. The background of the shaft has incised

holes approximately ¼ inch long. A similar cane by the same maker is known.

No. 86.
The handle has four ends: a mustached man's head is opposite a fox with a long body, and a carved dog's head is across from a bear's head. Knobs left by removed branches remain along the entire length of the shaft. The cane probably had an inserted metal ferrule.

No. 87.
The shaft, which appears to have been a broom handle, is pegged into the handle. The handle and shaft were probably originally painted green.

No. 88.
The stylized deer head has metal eyes and large (5 inch) affixed ears. On the shaft are stylized geometric carvings of vines or trees, a band with small holes, followed by a columnlike section and then a section decorated with crosses contained by double curved lines. Below is a band of small holes with glass(?) beads in them, followed by another band of cross motifs and another columnlike section. A carved swirl runs to the end of the shaft. The ferrule appears to be part of a brass cartridge case.

No. 91.
The creatures on this unusual cane, made of the galls that grew on the branch, are a parrot, bear with a rock, leopard, dinosaur, two cats, and bird in its nest.

No. 92.
The unadorned reverse side of the shaft is concave. The cane is Northwest Coast Indian, probably Kwakiutl or Haida.

No. 93.
This cane is Northwest Coast Indian, probably Haida. It was probably made for the tourist trade.

No. 94.
Below the lion handle, a vine winds down the shaft. Two cats, two squirrels, an owl, mouse, and bear sit on natural protuberances on the shaft. The paint is covered by a heavy varnish that has crackled with age. The ferrule was handcrafted.

No. 95.
Found in the Perkiomen Valley, Pennsylvania.

No. 96.
A squirrel with a flat incised tail reaches for an acorn just above its head. Below, a hummingbird, honeybee, and bumblebee approach flowers. Numerous elaborate carved and incised vines, leaves and flowers intertwine to cover the entire shaft, which has a background of punch marks.

No. 97.
A crosshatched vine entwines almost the full length of the shaft. Below the plain knob handle is carved Presented. to. J. Reynolds. On the opposite side of the cane are carved clasped hands, a five-pointed star, and crossed cannons with three cannonballs. Another cane by this maker is known.

No. 98.
The handle is an inverted acorn with a shell that extends the next 3 inches of the shaft. A crosshatched oak branch with off-shoots of green leaves and clusters of acorns winds up the shaft. Found in Chambersburg, Pennsylvania.

No. 99.
The cane was acquired at an estate sale in Louisville, Kentucky.

No. 100.
A large spider is at the top of the shaft opposite the head of a rattlesnake. Below is a vine with red berries. Another spider is followed by a centipede and a grape vine. All the creatures are carved and decorated by incising, and the background is punched. The shaft was broken in the middle and repaired with the loss of perhaps 1 inch.

No. 101.
The "butterfly" forms here may represent something else. The cane was acquired in 1990 at a home sale in Lancaster County, Pennsylvania. The sale included a post–Civil War nineteenth century photograph (reportedly accidentally destroyed) of a father and his two children, a girl with a handmade doll, and a boy with this cane. Other children's canes are nos. 74 and 261.

THE HUMAN FORM

No. 102.
The open-mouthed man has a snake around his legs and stands on a barrel. Apparently there were teeth or dentures in his upper jaw. Carved on the shaft are a drill, drawknife, saw, ax, chisel, square, and fishhook. Following are a saddle, horseshoe, turtle, anvil, awl, tongs, hammer, wrench, coffeepot, pitcher, gun, wineglass, ax, razor, scissors, knife, key, and a branch with four leaves. The figure may be a portrait of a politician or may refer to the antisaloon temperance movement, perhaps speaking with a "forked tongue." Found in Florida.

No. 103.
Found in New York State.

No. 104.
Found in northern Georgia.

No. 105.
The shaft has large incised diagonal cross-hatching. The separate handle is pegged to the shaft.

No. 106.
The upper 6 inches of the cane contain a full-length figure of a woman in a striped dress. Below her are a man in a bowler hat and suit, two horses, two chickens, and a rattlesnake with incised scales. All the carvings are on one side of the shaft.

No. 107.
Opposite the woman on the shaft is a hollowed-out, uncarved space containing the word Jack in ink, followed by a carved pointing dog labeled a fuuy(?). Below the woman are an alligator with carved scales called Joe/alagator, a pelican called Pojo, a frog with spots labeled rain frog and a rattlesnake with cross-hatching called ratler/diamond back. A space designed for a carving is without one. All the inscriptions are in ink.

No. 108.
Three women in two-piece bathing suits are carved along the length of the shaft, which also contains stylized roses, birds, a horse, dogs, and eagles. The 1 inch ferrule is missing.

No. 109.
The figures on the cane are carved in low relief and have features drawn in ink. At the top of the shaft are two men in profile (one possibly George Washington), facing each other. Below them are a lady in an evening dress and a man who is diving. Next are two women, one a nude and the other dressed in a sari, followed by a boxer and a hunter. The remaining figures are a man resembling Napoleon and a horse, followed by a man with a cap, a dog, leopard, lion, giraffe, and a seated jockey or boy. The 1 inch ferrule is missing.

No. 110.
Other buttons are missing from the man's coat. The entire shaft is carved in an undulating design. The hollow shaft is made from four pieces of laminated wood with an internal metal rod to which the separate wood handle and the ferrule are attached.

No. 111.
Although probably female, the figure could be male. A 1 inch pearl button is on top of its head. In the middle of the figure's back is an incised branch with leaves. A snake wraps around the torso, ending at the hips. The figure's legs and bare feet straddle a giraffe, which extends its tongue toward another branch with leaves. Farther down the shaft are a waving flag with *Old Glory* scratched below it, a sailboat, anchor, and hill with the sun rising above it. *Tedy Roosevelt President* is carved between two thin branches, which continue to wrap around the shaft to its end. Incised on the back of the shaft are a shield, a splayed alligator, the date 1903, and a branch with leaves. All the carvings except those on the handle are very shallowly incised. Another cane by the same maker is known.

No. 112.
On the four sides of the square shaft are various carved, incised, and punched decorations. On one side are a shallowly incised dove, duck, two sandpipers, and the initials *FLT* (for the Odd Fellows motto, Friendship, Love, and Truth). On the next side are a swastika, nude seated woman, 829, dog, and three Barney Google cartoon figures on a crosshatched background. The first is a horse wearing a blanket inscribed *Spark Plug*, followed by Barney Google himself and a black man. (For another cane using comic strip characters, see no. 215.) The next side has the date *May 1922*, a rabbit, a half-moon with a man's profile in it, IOOF (Independent Order of Odd Fellows), and *Loganton/Clinton Co Pa*. The last side is decorated with a branch with leaves, three chain links (Odd Fellows symbol), and five carved and incised "hex" signs with star and wheel-spoke patterns. Found painted on barns in Pennsylvania German communities, hex signs are geometric decorations of various designs, usually a star motif within a circle, that are popularly believed to ward off evil. The swastika, an ancient cosmic or religious symbol, was also a sign of good luck. This cane may have been a presentation cane.

No. 113.
The separate "pickax" handle is affixed with wire. Punched on the underside of the handle are the initials *F.T.* and on the buttocks of the 8 inch carved Chinese figure are the letters *CAM/ERA*. There is a cage on the shaft below the figure. The cane

may be a demeaning reference to the use of Chinese labor to build the Union Pacific Railroad (1862–69). Found in Corning, New York.

No. 114.
Below the cage on which the sailor stands are a carved sailboat and a flying goose, followed by a boot, the initial *G*, two fish, and a flower in a goblet. Next are a carved houseboat, fish, submarine with flag flying, an eel, and a man and a woman, each in either costume or period dress. He wears a pointed hat and a coat with tails and carries a stick in each hand; she has braids and wears a long dress with a large collar. Below are a booted leg, cat, rhinoceros, and barge. Carved swirls cover the last 1 1/2 inches of the shaft.

No. 115.
The handle of this delicate cane is a carved 4 1/2 inch full-length figure of a gentleman standing on a ball-and-cage, dressed in a suit and bowler hat. The shaft has four carved green leaves, pairs of eagles, bees with hearts between them, turtles, lizards, and snakes with heads pointing in opposite directions. These are followed by a monkey, a dog, and two rifles. The cane was broken in the middle and repaired.

No. 116.
The man, seated on a drum or stool, is African-American. The banjo, which descended from an African instrument brought to America by slaves, was popularized on the American stage in the 1820s and 1830s.

No. 117.
The man sits in a carved chair. Beside him on the extended handle is a dog, and opposite the dog is a fox with a bird in its mouth. The initials *E.M.* are carved on the underside of the handle. The end of the shaft is blackened where it was apparently used to poke a fire. Acquired from the Harry Geyer estate in Pennsylvania.

No. 118.
The coffin originally had a sliding removable lid. Similar Victorian carvings of miniature coffins that are unrelated to canes contain erotic male figures. The cane reportedly was acquired from an African-American family in Missouri.

No. 119.
Yellow paint is over a black ground. The cane was acquired from a family whose tradition has it that the cane was made by a slave ancestor. Found in Georgia.

No. 120.
The man, who appears to be Chinese, has a queue that winds around the shaft.

No. 121.
The ferrule is handcrafted. The cane was found in Buffalo, New York, with other carvings by the same maker.

No. 122.
The separate handle is shaped as a 6-inch-high curving horn, incised on the top with tiny squares. At the top of the shaft is a star, and below is carved *I.H Carter/born/1848/Dec/18*. Carved down one side of the cane is the full-length figure of a man with a mustache (presumably Carter), and descending the side are a

red heart; square schoolhouse(?); sword; gold-painted woman's high-buttoned shoe; green leaf; red, white, and blue shield; and rifle with bayonet. On the other side of the shaft are an alligator, cross, clasped hands (Odd Fellows emblem), snake, and a fish. Found in Maine.

The symbolic carvings on the cane may refer to the Order of the Little Red School House, founded in 1895 and popular mostly in New England. This group was open to persons of all races and religions, and its mission was to educate the young, to inspire reverence for the schoolhouse, and to promote Americanism.

No. 123.
The right side of the coat has a pocket and incised buttons running to the bottom. The man was carved without a lower right arm. Incised around the bottom of the coat is *Old Tip*. The initials *A.C.* appear on his right shoulder. Found in New Bedford, Massachusetts.

No. 124.
The carved figurehead handle was made separately. The dragon's tail ends in a trefoil.

No. 125.
The cane originally may have been painted. There is a similar cane by this same maker.

No. 127.
Part of the bottom of the shaft and one nail eye are missing.

No. 128.
In addition to the carved nudes, the shaft has a carved heart pierced by an arrow and a Masonic square and compass inside a horseshoe.

No. 130.
The 3 1/4-inch-high head is probably a portrait. This cane may be a maquette, or small model, done as a preliminary work for no. 131, which was carved by the same maker and is of the same person. Found in Ohio.

No. 131.
The man's head is 5 3/4 inches high. This cane was carved by the same hand as cane no. 130 and is a portrait of the same person. Found in Ohio.

No. 132.
The man's hair, eyebrows, mustache, and beard are incised to look like strands of hair. Written in ink above the collar is *Sierra Madre, Calif./'9 Mtn. Lilaz.* The handle is affixed to the shaft, and the collar covers the juncture.

No. 133.
Strands of hair are carved and incised. The top of the shaft is carved in a lacelike design resembling a formal shirtfront. Separated by rings of natural protuberances are two plain sections trimmed in the same lacelike design. The bottom few inches of the cane are missing.

No. 134.
On the shaft is a carved turtle with an incised shell, followed by an 11 1/2 inch snake.

No. 135.
The back of the silver collar has a small silver plate attached to it, engraved with the word *Cotton*.

No. 136.
The cane originally was probably painted.

No. 137.
The woman wears a carved and incised headdress. The shaft is carved with a stylized swirl, which is crosshatched near the handle. It is similar to college fraternity Indian-head canes, such as the "Dartmouth College canes." Although hand-carved, this cane may have been commercially made.

No. 138.
The shaft consists of five elongated carved swirls, which taper into a plain shaft. The cane was found in an old farmhouse in Connecticut.

No. 139.
A slender snake is carved on the shaft.

No. 140.
There is a hole through the shaft near the handle for a strap. Found in Pennsylvania.

No. 141.
There is some insect damage to the facial area.

No. 142.
Two holes in the head represent ears. The simply rendered body stands on three small carved segments of the shaft, which are followed by two long sections, all crosshatched, below which the shaft is plain and circular. Jim Wilson, a member of the maker's family in Florida from whom the cane was reportedly obtained, said a photograph of Fred Wilson unfortunately had recently been destroyed.

No. 143.
Found in western Virginia.

No. 144.
Below the handle is a metal collar on the shaft, and below that is a hole through the shaft with diamond-shaped metal eyelets. A snake with a red mouth winds up the length of the shaft. The metal ferrule is missing. A very similar cane by the same maker is pictured in Roger Ricco and Frank Maresca, *American Primitive: Discoveries in Folk Sculpture* (New York: Alfred A. Knopf, 1988), 184.

No. 146.
Below the handle are a running dog and the large face and small front legs of a cat. A snake is on the upper half of the shaft, and next to it is an open-mouthed alligator reaching toward the cat. Two more alligators follow the first alligator. Next to these two are a turtle and a fish. Another snake begins beside the second alligator. Below them is a Masonic compass and square with the letter *G*, followed by an ax, a turtle, the head of another snake, and an alligator. All but the second turtle have high-relief carvings representing scales or body parts. The eyes of the cat, the snake, and the first three alligators originally probably were beads or glass jewels.

No. 147.
Reportedly this cane and others like it were used in the Amish practice of "powwowing" or the sympathetic curing of illness. The bark has been left on the shaft.

No. 148.
The handle is a round burl knob with a working directional compass (marked with 32 points and 360 degrees) inserted in the top. On the sides of the knob, three tiny distinctly carved heads peek from small holes. On the shaft, carved men's heads face different directions. The knob in the middle is covered by heads of bearlike animals with colored glass eyes. Below are two men's heads, the second facing the opposite direction from the one above and resting on a long coiled snake. Below are another man, a small human face, and another bear with white glass eyes, whose head rests on a second coiled snake. At the bottom of the cane a small knob is carved with three human heads and a monkey head. Most of the men have dark brown beards or mustaches. Found in Denver, Colorado.

No. 149.
Four masklike stacked carved heads form the shaft (as in a totem pole), which is topped by a white knob handle. The masks are each painted and carved with different designs. *OEC* is carved down the top of the shaft, and the words *Portland* and *Oregon* form carved collars for two of the heads. There are also a swastika, horseshoe, and four-leaf clover. Two rattlesnakes encircle the bottom of the shaft. The rubber ferrule may be a replacement. There has been some paint loss and repainting, particularly just below the handle and at the tip. See no. 112 concerning the use of the swastika at this time.

No. 150.
The entire cane is carved and incised with intricate designs. A vine with green leaves and a brown rattlesnake with a black stripe intertwine up the shaft. A black collar studded with brass tacks encircles the shaft below the head, under which is carved *C.E. Smith*. Although plastics were available after 1860, the red tag just below the collar may not be original to the cane. Another cane by the same maker was reportedly made in a veterans retirement home in Dayton, Ohio.

No. 151.
The handle, which has split with age, is the large head (10 1/4 inches) of a bearded black man wearing a feathered Indian headdress. The indentation in the headdress once held a stone or ornament, now missing. The cane was found in New York.

No. 152.
The cane was carved from a branch with a burl.

No. 154.
The tail of one snake is missing.

No. 155.
The third man's head, with a black mustache, is carved at the junction of the handle and shaft. This cane may have been made by a European immigrant. Found in Pennsylvania.

No. 157.
Two gnomelike faces are on opposing sides of the burl below the eagle handle; a small owl is below them. The bottom part of the shaft appears to be missing. The cane was acquired at an estate sale in Columbus, Ohio. Reportedly the seller, an unidentified elderly African-American, said the cane came from her family in Tennessee.

No. 158.
The cane is probably made from a root. An owl's head with one eye missing is at the top of the shaft. The shaft has five carved masklike faces in addition to many human and animal heads along its length. A bear is formed by one of the gnarled growths, and other knobs also contain animallike shapes. A carved building with a high roof appears, and another area contains carved symbols. A slender snake winds up the bottom half of the shaft. This cane may be Native American.

No. 160.
Four monkeys climb the shaft, pursued by a snake, which is swallowing the last monkey. Found in Wisconsin.

No. 161.
The head is a human effigy. Bands of inked crosshatched triangles that touch at their apexes cover the top three-quarters of the shaft. One bead eye is missing. The cane was acquired around 1979 from a dealer in England.

No. 162.
The burl head was made separately and attached to the bark-covered shaft. This may be a human-head guardian figure.

No. 163.
Four deeply carved masquettes at the top of the shaft and two at the bottom are separated by a series of carved 1/4 inch rings. Probably False Face Society (see essay by David Penney, p. 229).

No. 165.
Below the man wearing a coat with tails, a roundhouse incised 1881 encircles the cane. A carved engine inscribed 3 and a loaded coal tender pull out of the roundhouse and head down tracks on the shaft. Incised on the engine is *The [indecipherable] work 1881*, and on the coal tender is incised *Nor. 3 Desmones* (Des Moines?). A wheelbarrow is beside the freight car, and an alligator is in front of the engine. A cow's head protrudes from the tracks, her body wrapping around the rest of the shaft. At the end of the tracks a flagman holds his signal flag in one hand and a shovel in the other. A sledge hammer and a wrench are beside him. At the end of the shaft are a horse, a weasellike animal, and a rattlesnake. The 5/8 inch ferrule is missing. The parrot-head man is probably Chauncey M. Depew (1834–1928), whose face, it was said, resembled a parrot and who was portrayed as such by political cartoonists of the day. Depew was the attorney and legislative contact for Commodore Cornelius Vanderbilt's railroads. Later he became president of the New York Central Railroad and U.S. Senator from New York. Depew was called a charming and influential speaker and politician, although he was later said to have been unfeeling about a railroad accident in New York. This cane was made by the same maker as no. 184.

No. 166.
On the back of the man's head is the head of a snake with a small carved heart between its eyes.

No. 167.
The head appears to be a portrait. The cane has a 1 inch copper collar and an unusual ferrule with high, sharp points, decorated

with a circle of vines. The shaft is covered with natural diamond-shaped depressions (see no. 270). The cane was found in Geneseo, Illinois.

No. 168.
A stylized man's head tops the polychromed shaft, which has high-relief full-length figures of men with swords, a horse and rider, monkey, crown, animal heads, and a snake eating a man. Four groups of wooden rings in loops appear to have been cut out of the shaft. Crown motifs are also found on Pennsylvania German blanket chests and frakturs (paperwork illuminated with decorative motifs). The many colors on this cane are in contrast to European folk art canes, which were rarely painted. Found in Lancaster County, Pennsylvania.

No. 169.
The brim of the hat is broken, and the end of the cane is wrapped with black electrician's tape. There is a hole for a strap above a shallowly carved snake. The cane was found in Scott County, Kentucky, where it was reportedly made.

No. 170.
The sensitively carved head is fastened to the shaft by rope sailor work (decorative or fancy rope work done by sailors, generally when off duty). The brass tubing ferrule is also attached with a rope sailor knot. The bark is intact on the varnished shaft. This cane was done by the same hand as cane no. 171 and was found at the same time reportedly in a former sea captain's home in Farmingale, Maine.

No. 171.
See description of no. 170. What is probably gold radiator paint was added later.

No. 172.
On the shaft are a crudely incised *A* next to a *Y* enclosed in a square. Below, in gold lettering on a black background is *Aug. 26, 1926/presented [to]/Capt. A.E. Rawley by/Ex. Judge C.K. Willer Camden/over 100 yrs. old*. Deep holes form the ears. Captain Alfred E. Rawley (1870–1941), who lived in the Rockland area of Maine, was from 1903 to 1935 master of the 320-foot passenger steamer *Belfast*, which ran from Boston to Bangor. The inscription "over 100 years old" may refer to Judge Willer or the cane itself. It probably does not refer to Rawley, who would have been only fifty-six in 1926, the date on the cane. There apparently is a New England tradition of giving a cane to the oldest person in a town. In Maine, the cane that is given is called the "Boston Post Cane."

No. 173.
The hand is carved separately and attached to the shaft. A 9 inch, two-headed snake is on the shaft below the back of the hand. Found in New England. The hand is a universal symbol, used in early Christianity and other religions. It is also used to portray friendship. Ulrich Klever described its use on walking sticks in "Hand to Hand: Thoughts about Hands Figuring as Stick Grips," *The Cane Collector's Chronicle* 3, no. 1 (January 1992). See also Frederika Alexander Burrows, *The Yankee Scrimshander* (Taunton, Mass.: William S. Sullwold Publishing, 1973), 45, and E. Norman Flayderman, *Scrimshaw and Scrimshanders, Whales and Whalemen* (New Milford, Conn.: N. Flayderman, 1972), 124.

No. 174.
A sleeve with incised pen and ink triangles forms the handle, and a particularly graceful hand extends from the sleeve to hold the rest of the shaft, in a design that cleverly repeats the gesture of the bearer's hand. Eight ball-in-cage motifs form the shaft along with a spindle in an elongated cage toward the bottom. Above the cages, on each side of the square shaft, are small incised drawings—three birds and one deer head. Between the cages on each side of the shaft are lightly incised five-pointed stars in circles, and a circled star ends the design on the shaft.

No. 176.
The shaft is pegged into the separate handle, and the joint is covered by a collar. The tips of two fingers are missing. Found in northwestern Iowa. Catlinite, or pipestone, a red clay, was named after explorer-artist George Catlin (1796–1872). It was frequently used by the Sioux for carvings, particularly pipes.

No. 177.
A snake with natural markings winds up the full length of the shaft. Holes just below the hand and on the end of the stick probably contained beads or nails.

No. 178.
Four evenly spaced snakes with cuts for scales wind up the upper two-thirds of the shaft. The cane may have been an Iroquois speaker's staff.

No. 179.
Below the hand and cuff are an earth-colored band and a darker band, each with a sawtooth edge. Around the shaft is *WB 1888*. A branch of carved oak leaves and acorns is on the upper part of the shaft. Immediately below it, a grape vine begins with blossoms, leaves, and grapes that wind down the shaft. Between is carved *Whosoever shall call upon the name of the Lord shall be saved*. The lower third of the shaft was broken and repaired.

No. 180.
The torch has some breaks.

No. 181.
The mahogany handle is separate. On each side of the top 8 1/4 inches of the square shaft are inlays of different materials. They are in the forms of hearts, diamonds, stars, rectangles, and four buildings (churches?) viewed from the front, including one with a cross. The central portion of the shaft is hexagonal and the lower part is round. Similar inlays are seen in scrimshaw canes (see p. 181).

No. 182.
The handle is a laced Victorian shoe. The ankle is clad in a stocking indicated by inked lines. Three carved classical nude muses are enclosed in a circle made by a coiled serpent, which bares its fangs at a snarling lion. With the lion are two cobras and two birds, one looking at a nest full of eggs. A mother lion has one cub on her back, a second nurses, and a third wanders away. A nude woman dumps wine from her glass as Cupid hovers nearby. At the bottom of the shaft is a monkey or baboon wearing a vest and holding a screeching cat.

No. 183.

The handle of this cane has a snake across the top and another poking its head from a carved hole. Descending the shaft are the shield and eagle of the Knights of the Golden Eagle, then a larger shield bearing a compass, an arm and hammer, and the inscription *Virtue/Jr. O.U.A.M.* (Junior Order of United American Mechanics)/*Liberty/Patriotism/Founded/1853*.

Next on the shaft are a compass and square with the letter *G* of a Masonic Blue Lodge; a three-barred cross, which is the Patriarchal Cross of Masonic Scottish Rite; and a ladder and boat with the letters *MOI*, for the Independent Order of Mechanics. Next are a round shield with an ax, maul, and splitting wedge of the *WMA* (Modern Woodmen of America) and three interlocking rings marked *FLT* (Friendship, Love, and Truth), from the motto of the Independent Order of Odd Fellows. Next is the head of an armored knight above a shield with the letters *FCB* (Friendship, Charity, and Benevolence) for the Knights of Pythias.

Continuing down the cane are a six-pointed star containing a triangle, which in turn contains a pi symbol. Following is a large *E* within a *C*, for Christian Endeavor, with *mizpah* carved on the *C*. A banner reading *For Christ/and the church* threads between the *C* and *E*. The next shield has *D of A* (Daughters of America) across the top, then an open book, and clasped hands at the bottom. Below that are two more Masonic compasses and squares. A *G* surrounds one compass, and a second *G* intertwines the arms of the other. Found in Iowa.

No. 184.

A plain handle leads to a heart. A locomotive and a coal tender are on tracks that lead from a roundhouse down the shaft. Beside the tracks is a signalman with a shovel and a raised flag. His wheelbarrow, pliers, and mallet lie beside the tracks. At the end of the tracks are a protruding deer head, lion, shovel, owl and squirrel in a tree, and an alligator or lizard. Also depicted are a boat (ark?) on water and a carved frog with traces of paint. The lower part of the shaft was broken and repaired. Found in Pacific, Missouri. Made by the same hand as no. 165.

No. 185.

One side of the handle is a bust of a man wearing a cap, while the other side has an attached leather stacked heel. At the top of the shaft is a cobbler's bench, followed by a shoemaker holding a boot and an oversized hammer. Additional tools carved on the shaft are pliers for attaching soles, knife, punch, awl, another hammer, scraper, bracket, mallet, boot last, ruler, and rasp. The initials JB and 1888 are deeply carved above twistings near the bottom of the shaft.

No. 186.

Crossed axes and a fireman's helmet are carved at the upper end of the shaft, followed by low-relief portraits of firemen connected by carved fire ladders. Each portrait is completed in ink. From top to bottom the men are named *G.H. Thompson, James Farrell, Andrew O'Day, H.C. Anderson, J.B. Listman,* and *N.S. Bauer.* The top of the handle may be missing.

No. 187.

The knob handle contains the initials *O/P/WE*, and a relief portrait appears on the shaft. Below it a piece of glass covers an opening that contains a slip of paper with the initials *G.H.* Carved in high relief down the shaft are the words *Boy. D. Safty.* A snake winds up the length of the cane, its head next to a book decorated with what appear to be a Masonic square and compass, a *G*, and a pencil. These are followed by sticks of dynamite(?), a miner's lantern, shovel and pickax, hand, lumps of coal, and a loaf labeled *bread*. At the end of the shaft is a carved turtle. Reportedly the artist was an African-American from West Virginia.

No. 188.

A lead handle is affixed to the wooden shaft. A metal band and two rows of seven metal circles are below the lead cap. This is followed by four diamondlike forms, of which the two opposite ones serve as an eyelet. The shaft is decorated with nailed tin cutouts of hammers, chisels, adz, square, saws, ax, penknife, calipers, clamp, drill, drawknife, auger, plane, level, pliers, tin snips, oil can, ruler, and bottle. A few of the cutouts are broken. The lower part of the shaft has additional metal circles. Newhall was a carpenter.

No. 189.

A farmer dressed in a suit and carrying a cane is at the top of the shaft. A crowing rooster next to him is followed by a scene of the farmer behind a plow pulled by a team of mules. In the next section the farmer digs with a spade. A basket is beside him, and nearby is a snake. The last part of the shaft portrays a barnyard with carvings of a goose, cow, duck, horse, and sheep. Found in Michigan.

No. 190.

The cane's handle, shaped as a claw hammer, is a separate piece glued to the shaft. The hammerhead has cork attached. The tool's handle is the shaft, which contains a 14 inch ball-in-cage. The 1½ inch ferrule is missing. Found in Pennsylvania.

No. 191.

The separate elongated handle with two large holes is pegged on the shaft. Attached to the broad shaft by wood pegs are large wood cutouts of scissors, razor, brushes, comb, soap (labeled *soap*), and other barber's implements, one of which is missing. Acquired at an estate sale in Beatrice, Nebraska.

No. 192.

The shaft has a low-relief carving of the front of a locomotive with 7 and *W*S* carved below it (a possible reference to the Winona and St. Peter [Minnesota] Railroad).

Carved on the reverse side of the shaft are a horseshoe around an anvil and hammer, a rose, shield with a star, dog's head, and the three chain links of the Odd Fellows. The rest of the shaft is carved with a horse head, a pig inscribed 10B, a heart, decanter and glass, circle with a triangle in the center, cross, acorn, Masonic anchor, sword, square with an ax, bridge, another ax, bowler hat, pointing finger, 1890, fish, pipe, and vine with leaves. There are two painted rings around the bottom of the shaft, followed by a black uncarved area. The 1 inch ferrule is missing. There is another cane (not illustrated) in the Meyer collection by the same maker, dated 1891 and with the initials *L.D.*

No. 193.

The design is a painted mottled background with detailed inked Masonic emblems. The handle is carved separately and pegged to the shaft. The initials *G M B W L I* encircle the top of the shaft. Descending the cane are an elaborate "all-seeing eye," a red-cheeked face of a sun beside a small five-pointed star in a circle, a crescent moon with a face, three crowns, a stick on a pedestal with a climbing snake (the Brazen Serpent), and a skull and crossbones. Several natural knobs in the middle of the cane have been incorporated into the design.

On the lower half are crossed keys, an arch over a column, ladder, square, compass, open hand, plumb, level, decorated box, sign with a geometric drawing, rooster, compass lying on an open book, Masonic apron with a compass and square drawing, two columns topped with small candles, and a gauge. (The gauge divides the day into three equal eight-hour parts for work, sleep, and refreshment.) Drawn below are a small mallet, trowel, chisel, more knobs, and an armored head of a knight with a shield, followed by two indistinct shields.

No. 194.
The handle of this cane is a carved head of a man with a full beard. A ³/₄ inch ring encircles the top of the shaft. The carved symbols are a mixture of professional and fraternal memberships. At the top of the shaft are a Bible on one side and a compass and square with a *G* on the other. Descending the cane are a beehive, plumb, ruler, crossed quills, crossed keys, crossed swords, triangle (alluding to the Trinity), frog, a Masonic chapter Mark Master, interlocking triangles of King Solomon's seal (also a symbol of Masonic Scottish Rite), heart, rifle, powderhorn, ruler, dog chasing a deer, ellipse, eagle carrying a rabbit, squirrel, and horse collar.

J. A. Mell is carved on a carpenter's jack plane, and *Mich* is below. A saw contains *March 19*, and a marker is inscribed *1899/Moline*. Continuing below are a fish, turtle, rattlesnake, skull and crossbones, bottle, fat man with a bottle wearing a sash inscribed *Oldrye*, a barrel, pointing hand, arrow, and saddle.

Mell was a blacksmith and an inventor, who patented an oarlock and a wrench. The cane was acquired in Michigan from Mell's granddaughter.

No. 195.
The handle is inscribed *1936 Governor Fred P. Cone/Florida 1940* on one side, and *Fred P. Cone* on the other. Cone (1871–1948) was the Democratic governor of Florida from 1937 to 1941. He was a member of Lake City, Florida, Lodge 27 and various Masonic bodies, including Mystic Shrine, Royal Arch Chapter, and Knights Templar Commandary.

On the shaft below the handle, a carved crescent moon with a Sphinx face curves around a star, the emblem of the Ancient Nobles of the Mystic Shrine. On the other side of the shaft is a lyre containing the head of a mustached man wearing a crown. Below the head is carved a rectangle resembling a brick wall. Below the moon are a triangle labeled 32 (32nd degree), and then, continuing down and around the shaft are two columns with rocks on top, a sword between them on one side, and a rectangle with the fraction ³/₇ on the other. One column is inscribed *Boaz*, and the other *Jachin*, the names given to the brass pillars erected on the portico of King Solomon's temple.

Circling the next level are a ruler, square, and compass and square with a *G*. Below this are a crossed ax and shovel, pick, ladder, spade, square with two smaller squares balanced on it (a Euclidean problem), and scythe. Below these are the keystone of the Mark Master (4th degree) and the initials *TKSHTWSS* around a circle with a dot in its center. Next to the keystone is a skull and crossbones. Below are the "eye of God" and an urn. Below

that is a Knights Templar cross and a Hiram's coffin. This is followed by crossed keys and a Masonic apron. At the bottom of the shaft is a book lying face down with *AD 1032* written on one side and *Holy Bible* on the other.

No. 196.
At the top of the shaft is a carving of the upper torso of an African-American(?) man who appears to be a boxer. Below, on the same side of the shaft, carved in ovals are a fish, a pelican, and a snake that coils up the bottom of the cane. At the top on the reverse side is a compass and square with a *G*, a dog, alligator, and cat.

The cane was found in Louisiana, where the pelican is the state bird. The long history of African-American Masonic chapters dates from 1787.

No. 197.
Under the elk's throat at the top of the shaft is carved *Ho/Bill/B.P.O.E.* (Benevolent and Protective Order of Elks). Also carved are *Phila. July 15th to July 20th./1907* and *The best people on earth.* Outlined in nail heads is *N.M. Kuctly(?)*, who may have purchased the cane, probably as a souvenir of an Elks convention. The ³/₄ inch metal ferrule is missing. Found in Pennsylvania.

No. 198.
A green knob forms the handle of the cane. Three interlocking Odd Fellows links (one missing a section) are carved on one side of the shaft, and *IOOF* (Independent Order of Odd Fellows) is carved on the other. Two green snakes coil up the length of the shaft. The tip of the shaft is painted green in imitation of a ferrule.

No. 199.
The separate handle is shaped like a short horn. Carved on the shaft are various Odd Fellows symbols. First is the Bible encircling half the shaft, with an elaborate "all-seeing eye" on the other half. Lines radiate from the eye, which has drapery around it. Descending the sides of the shaft are a carved skull and crossbones, coffin, three interlocking rings, ax, mallet, heart on a hand, bow, bundle of three-feathered arrows, beehive, and scythe. A ribbon-bound fagot encircles the cane slightly short of its midpoint.

Near the middle of the shaft is carved a vine with green leaves encircling a turtle. Below are a carved Maltese cross, red ball on a column, two crossed canes, hourglass with wings, shield, and another column topped with a ball. These are followed by another branch with green leaves and a sheaf of wheat on the opposite side. An alligator descends the shaft. Opposite it are a snake, star cross, balance, crescent moon with a face, church, cup, and two tents. The base of the shaft has carvings of a coffeepot, an owl sitting on a stump, and a fish. Written on the coffeepot is *Trade mark/R.M. Foster/Sparta Mo.*

The lead ferrule is handcrafted. The strong similarity of subjects and design on this cane and nos. 200 and 201 suggests a common source.

A number of canes by R. M. Foster, signed in this same fashion with a carved owl and coffeepot, have been found. Three are in the Meyer collection (see no. 213 for a cane on a different subject), and at least three others are known. On one cane with an Odd Fellows theme there are a signature and a verse in which Foster refers to himself as a Confederate veteran. The 1900 official census of the United States lists Robert M. Foster as a farmer, born in Virginia.

No. 200.

The silver handle is engraved on the top, *Presented to Herm[an]. Dick by the employees of the Dick's Brewing Co.* Dick's Brewing Company, Quincy, Illinois, was in business from 1857 to 1952. On the sides of the handle are a set of columns, a flame over the connecting arch, and above it a six-pointed star inscribed *UPC* in the center. There is also a beer barrel over a crossed broom and spade. The third panel contains a lyre. The last section has the intertwining initials *DBC.*

A carved, open Bible encircles half the shaft, and an "all-seeing eye" is on the other half. Below, carvings descend the shaft's sides: an ax with the Odd Fellows rings, hourglass, beehive, bow and arrow, scale, skull and crossbones, dove carrying a leaf, crossed shovel and pick, crescent moon with a face, heart on a hand, scythe, coffin, and three triangles. A fagot forms the middle of the cane, followed by a carved powder horn with a rope, rifle, two powder horns, snake, saddle, and anchor and rope.

The handle was made by a skilled silversmith and engraver. The ferrule was handcrafted from a piece of sheet metal. Herman Dick (1853–90) was vice-president of Dick's Brewing Company and probably a member of the Odd Fellows.

No. 201.

Below the plain handle is a high-relief carved Bible that takes up three sides of the shaft. On the fourth side are three intertwining rings. Descending the shaft are carvings of an "all-seeing eye," a snake, stick, mallet, alligator, and large C shape (or a very simple ark?). Continuing down are a scythe, ark, coffin, heart in hand, and ram. The middle of the cane has a fagot tied with a ribbon. Below are a carved anchor and rope, bow and arrow, branch, shield in a three-sided rectangle, beehive, plain banner, head of a dog(?), and frog. The cone-shaped ferrule was handcrafted; it was closed up around a steel end and seamed with lead solder.

No. 202.

The gold-colored metal handle is highly decorated. On one side of the body of the cane is carved *No 105/Im. P.O.R.M* (Improved Order of Red Men). On the other side is *Sam. Crew./ Navajo. Tribe.* Below a carved ball-in-cage are two Indians, one holding a gun and the other a hatchet and spear, who stand on a band of the carved words *Redmen. Tribe.* A snake coils up the bottom of the shaft. Between the coils are an Indian on horseback, bow and arrow, dove, anchor, and smaller snake. Almost all the carvings have incised dark stripes.

No. 203.

The separate maple handle is shaped as a woman's leg. Inlaid in the shaft is *TOTE*, standing for Totem of the Eagle, the mystic anagram of the Improved Order of Red Men. Five mother-of-pearl inlays are missing. The use of a woman's leg as a handle along with various mother-of-pearl inserts is a common motif on scrimshaw canes, on which fraternal symbols are also found. See p. 181 for an example of inlays in scrimshaw canes.

No. 204.

The tip of the handle is a small carved Indian head. The rest of the slender handle is decorated with an eagle with wings spread (carved in what the maker may have considered an "Indian style"), the word *TOTE* (Totem of the Eagle), and a bow and arrow. At the base of the handle is a shell Indian head inserted

into a framelike opening in the wood. On the other side is a carved pig. The bark is still on the shaft.

No. 205.

This presentation cane has a Masonic compass and square with a *G* at the top of the shaft. On the other side of the shaft are three wheels driving a chain. All the printing on the shaft is borne on the chain, which winds around the natural protuberances in the wood that act as gears directing the chain. The carving between the part of the chain going up the cane and the part returning states, *J[onathan] D. Mawhood, Richmond City, Ind., mill expert, carved and presented by G.W.B. McKnight, Columbus, Ga.* There are small carved vignettes of Mawhood's office, of Mawhood holding a banner reading *RRR*, and of twelve seated men, possibly a jury or mill committee. In the last scene, the meaning of which is unclear, a man kicks Mawhood in the seat of the pants. Jonathan Mawhood (1843–92) was "one of the main men in the mechanical department of the mill works," according to his obituary in the *Richmond Evening Item,* December 8, 1892. The Richmond City Mill Works manufactured flour mill machinery. G.W.B. McKnight was the head miller at Empire Mills, Columbus, Georgia, a steam-powered grist mill, which was established in 1854 and closed in 1931.

No. 206.

The bust on the handle is probably a portrait of Snyder. Carved down the length of the shaft is *C.F. Snyder Alburtis Pa. 1900/Dax E. Lax Sprine No. 398. O.R.M.* (Tox-E-Lox Tribe No. 398, Improved Order of Red Men)/*Patriotic Jr. O. of U.A. Mc. No. 1014.* The Junior Order of United American Mechanics split from its parent organization of United American Mechanics in 1885 and soon became a strong organization in its own right. A Clinton Snyder was listed in the Alburtis city directory as a butcher. The Alburtis chapter of the Improved Order of Red Men was formed in June 1900, and the cane may commemorate this event.

No. 207.

The separately made handle has three intertwining rings with *FLT* (Friendship, Love, and Truth) carved on one side and *DC10* in three rings on the other side. At the top of the square shaft are a white skull on one side, a hatchet on the next side, a sickle on the third side, and a scale on the fourth side. Around the sides of the shaft is carved *W.A. Spotts/Foutain/Lodge* (for Fountain Lodge, Harrisburg) *1120/IOOF* (Independent Order of Odd Fellows) *1882.*

Carved in a band around the shaft are a heart in hand, an "all-seeing eye," a serpent, and pavement. Below this are several scenes that may be of initiation rites. In the first, two men wearing white robes hold wands or staffs over a coffin while two others in suits observe. On the other side of the shaft a man dressed in white stands between two men dressed in suits. He appears in the next scene leading a man carrying a spade, followed by a white bird (dove?) and a third man. In the last scene on the opposite side of the shaft, three men dressed in black watch a man in red who holds a red wand toward a silver object (an ark?) on a stand. Opposite him, one of the men from the previous scenes points a sword or long silver staff at the ark. At the bottom of the cane are the initials *LO/OM/FOE/ORG* (for Loyal Order of Moose, Friends of Elk, Organizations?) and a compass and square with a *G* for the Masons.

No. 208.

The handle appears to be the head and snout of a pig. Opposite is a carving of a blond man, possibly the same person as the one portrayed throughout the cane. Lower on the shaft are a star with a nail in the center, two small holes with drawings of the sun and the moon, and a jackknife(?). Carved on the shaft are a camel, rooster, bugler, crow, jockey(?) on horseback, and goose. Next are carved busts of a brown-haired man and a blond man wearing glasses. A knife, a two-door car, a cube, and Pegasus appear (a possible reference to the Mobil gasoline sign).

In the central scene a car and driver are pulled by a horse, a dog chases a rabbit, and an Indian head is depicted, which might refer to Chief Pontiac and the General Motors nameplate of the same name. Carved on the end of the shaft are a spotted pig, an arrow, small portraits of a bearded man (Lincoln?), a woman, jockey on a cow, dog, rifle, and deer head with antlers. The last two carvings show a woman in a two-piece bathing suit, hat, sunglasses, and high-heeled shoes facing a man dressed in a formal morning suit and top hat. A sword is between them.

No. 209.

The handle is carved as an Indian with feathers and beads. A Silver Beaver medal, one of Scouting's highest adult honors, hangs around the neck of the Indian. Below are a red arrow (for the Brotherhood of the Order of the Arrow, an honorary Scout camping society) and the date 1949. On the other side of the shaft is an Order of the Arrow lodge emblem with the initials *WWW*. Across from it is a green adult Scout's key, below which is carved SMTC (Scout Master's Training Course). A painted silver rope tied with Scout knots winds down the shaft. A red camp attendance ribbon, resembling a pennant, is inked *Flight/Springfield. Massa* and *Mont* are carved above and below a cabin indicating campsites. An arrow marked P symbolizes the Philmont Scout Reservation in Cimarron, New Mexico. At the end of the shaft is carved *Jamb/oree/19/28/Aug.27./3.11./27*. The shaft also contains numerous merit badges and other awards. The word *Easton* is carved in a square, and *M.E.Z.* and 1934 are around the end of the shaft. The cane, which may have been carved over several years, probably should be read from the bottom up.

The cane was carved and carried by Edward M. Zopff (also known as M. Edward Zopff), who at one time lived in Fraser, Michigan. A design engineer in Detroit, he was an active participant in the Detroit Area Council of the Boy Scouts of America. The cane reflects the personal Scouting history of Zopff, who was a Life Scout and a member of the Order of the Arrow, where the cane may have been used ceremonially.

Adult Scouts in the first quarter of this century sometimes carried canes. Boy Scouts today carry 6 foot "hiking sticks" on camping trips which are also used as poles for shelters and as tripods for cooking pots. Boys often carve these sticks with their personal history as Scouts, just as a Scout troop or other unit may carve its history on a totem pole (conversation with Thomas D. Trainor, Director of Administrative Services, Detroit Area Council, Boy Scouts of America, November 5, 1991).

No. 210.

The top of the removable handle, which was made on a lathe, has JKK engraved on it. A carved train, consisting of engine, coal tender, boxcar, and caboose, winds around the upper part of the shaft. A flowering thistle is at the end of the tracks. Below are a Civil War soldier holding his rifle at ready and a man sitting in a chair drinking a mug of beer. Near a wood stove a woman is reading *The Times*, while a cat rubs against her skirt. A man behind a bar drinks from a glass, the bottle on the bar beside

him. Above the man's shoulder is a bird, probably a parrot, in a ring. A jester blows his horn, and a girl swings from a trapeze. Finally, a man sits astride a beer barrel drinking a foaming mug of beer, watched by a goat.

No. 211.

A woman's elegant hand forms the handle of the cane. Four ball-in-cage motifs divide the cane, which is deeply carved with figures and animals. Carved sayings with related pictures along the shaft include (see details) *wicked children/two/bears destroyed/forty two of them* and *Hebrew children* (2 Kings 2:23–24), below a carved angel; *Daniel in a den/of/lions* (Dan. 6:16–23); *Jonathan and/David* (1 Sam. 18:1); and *Moses in the/wilderness* (Num. 20–21). Found in Minnesota.

No. 212.

The ferrule is handcrafted. Carved inscriptions state that the cane was made in 1884 for *James Francis, Pittsfield, Mass.*, who was *born Nov. 8, 1805*. The handle has a carved woman astride a dragon and a snake with *mythology* carved on the side. A snake winds below the main part of the handle to face a carved lion. Carved beside the lion is *Beautiful are the/admonitions of him/whoes life accords/with his teachings*. On the opposite side of the shaft is carved: *These are the wants of mortal man. I cannot want them long./ For life itself is but a span, and earthly bliss a song,/My last great Want-absorbing all, Is when beneath the sod,/And summond to my final call, The Mercy of my God*. The initials *J.Q.A.* appear in a half circle, and below is *James 3:7*, the Bible passage that is quoted along the length of the shaft. This passage is broken by another phrase that winds around the cane, *For/every kind/and of/and of things in the/sea/is tamed; and/hath been/tamed of/mankind*. Carved near the word "sea" are a flying fish, a shark, and a walrus. The cane has carvings of other finely rendered animals with carved first initials of their names: L for lioness, F for fox, S for squirrel, B for buffalo, W for wolf, D for deer, B for bird, O for owl, E for eagle, P for parrot, C for canary, and P for two pythons.

Also carved around the shaft in a spiral is *A true and faithful friend; a comfort in solitude, and a sanctuary in distress*. In a circle around the shaft are the words *A. P. Dean, Owego, N.Y.* Below, spiraling in the opposite direction, is *Life! We've been long together, through pleasant and through cloudy weather; Tis hard to part when friends are dear; Perhaps 'twil cost a sigh a tear; Then steal away, give little warning, chose thine own time; Say not good-night, but in some brighter clime bid me good morning. Vive. Vale*.

James Francis, the owner of the cane, was born in Pittsfield, Massachusetts, November 5, 1805, and died there July 31, 1894. His extensive obituary in a Pittsfield, Massachusetts, newspaper of August 5, 1894, reveals that he was a cabinetmaker with his own shop and a deacon of the Baptist Church in Pittsfield for many years.

Dean was in the lumber and the tanning businesses, both in Owego and Berkshire County, Massachusetts. Using only a jackknife, he carved canes that he presented to men he admired, including Presidents Hayes and Garfield as well as Francis Murphy, a temperance movement leader, and P. T. Barnum.

No. 213.

The handle is a carved black boot with toes protruding from it. Below it is a banner inscribed in ink *My first drink/only wine*. A carved man with a goblet in his hand stands next to a sheaf of wheat and a vine with grapes. A barrel encircles the shaft. Next are another banner with illegible writing and then bottles and jugs labeled with inked names of various drinks and containers: *Tickle, water cooler, apple brandy, old [illegible] little brown jug, rum sherry wine, brandy, pocket flask, poz worse, cherry herring, and in sure death.* Also pictured are a carved tap for a beer keg, a beer stein, a pitcher, and a goblet.

Near the bottom of the shaft there is a carved pair of black boots with snakes coming out of the tops. Below is the same man who appeared at the top of the cane, this time in his coffin, which is held by the devil. The last banner reads *T'was sparkling wine/but led me to an endless hell.* On the other side is an owl sitting on a coffeepot on which is inked *Trade mark/R.M. Foster.* See no. 199 for another cane by the same maker. The cane, which was found in California, once had a 1/2 inch ferrule. Similar temperance themes were expressed in the snake jugs made about this time at the Kirkpatrick pottery in Anna, Illinois.

No. 214.
The handle is carved with a platypuslike animal. At the top of the shaft in large lettering is the name *Rosey*, and on the opposite side is *The rum one.* A 7 inch carved eagle and many carved flasks, bottles, decanters, and glasses cover the shaft. Carving down the shaft reads *Grub Hoe/Coal Black/Pick Axe, E Pluribus Unum* (over the wings of an eagle), *Brandy/Jew Lips* (juleps), *Old/Jamaica/Whiskey/ Pandemonium/Gin/Cocktail, Brandy.* There is a carved square and compass surrounded by *5 points.* At the end of the shaft is another carved eagle with *Lieut. Gen Cuffrage* etched over the wings and *Martha's Vineyard* under them. *Nantucket* is carved on the other half of the shaft.

No. 215.
The separate, plain wood handle is pegged into the shaft. All the figures are carved and have details drawn in ink. At the top of the shaft is an eagle standing on an 8 1/2-inch-tall Uncle Sam. On the reverse side are the head of a man wearing a hat, the bust of a woman with her hair in a bun, and a bald bearded man. Below are a woman in a rocking chair, Happy Hooligan in a plaid jacket and a topknot, a hand, and Happy's brother, Gloomy Gus, holding a little girl. A round-faced woman with her hair in a bun sits in a chair, holding a cane.

In the next carving, Gus sits in a chair, and a large dog, Flip, licks him. A man's head and arm are carved nearby. Following this, Gus stands on the chair, trying to get away from the licking dog. Below are the Happy Hooligan with a topknot and a woman with a bun. A carved boot is at the end of the shaft.

Another cane (not illustrated) with cartoon characters by the same maker is in the Meyer collection. See no. 112 for an additional cane with cartoon characters.

No. 216.
The shaft has shallow carvings with inked details and designs. A banner at the top of the shaft states *Famous/Actresses.* An eagle gripping a shield and arrows in its claws holds the middle of the banner in its beak. Painted decorations include a flower, a heart with a cross, a heart with crossed arrows through it, and a sunburst. The first shallowly carved bust is entitled *M[ary] Pickford* (1894–1979), and the next bust, with painted flowers beside it, is identified as *Pola Negri* (1899–1987). The third actress is *C[lara] Young* (1890–1960), who has an American flag and a flower painted beside her. The last picture is of *B[ebe] Daniels* (1901–71). The name *E.P. Mares* is inked around the bottom of the shaft, followed by a painted American flag, a black inked flower, and a black band. A similar cane is at the Cooper-Hewitt National Museum of Design, Smithsonian Institution, New York.

No. 217.
The separate handle is attached to the shaft. The cane is decorated with halftone photographs, probably cut from magazines, decoupaged on the shaft, and then carved away from the background. First is a black eagle, then the upper half of a little girl holding a trophy, and then a nude boy. Below is an egret on a log, next to a woman wearing a 1940s playsuit and a sash from shoulder to hip. They are followed by a woman in a two-piece bathing suit next to a little blue heron. Next are the head of a woman holding her hand in front of her chin and a woman in shorts and a scanty top holding a glass(?). Below are a green heron, a black-crowned night heron, and a yellow-crowned night heron. The shaft has a punchwork background.

No. 218.
This cane seems to be a blend of ancient and modern mythology. The handle is followed by a bold 6 inch carving of a gorilla (King Kong?) with glass eyes. On the opposite side is the carved head of a woman (Fay Wray?), and below her are three intertwining Odd Fellows rings. In the middle of the cane a man (Hercules?) stabs a centaur. Below him are a skull and crossbones followed by a fierce griffin. *Carved by Leonard Taylor* is inscribed on a banner on the shaft.

No. 219.
The hand and ball form an apparently separate handle. Underneath the carved band is *Pos. FAIORM* (Positively Our Son Fraternal and Improved Order of Red Men). Beneath it is a shield inscribed *TOTE* (Totem of the Eagle). Below is the name *C. Kocher.* All the lettering is carved and painted black. On the side opposite the shield is a star with a face. A carved leafy vine extends from a crosshatched section at the bottom of the cane and twines up most of the shaft. A black snake winds up the cane, crossing the vine at regular intervals to give an overall appearance of large cross-hatches.

No. 220.
Fitz and Corbett is lightly incised above the boxers, identifying the carved figures as Robert "Fitz" Fitzsimmons and James J. "Gentleman Jim" Corbett. Fitzsimmons defeated Corbett on March 17, 1897, in Carson City, Nevada. At the top of the shaft, opposite the tiger, is carved the name *Geo. J.P.* The carved tiger probably depicts the pet tiger owned by Fitzsimmons which he reportedly led on a leash.

No. 221.
At the top of the shaft is an ink drawing of an eagle holding a banner reading *Champion of the World.* Below is a drawing of a boxer, and beside him a carved outline of a head is labeled *James J. Corbett.* This is followed by an ink sketch of two boxers and another carving labeled *John L. Sullivan*, while below him is a sketch of one boxer punching another. Beside them is a third carved head titled *Charley Mitchell.* All the portraits have details such as hairstyles, ties, and collars finely drawn in ink.

Next, two crossed punching bags are followed by decorations and the words *Corbett Mitchell/The Great Nine Minute Rage/ 1 2 3.* Below this, carved and detailed in ink, is an outline of the two boxers inscribed *First Round*; Corbett is shown hitting Mitchell. The next carved picture, labeled *Second Round*, again shows Corbett punching Mitchell. Beside them are two large boxing gloves drawn in ink. The last carving, *Third Round*, has Corbett with *American* printed over his head standing over the prone Mitchell, *England* written under him. An ink decorated section with a scallop edge ends the shaft.

This cane commemorates the January 25, 1894, fight between Corbett and Mitchell in Jacksonville, Florida, which Corbett won in three rounds. Previously Corbett had defeated Sullivan in twenty-one rounds on September 7, 1892. The 1892 fight was the first professional bout in which boxing gloves were used. See no. 222 for another cane that may have been made by the same hand. The use of shallow carving, inked design, and popular subjects of the period is similar to no. 253.

No. 222.
T W Moore is carved in a banner at the top of the shaft. Below are an inked drawing of a peacock and a carved horseshoe with daisies inscribed *Good Luck*. These are followed by a carving of a trotter and driver in a sulky. Below the horse are the time *2 04* and the name *Nancy Hanks*. Below are more carved horses and their times: *Flying Jib*, 2 05 1/4; *Director*, 2 17; *Directum*, 2 11 1/4; *Guy Wilks*, 2 15; *Stamboul*, 2 07 1/2; *Salvator*, 1 35 1/2. A sulky seat is drawn next to Director, and a dog is sketched facing Stamboul.

Below are a carved and inked western saddle, a racing cap, and a carved scene of a horse with a colt and a cow with two calves in a field; another saddle is above them. An unadorned area of the shaft ends with a serrated band. See also no. 253.

T.W. Moore is probably Trotwood Moore, a noted Tennessee writer. Before Moore made pacers popular, only trotters were favored in harness racing. Nancy Hanks was one of the first trotters to pull a sulky with low wheels as is used today. She ran a 2.04 mile in 1892. Director, 2.06 in 1891, was the sire of a long line of famous pacers including Directum and Flying Jib, who won $13,700 in 1892. Stamboul, a trotter, became famous when he won a large purse in San Francisco in 1888. This cane is probably by the same hand as no. 221.

No. 223.
The handle is a bird head with a carved diamond and cross. *The* is inscribed between the carvings of the boxer and the schoolboy. Below the boy is a carved alligator with incised scales. On the back of the shaft the bird's feathers swirl down, ending in what might be a tail. Below is the carved face of a young long-haired woman. Two leaves and a small snake are also carved. The ferrule was chiseled by hand and the ends simply bent over. Found in Rochester, New York.

No. 224.
The shaft is carved in interlocking turnings that appear to represent an auger and a reamer. The natural protrusions at the bottom of the shaft have been shaped to look like bolts. Found in Georgia.

The ball-style handle and twisting shaft are similar to forms of American glass whimsy canes (see p. 181). Made generally before 1920 by glassblowers between shifts or during the lunch hour, glass canes were both hollow and solid and of varying colors and lengths. See Joyce E. Blake, *Glasshouse Whimsies* (East Aurora, N.Y.: Joyce E. Blake, 1984).

No. 225.
A stylized flat circular cap made of a button is attached to the handle with brass tacks. The shaft consists of pillars and cross-hatched ball-in-cage motifs. The cane was acquired from a grandson of Amos Fisher, who owns a second, similar cane also made by his grandfather.

No. 226.
A rounded handle expands into a squared shaft, which encloses a whimsy ball, three rings, and another ball, all painted gold. Each cage is separated from the next by blocks of the shaft with gold painted banding on each end. A slender black crosshatched snake twines around the bottom part of the shaft. Zaunheiser, whose first name is unknown, reportedly was a Union Civil War veteran.

No. 227.
The delicate cage handle, which contains two balls, sits on a slender pillar with a partial collar. A carved ball crowns a turret-like section housing under glass four colored lithographs of Victorian scenes. The first is of a skipping boy with long hair in a short jacket; the second depicts a young girl in a pink dress standing by a pink rosebush; the third shows a girl with long blond hair in a mob cap and apron; and the last pictures a woman dressed in a Victorian coat and bonnet. Below these scenes another cage holds a square with glass inlays. Behind the glass can be seen some material, possibly hair or straw. Below this cage are mirrors in rectangles on each side of the cane. The rest of the shaft is carved in various geometric designs ending with cross-hatching.

No. 228.
Carved on the top of the shaft are the words *Beer/sheba/ Springs/Tenn.*

No. 229.
The handle is a buffalo horn attached with hand-forged nails.

No. 230.
Carved on the shaft is *Made by/NC Woolley 1895.*

No. 231.
The attached squared handle with cap and the hexagonal shaft are completely covered with cut pieces of Bakelite (first patented in 1906) of various sizes and colors, glued in a pattern resembling a crazy quilt. A few of the Bakelite pieces have been lost. Found in Tulsa, Oklahoma.

No. 232.
Written in ink on the shaft is *Pine Ridge 1885/CB*, followed by a small triangle. Pine Ridge is in Sioux County, North Dakota. Part of the wooden circular tip of the shaft is broken.

No. 233.
The knots are in designs similar to the rope motifs often found on scrimshaw canes. For another example of knot work see 111 171

POLITICS, PATRIOTISM, AND THE MILITARY

No. 234.
The extended handle of the cane is formed by the soldier's beard, which is inscribed on the underside with the initials J.B. Clover and star corps badges are carved on the top of his cap. Carved inscriptions include *(Company) F 125 N.Y. Vol* on the pack, *US* on the regular-issue standard ammunition box, and

W.F.M. on the canteen. Lightly carved on the top of the shaft are a G.A.R. (Grand Army of the Republic) badge and the carved intertwining initials GAR. The roll, pack, and standard bayonet identify the figure as an infantryman. A metal collar covers the juncture of the handle and the shaft.

No. 235.
The separate handle is the head of an eagle. A shield is at the bird's throat, and its wings are folded down the shaft. The eagle grasps an officer with epaulets by the seat of his side-striped trousers. Below the soldier's outstretched arms is a cannon. Facing down the shaft are a lion, rattlesnake, goat, red stag with black antlers, doe, fox, and an eagle clutching a snake that has a winged man as a head and a pointed tail.

In the middle of the cane is a five-tentacled scorpionlike creature with *Serpent of Rebel[lion]* written in yellow paint along its length. Each tentacle holds a tiny human head. Below this creature are a red animal, two flying eagles, turtle, coiled snake, lizard, eagle clutching a snake, and alligator. Holding a raised red saber, an upright soldier wearing an early-style Union uniform is astride a horse. Beside him is a red steer standing on its hind legs. Following is a monkey dangling a boy from one hand and holding an American flag in the other. Below the flag is a soldier with the head of an eagle wearing a hat marked US. He holds a saber in his right hand, while his left hand grasps a horn protruding from the hat (marked BU) of a man in a yellow coat, who holds a leash attached to the tail of a dog or lion. Below are a dog, two flying eagles, a rabbit, and an enlisted man holding a flag and a rifle with bayonet. The animals and human figures with animal features are probably references to specific leading secessionists in the Confederate states. Similar symbolism is used in a lithograph entitled *The Eagle's Nest*, published by E.B. and E.C. Kellog in 1861, pictured in Geoffrey C. Ward with Ric Burns and Ken Burns, *The Civil War* (New York: Alfred A. Knopf, 1990), 32.

According to family tradition, this cane was a gift from Union Secretary of War Edwin Stanton to a member of the Dana family in Massachusetts. In addition to the symbolism, the absence of corps badges or symbols of a veterans organization supports the dating of this cane to the early period of the Civil War.

No. 236.
A building with polychromed windows and two chimneys is above a carved eagle with a snake in its claws. Regimental symbols of a heart and shield are on the opposite side of the shaft. A cannon straddles the shaft, with its wheels on either side and its carriage projected through the shaft. Below the cannon is a pair of carved corps badges of crescent moons and stars. A snake coils up from the bottom of the metal-tipped shaft.

No. 237.
A round, decorated, commercially cast pewter handle caps the wooden shaft, which is completely covered with carvings of figures and calligraphy. Below the name *H. Keller* are two branches with leaves, a 6-inch-high soldier carrying an American flag, and a 3 1/2-inch-high mounted soldier. Deeply carved calligraphy, in which some of the letters are backward, covers the bottom half of the cane: *From 1862/To 1865/2B47OVC/Boycnk/Nashvi/Nayyya/Cheryn/MON5OM/Massey/Macon/Aveyrp/Morish/Fridom*. Although the inscription seems to be in code, some of the information may refer to battles in which the Second Battalion of the Fourth Ohio Volunteer Cavalry was involved. This cane may have been made during the later part of the Civil War or very soon afterward.

No. 238.
The handle is the carved head of a man with a painted red face and long black hair. A snake, coiling up from the bottom third of the cane, bites at his throat. On the back of the man's head are a painted shield and a carved G.A.R. medal that extends down the shaft. Descending the shaft between the coils of the snake are a clover, dog's head, Maltese cross, crossed cannons, ramrod, trumpet, crossed swords, ram, red diamond, red six-pointed star, red and blue cross, and another dog's head. The snake's tail ends in a carved alligator's mouth.

Some Civil War regiments had large concentrations of Native Americans to which the handle and the alligator could refer. The cane reportedly descended in a Massachusetts family.

No. 239.
The bone handle is inscribed *Pvt/Alonzo Smith/Co C/7th Michigan/Inftry/Hero of/Hatcher's Run Va/Oct 27, 1864*. There is an engraved eagle with a striped shield on top of the handle. The unadorned shaft is a branch. The 3/8 inch ferrule is missing.

The engagement at Hatcher's Run actually took place at Burgess's Mill. Part of Grant's encirclement of Petersburg, Virginia, the battle achieved little of significance in spite of 166 dead, 1,028 wounded, and 564 missing.

Alonzo Smith, a farmer born in Heartland, New York, joined Company C, Seventh Michigan Infantry, in August 1861. On October 27, 1864, he captured a Confederate flag by waiting behind a tree and ambushing several passing Confederate soldiers. He received the Medal of Honor (then given to men who captured an enemy flag) on November 14, 1864. By the time Smith was discharged he was a lieutenant commanding a company. He returned to Middleport, New York, to live.

No. 240.
The handle is the head of an eagle wearing a cap that is a shield with stars and stripes. The back of the eagle's neck is carved with a scene of two uniformed soldiers standing under trees. One soldier has his hand upraised as if waving. His roll and pack and the standard bayonet indicate he is an infantryman. The uniforms, with buttons on both sides of the coats, are somewhat stylized. The throat of the eagle has a large carved swirl. The shaft is painted black with occasional brown mottling. This cane could have been made during the Civil War rather than after it.

No. 241.
This cane, carved to show stages of the battle at Antietam, is inscribed at the top of the shaft, *Cut from the battle/field/of/Antietam*. Listed sideways down the shaft are (Generals) *Hancock Meade/McClellan/Hooker Reno*. In the scene entitled *Siege*, a soldier stands behind a cannon aimed at the Dunker Church; a tree is on either side of the church.

In the next section, *The Charge*, two lines of Confederate soldiers are led by an officer with an upraised sword under a Confederate flag. Opposing them, a Union officer leads six men with rifles and fixed bayonets. A soldier carrying a large American flag marches behind, followed by others—some on foot and others on horseback—and two cannons.

The next section shows a bridge labeled *Burnside*, at which standing and kneeling soldiers shoot. A man rides up an incline labeled *hill*. In the scene called *Rebs* there are several soldiers, two on horseback. One carries a small pennant, and the other holds a sword. In the last tableau, called *Wounded*, two men carry a man on a litter, while a horse draws a hospital cart.

G.A.R. and other veterans reunions were frequently held at battlefields, and carvings, including canes, were often made from wood gathered at the battlefield. This cane may have been made during the war or soon afterward. A similar Antietam cane is pictured in Marian Klamkin and Charles Klamkin, *Wood Carvings: North American Folk Sculptures* (New York: Hawthorne Books, 1974), 82. Found in Milbain, Centre County, Pennsylvania.

No. 242.
The handle, a carved head of a Civil War soldier with a kepi (hat) and faintly carved mustache and goatee, may be a portrait. The handle is made of a different wood than the shaft. The collar, which is iron, may have been formed from the spout of a "drum" canteen. This cane was probably made during the Civil War rather than afterward.

No. 243.
The top of the handle has an inlaid metal cross. A drapery encircles the top of the shaft. The first major figure is a drummer boy. On the opposite side, two Zouaves with crossed bayonets face each other. Above them are corps badges of a Maltese cross, a six-pointed star, clover leaf, five-pointed star, circle, and crescent moon. A band that looks like a belt with an oval buckle inscribed US divides the upper part of the cane from the rest of the carvings. Included is a G.A.R. medal of an eagle sitting on crossed cannons that hold a flag, below which hangs a five-pointed medal.

On the side opposite the G.A.R. medal, a soldier wearing a uniform with double rows of buttons stands at attention, holding a flag. A cross, diamond, five-pointed star, and cross in a circle are carved next to the flag. This flag and the one in the G.A.R. medal each have seven stripes and thirteen stars in four rows. Descending the shaft on either side of the soldier and the medal are an arrow, diamond, four-leaf clover, and heart. Three crossed rifles with bayonets are under the heart.

Below the soldier are a shield and a shield-shaped medal with a hanging Maltese cross. (This may be the Kearny Medal, named in honor of General P. Kearny, given only to his troops.) A piece of hardtack is next to the medal. Below this is a cook pot hanging from a stick suspended at each end from crossed logs. This is followed by three corps badges—a diamond, an acorn, and a shield with an anchor and a cannon on it.

Below the crossed rifles is a canteen with the initials *N.M.H./Va.* (New Market Heights, Virginia, was the location of a successful Union action on December 10, 1864.) Finally, there are crossed swords, a saddled horse, a cross, a diamond with a triangle in it, a crescent moon with a star in it, crossed cannons, and a coiled strip of bunting.

This cane was found in Reading, Pennsylvania, in the home of a descendant of the drummer.

No. 244.
The upper tableau portrays Lincoln standing on a platform flanked by two flags. A large wreath frames a kneeling man. *Lincoln* is written under the scene. The second scene is lettered *Gen Grant for/Richmond* and depicts a mounted uniformed soldier holding an upraised sword. The last carving is a Union soldier wearing a plumed hat and standing on a shieldlike platform, gazing at the distance. Gloves indicate he is an officer, and the short sword may show he is in the cavalry. Found in Ohio.

An almost identical cane was given to the Smithsonian Institution by Ida Honoré Grant, the wife of General Frederick Grant, Ulysses S. Grant's son.

No. 245.
The upper 18 inches of the cane is carved in the round as a full-length figure of Abraham Lincoln standing on a platform. Below Lincoln is one side and the complete roof of a log cabin. Farther down the shaft is a protruding tree stump, and near the bottom of the cane is a felled tree. The cane is reported to have been made by an African-American in Kentucky, where it was found.

No. 246.
The upper 14 1/2 inches of the cane is a full-length carving in the round of Abraham Lincoln standing on a block of wood decorated with round punch marks. His trousers are incised with diagonal stripes. Lyle Maynard, the daughter of the maker, from whom the cane was reportedly acquired, later added a metal and plastic tip to assist her in walking. This cane was exhibited at the Kentucky Art and Craft Foundation Gallery, Louisville, in 1988 as part of the exhibition *Sticks: Historical and Contemporary Kentucky Canes.*

No. 247.
All three canes (nos. 247–49) in this group are very similar in theme. An eagle head forms the handle. The first carving on the shaft is a shield flanked by flags, below an eagle with uplifted wings. Below on the shaft are several relief portraits—a man in a brimmed hat, a man with a mustache wearing a suit, another mustached man in a uniform, and a sailor. There are a horse head in a horseshoe, two birds with folded wings on either side of a flying bird, an anchor, an antlered deer's head, a monkey with a clenched fist, a fox chased by two dogs, clasped hands, and a cat and fiddle. (The cat and the fiddle may be based on the well-known nursery rhyme.) Last is a woman wearing tights, holding a flag. The metal ferrule is missing.

No. 248.
In addition to an alligator, which is carved on the handle, the cane has a G.A.R. medal, clasped hands, deer head, lion head, horse head in a horseshoe, and a woman in tights holding a flag (see also description of no. 249).

No. 249.
This cane and no. 248, although not made by the same person, have very similar themes. Both have a central carving of a soldier facing a sailor framed by a thin circular line. The decorations on both shafts start with eagles with outstretched wings. A shield with a flag on each side sits below. Both canes have running dogs chasing a fox that is halfway in its hole, a cat playing a fiddle, and an owl and a squirrel.

The shaft also has carvings of a monkey, dog's head, dog sitting up, mermaid, peacock, hawk, and hand holding a snake.

No. 250.
The handle, which was made separately and pegged to the shaft, is a fat bird with a large tail; a brass tack decorates the middle of its breast. At the top of the shaft are four corps badges—a green clover (second corps), black diamond (third), green triangle (fourth), and white Maltese cross (fifth). A flag with seven red stripes and six white ones sweeps down the shaft.

Below are many other corps badges—a Union Signal Corps badge of green crossed flags, black cross (sixth), red crescent moon with a star (seventh), black five-pointed star (eighth), white shield (ninth), and yellow dove carrying a banner. The bottom of the white flagpole divides the upper part of the shaft from the lower, while below it are a gold and black acorn (four-teenth), red "four bastion fort" badge (tenth), black star (twentieth), white horse, and red diamond (third).

A black banner swirls down the rest of the shaft. In between the swirls are the heads of a cat and other animal, a white arrow (seventeenth), black four-leaf clover (eighteenth), white Maltese cross (fifth), yellow duck, black star (twentieth), red shield (twenty-third), long-legged bird, yellow bird, black shield, red heart, playing card symbols of a heart, club, spade, and diamond, a fish, and a scorpion. The Union army often had mascots, which may help explain the animals on this and other Civil War canes.

No. 251.
A brass button with an eagle and the initials NDVSH (National Home for Disabled Veteran Soldiers) is placed in the top of this cane. The American flag that wraps around the upper part of the shaft has a design similar to that of no. 250. The blue field of the shaft contains twelve stars arranged around the outside with one larger star in the middle. Above the flag is carved In/God/We/Trust/* * */Liberty. Below the flag is inscribed We/will/stand/by the/* * */flag. A black belt with a buckle marked US also separates the cane into parts. A carved banner winding down the length of the cane is inscribed *To. Capt. P.R. Schuyler. Post. No 51 G.A.R. by. Comrade. J. McClarnen. Sept 4th 1888.

Around the shaft under the belt are corps badges, including a three-leaf clover, diamond, triangle, and circle. Descending the cane, alternating with the winding banner, are a Maltese cross, cross, crescent moon with a star, six-pointed star, a shield with an anchor and small fish on it, a "four bastion fort" badge, a half-moon, an anchor with a small castle and turrets above it, an acorn, a diamond with a shield inscribed US, a circle with an X in it, an arrow, a Jerusalem cross, a Maltese cross, crossed flags with a baton, a five-pointed cross, a shield, a heart, and a square with a diamond in it.

There is a nearly identical cane in the Meyer collection (not illustrated), which is inscribed To Richard. Edwards. Co. H. 148 Regit N.Y. Vol INFIT/From. Sam. Garner, Dec. 25, 1891, probably indicating that a person other than those named made both canes.

No. 252.
This cane is similar to two others in the Meyer collection (not illustrated), one of which has inscribed on it C. Teale, maker, Bath, N.Y. Several others by the same maker are known. The top of the knob handle has a circular ivory inlay containing a red polished stone circle and a brown five-pointed stone star. A wooden collar in the form of a rope tension drum separates the knob from the black shaft.

The shaft is decorated with various carved military and patriotic emblems finished with pen and ink. First is a shield with seven red stripes and thirteen stars, then the U.S. eagle on a shield holding three arrows. Below is a G.A.R. medal, followed by a smaller eagle with a shield.

The rest of the shaft contains individual interpretations of various Union corps badges, most of which are decorated in pen and ink. Numerous corps are represented: an acorn (fourteenth corps), a six-pointed star (eighth), a clover (second), a scalloped circle holding a square within a diamond (twenty-fifth?), a Maltese cross (fifth), a circle with four minié balls (sixteenth), a diamond with three diamonds drawn inside it, and an upside-down shield with crossed swords.

Next are a heart with crossed arrows (twenty-fourth), a fan-leafed cross with an octagonal center (nineteenth), an anchor

and crossed cannon on a shield (ninth), a diamond with a clover, a shield (twenty-third), an arrow (seventeenth), a diamond (third), a circle with a star and crescent (seventh), a diamond with US inside it (fifteenth), a triangle (fourth), a circle with a cannon and crossed swords, a cinquefoil (twenty second), a cross (sixth), and a circle with a star in it (first).

C. Teale is probably Charles W. Teale (1817–95), who lived in the New York State Soldiers Home and is buried in the Veterans Administration National Cemetery in Bath, New York.

No. 253.
The shaft is carved and etched with detailed portraits of Spanish-American war heroes. Below the detachable screw-top handle (which has a concealed 13¼ inch knife attached) is a scene of two battleships, one labeled Olympia. Two sailors stand on either side of a raised carving of a small eagle carrying a banner in its beak reading Favorites of Our Navy. The eagle carries in its claws a circular plaque that contains a finely drawn portrait of George Dewey. Below him in differing sizes are similar pen and ink drawings of Winfield S. Schley, the ship Oregon, William T. Sampson, an unnamed ship, Charles T. Clark, an unnamed soldier, Robley D. Evans, a battleship, a woman greeting a sailor, and another warship. Each section of the shaft is covered with drawings, either a design background or pictures of sailors and soldiers ready for battle.

Commodore Dewey (1837–1917) defeated the Spanish fleet in Manila Bay. The ships under the command of Commodore Schley (1839–1909) and Rear Admiral Sampson (1840–1903) defeated the fleet of Admiral Cervera outside Santiago Bay. Charles E. Clark (1843–1922) commanded the battleship Oregon, which helped blockade Santiago and was a major force in the battle against Cervera. Robley "Fighting Bob" Evans (1846–1912) was commander of the battleship Iowa and fired the first gun at Cervera's fleet as it came out of Santiago Bay in July 1898.

A similar cane, probably by the same maker, is pictured in Larry Hackley, Sticks: Historical and Contemporary Kentucky Canes (Louisville: Kentucky Art and Craft Foundation, 1988), no. 15. Although by a different artist, a very similar cane in the Meyer collection was owned by Thomas Gumbell of Brighton, Iowa, who served on the gunship Marblehead in the Spanish-American War. Other canes were made using this same approach and technique with popular subjects of the time, indicating the possible existence of a school or "factory." See also nos. 221 and 222. The technique is similar to that used on scrimshaw canes.

No. 254.
The knob handle has deep lines and cross-hatching. The shaft has low-relief carvings of an eagle with a shield on one side and US/A above crossed cannons on the other. A turtle and Nov/14/1917 are below the cannons. The name B.B./Wilmoth is carved on the other side of the staff, followed by a band, triangles, and a rattlesnake. The 1½ inch ferrule is missing. Wilmoth, who reportedly carved the cane himself, was from West Virginia and served in the U.S. Army during World War I. The cane was found in Elkins, West Virginia.

No. 255.
Dewey is carved around the top of the shaft. The length of the shaft is carved to read Patriotic Order Jr. Mc. of America./Remember the Maine 1898. &/Our Heros Dewey, Schley and Hobson. The Junior Order of United American Mechanics was a fraternal organization with great patriotic zeal (see also no. 206). For more information on Dewey and Schley, see no. 253. Richmond P. Hobson

(1870–1937) sailed the *Merrimac* into Santiago Harbor, June 3, 1898, planning to sink her and block the harbor's channel, but the Spanish opened fire and prevented the plan from succeeding. Hobson and his men were captured by Admiral Cervera. After his release, Hobson returned home a hero.

A similar cane of Admiral Dewey by the same maker is pictured in Lynda Roscoe Hartigan, *Made with Passion* (Washington, D.C.: National Museum of American Art, Smithsonian Institution, 1990), 115. There are other known examples of this subject, at least one by the same carver.

No. 256.
The handle of this campaign cane is the bent-back full-length figure of William Jennings Bryan (1860–1925). A small bird sticks its head out of Bryan's side pocket. Deeply carved block lettering on the shaft reads *W. J. Bryan Hero for Free Silver/Democratic President Champion 1896/The Solon of the 19th Century J.M.*

This cane is by the same maker as no. 257 and probably no. 259. Other examples are known. Most of these canes reportedly have been found in Pennsylvania.

William Jennings Bryan, a populist, ran unsuccessfully as the Democratic party presidential candidate in 1896, 1900, and 1908. In 1896 he campaigned on the issue of free silver. Bryan assisted the prosecution in the 1925 Scopes "monkey" trial, opposing the teaching of Darwin's theory of evolution.

No. 257.
Deeply carved block lettering on the shaft reads *Wife of W. J. Bryan Hero for Free Silver/Champion for the Democratic Rules/Solon of the 19th Century J.M.* William Jennings Bryan's wife was Mary Baird. Found in Pennsylvania. See no. 256.

No. 258.
The handle is a thick human leg wearing a boot. A dove holding an olive branch sits on the handle. This is followed on the shaft by a 10-inch-high soldier with his hand on his sword. He is followed by a 10 1/4-inch-high mustached man wearing a hat, bow tie, and suit with six buttons and wide lapels. The carved letters at the bottom of the shaft read *President. U.S./In God and You — /We Trust 1896.* The reference is probably to William McKinley and his successful 1896 presidential campaign against William Jennings Bryan. Found in Pennsylvania.

No. 259.
Carved in high relief underneath the full-length figure of William Jennings Bryan are the words *W. J. Bryan Hero for Free Silver/Democratic President Champion/The Solon of the 19th Century.* See no. 256.

No. 260.
Carved block lettering on the shaft reads *Clayton C. Adams Fen. Sec/of P.O.S.O.A.* (Patriotic Order Sons of America) *No. 531 for 13 Years/Tax Collector of Lenhartsville for 15 Years.* This was probably a presentation cane.

No. 261.
Carved in high relief on the squared shaft; *WF. Donahue/NY* and the complete alphabet. Many of the letters are reversed in the way that children sometimes print. Geometric designs are below the initials NY. Donahue was probably the child owner of the cane. It is possible that he carved the cane. For other children's canes, see nos. 74 and 101.

No. 262.
A formal relief bust of Theodore Roosevelt (1858–1919) in his army uniform (inscribed *Our President*) and portraits labeled *Lawton, McKinley, Sampson,* and *Dewey* are carved on the shaft between the natural diamond forms in the wood (see no. 270). Crossed swords are carved under Roosevelt, and two doves and a leaf are lightly incised on the shaft of the cane.

Roosevelt became president when William McKinley was assassinated in 1901. Brigadier General H.W. Lawton (1843–99) commanded troops in the Spanish-American War, including the Rough Riders, who were recruited by Roosevelt. For information on Dewey and Sampson, see no. 253.

No. 263.
The handle of this campaign cane is a ball with ivory inlays. The shaft has inserted lithographic portraits of William Howard Taft, Lincoln, and Washington, followed by a movable coiled snake carved free from the shaft. There are additional small geometric inlays of wood, ivory, obsidian, silver, and shell. Inset in pewter is 1909, the year Taft was inaugurated as president.

No. 264.
The top of the six-sided stylized handle has an incised eagle with a shield and the date 1817. Incised into the shaft is *Equality/Columbia/Freedom. U.S./Liberty. July 4/Independence/Union 1776* (then thirteen stars)/*Harmony. G.W./Strength 7239903/962573/ Justice. N.H./Power & Truth. Genesee* is carved around the shaft above the numbers 71285640/31706954. The remainder of the shaft is unadorned except for carved coils around the bottom. "Genesee" followed by "G.W." may refer to the carver, owner, or possibly even George Washington.

No. 265.
This cane was carved as a souvenir of Monticello, Thomas Jefferson's home in Virginia. Although Jefferson was not a Mason, the top of the cane is ringed with Masonic symbols: a compass and square with a *G,* a horseshoe, and a square shaped like an hour-glass with an arrow in it. Below is a flying eagle holding a Knights of Pythias emblem. Carved down the shaft is *Thos. Jeffer/son of Va. Born Apr. 13. 1743. Was president. USA. 1801 to 1809. Wrote Declaration of/Independence/Founder of the University/Died July 4.1821 Va. 1819* (founding year of the University of Virginia)/*This cane was cut near/Jefferson's tomb.* A carved replica of Jefferson's home is titled *Monticello.* An additional inscription reads *Jeffersons dying/words. I resig[n] my spirit/to God my daughter to/my country.* There are also carvings of a fish, sheep, duck, another fish, and a snake.

A large number of similar canes are known, some probably by the same carver. An 1892 inventory of the canes owned by Thomas C. Yarnell, D.D., listed a "cane with carved work (from near President Jefferson's tomb)"; *Bits of Wood: Walking Sticks* (Philadelphia: Press of Allen, Lane and Scott, 1892), 8.

Unlike European canes, American canes made from historical structures and artifacts seem relatively common. Interesting earlier examples are the wooden canes made in 1844 from the temporary coffin in which the body of Mormon prophet Joseph Smith was returned to Nauvoo, Illinois. See Steven G. Barnett, "Canes of the Martyrdom," *Brigham Young University Studies* 21, no. 2 (1981), 205–11.

No. 266.
This cane was probably inspired by the erection of the Statue of Liberty in the United States in 1886 and the Eiffel Tower at the

1889 International Exposition in Paris. A carved five-pointed star is on the top of the crosshatched handle. This is followed by the incised words *Made by/E. Dasse/1890.* A rope with an attached anchor circles a small natural diamond-shaped indentation in the wood. On the opposite side are crossed French and American flags with the word *Union* and a five-pointed star over three cannonballs. Below are the Statue of Liberty, next to her the Washington Monument, and then the Eiffel Tower with inked details. A shield with stripes and two rows of five stars is carved above a second shield with the inked initials *R.F.* and *Patrie* underneath. Next is a horse head in a horseshoe and the bust of a woman in a toga holding a palm branch. Below are raised portraits of two men in carved square frames; one appears to be Washington and the other Lafayette.

Below the portraits are many small detailed carvings. A banner stating *E Pluribus* is followed by a five-pointed star, an eagle, crossed cannons, and swords. Opposite is a branch in an urn. Next are a crescent moon (broken) and four stars, a small drum, and two women dressed in classical robes—the one holding a flag is apparently Columbia. There are also an owl, clasped hands, a lion, nude woman, frog playing a banjo, and finally, an artist (below Columbia and the clasped hands) who stands before his easel, head in hand as if he were thinking. The last 5 inches of the staff are covered with bands of lacelike designs.

No. 267.

A Chinese man's head forms the handle of the cane. *Confucius* is carved on the back of the head, and a perpetual calendar is carved on the top. [Indecipherable] *Fayette, Ind.* is engraved on the metal band around his head that forms his cap. A farm scene is drawn in ink on one side of his neck, and a rooster is pictured on the other. Written under the figure's chin is *Only 3 pieces/glued on this cane.* A carved miniature cane is glued on the shaft, next to which is written *Piece of table/106 years old.* Nearby is carved *Cedar wood carved by/Joel Peffley/Colburn Ind.*

Carved down the shaft are the arms of Confucius holding a frog, a tiny dog, a bird, the three Odd Fellows rings with an ax through them, a Masonic square and compass with a *G,* and a carved scene of two men labeled *Wm. Penn laying out/Philadelphia.* Below the scene is a carved man titled *John Hancock/head of the/Provincial Cong[ress].* On the opposite side is a rectangle containing *Centennial/1876,* followed by two snakes, one emerging from a hole. Below Hancock is carved a battle scene labeled *Bat. Lexington 1775,* followed by an armadillo and a turtle.

Another set of interlocking Odd Fellows rings and a book are suspended from an ax, which is glued to the shaft. Written beside these objects is *Piece of/wood from/the largest/tree in the/world-Cal.* Shaking hands through the rings are two men labeled *Washington/South* and *Grant/North.* Beside them a rectangle is carved *Dedicated to the/Columbian Worlds/Fair Chicago Ill. 1893* and *Carved for/the Centenni-/al Phil. Pa. 1876.* The book glued to hang from the three rings is inscribed *Hachmetac/wood/from East/port Me.*

Carved below are an owl, swordfish, shield, squirrel sitting in a knothole, two oak leaves, scissors, razor, pipe, and a scene of people walking entitled *Going to the/Centennial.* Two babies are saying, *Ise comin.* Railroad tracks lead to a knob which is drawn as a building labeled *Depot.* Farther down the shaft is a man riding a grasshopper labeled *Kansas/goes to the/Centennial.* The carvings end with a man on an elephant.

Peffley, who was listed in the census as a farmer, made several penmanship drawings in the 1850s. He also carved at least two small wooden owls.

Penmanship drawing, Joel Peffley, February 29, 1855. Collection of George H. Meyer.

No. 268.
The shaft is pegged into a separate handle, probably made of gumwood.

No. 269.
The skull handle is 7 inches high. In white paint on the shaft is *Okinawa/Japan/Hawaii/Phillippin's/Hong Kong/Vitnam.* Above the word "Japan" is a painted mountain with snow on it. This cane was found at a garage sale in 1981 in Lafayette, Indiana. The cane probably relates to the anti–Vietnam War movement. It may have been made by a sailor or soldier on a tour of duty.

No. 270.
The carver used wood from a tree called the diamond willow (*Salex missouriensis*), which has diamond-shaped indentations caused by fungi that erode the scars left by fallen diseased branches. These natural formations may be further shaped and carved to create a pattern on the cane. See Karen Bingham, "Carving Diamond Willow Canes," *Creative Crafts* 8, no. 3 (June 1982), 49. See also H.J. Lutz, "Observations on 'Diamond Willow,' with Particular References to Its Occurrence in Alaska," *The American Midland Naturalist* 601, no. 1 (1958), 176–85.

The extension of the plain elongated knob handle is a hand with painted black fingernails. On the back of the hand are a carved eagle with spread wings and the date 1900. In incised lettering on the inside of the wrist is *Ypso/Facto.* The hand holds an arm with a second hand, this one having two black fingernails and three fingers turned under. Carved on the arm are a painted black horse drinking from a trough, a black-spotted dog, a black flag, an ax, two black rifles with bayonets, and 1861. Also carved are a black ladder, black cow, and the names *Mike* and *Orion*.

Two carved and painted snakes face the bottom of the shaft, and the head of a third snake emerges from a natural opening in the wood. *From D. Young/To/C.Y. Young* and a Masonic square and compass are carved at the end of the shaft. The backgrounds are all punch marked. The ferrule is handcrafted.

No. 271.
The elongated knob handle is painted black with gold dots. Below a carved collar painted gold is a section decorated with punched stars and quarter circles. The section ends with a serrated edge around most of the shaft. A carved branch descends the shaft behind the face of a man which is made from the natural shape of the wood. An animal sits on a natural concave diamond formation in the shaft and encircles part of the man's head with its tail. Both man and animal have bead eyes. Below the animal is a carved rectangle with the name *Orion* carved on a punched background. Below the end of the branch are an American flag and then a similar carved rectangle with the name *Mike*. Both words are painted gold.

In a rectangle below *Orion* is a carved fish with bead eyes. At the end of the shaft are an animal with bead eyes and an intentionally omitted front paw, a natural diamond carved to resemble a flower with a pistil and a leaf, and a small animal's head looking at the end of the cane. The ferrule is handcrafted. Found in Manchester, Michigan.

No. 272.
Natural empty spaces and indentations in the wood are used along the shaft's length. A 6 inch hand extends from the plain elongated knob handle, with natural divisions in the wood forming a separate thumb and second and fifth fingers. The third and fourth fingers are together on a different extension of the wood. Carved nails on each finger are painted gold, and a simple gold band on the ring finger is decorated with crosshatching. On the back of the hand are two carved rectangles with punch-marked backgrounds containing *Orion/Mike*. Opposite them is an irregular rectangle containing a rifle with bayonet. Below, along the shaft in raised lettering painted gold is *Capt.O.B./Weed/U.S.A. MD/1898/14.US.Inft/22.ond.Mich/Vol.Inft/1902*. At the bottom of the cane are a carved bass, a Masonic square and compass, and a horse and rider. Below the feet of the horse are the words *Comeing/Home*. Various creatures emerge from openings in the shaft. The ferrule is handcrafted.

No. 273.
Along the length of the shaft are carved separate rectangles with punched backgrounds and the carved words *Orion. Mike/Mrs. S.A. Walton/Pontiac/U.and I.* There are incised decorative lines and dabs of silver paint. A rabbit's head is carved at the bottom of the shaft. The ferrule is handcrafted.

No. 274.
The elongated knob handle is painted black and dabbed with gold paint, probably representing stars. Inside incised rectangles, block lettering raised from punch-marked backgrounds reads *Mike. to/Adelbert. C./Kelley/1861*. Other carved rectangles contain an upright heron, a fish and a heron bending over, and a black crow. The natural diamond-shaped openings in the wood have been incorporated into the design. Punch marks cover the surface except where raised areas, such as the heron and fish, are decorated with less dense markings. Several otherwise plain

surfaces are decorated with punched-in tiny stars painted gold. A small spotted snake faces the bottom of the shaft. The ferrule is handcrafted.

No. 275.
The elongated knob handle is painted black. The shaft has many natural openings and indentations—an animal peaks out of one. The carved areas have punch marks for backgrounds and excised carvings of a shield with wings, horse, fish, rifle with bayonet, and small animal's head. Two naturally formed ovals are decorated with vines formed by punch marks, and one is ornamented with a line of punched stars. The ferrule is handcrafted.

No. 276.
Carved on the shaft below the green elongated knob handle are a turtle, four fish (one a swordfish), and an eel with a worm in its mouth. Two green snakes coil around the main part of the shaft, and a snake with a missing head is on the other branch. Above the latter snake is a circle of tiny humans with their hands clasped over their heads, and below is the sole of a shoe. A carved lizard faces the end of the shaft. The ferrule is handcrafted.

No. 277.
Viewed from a distance, the cane is a one-armed soldier whose faceless head is the cane's handle. The 7 inch arm is uniformed in a sleeve with corporal's stripes and terminates in a carved hand with individually carved fingers. On the back of the hand is a large green leaf with incised veins. The shaft has carved rectangles containing raised lettering on a punched background. *Mike* is on what would be the front of the jacket; *1861* appears above the sleeve; *Orion* is carved in the middle of the back. At the bottom third of the shaft is carved *To/E.C./Eldred/Montrose*. The maker incorporated all the twists and knobs and holes of the wood into his design. There is a face that could be a wolf or an owl; a fish is carved in a square; an animal, possibly a rat, faces the bottom of the shaft. In a carved rectangle opposite the rat is a badge of a trefoil with a star in each of the three leaves (second corps). Punch marks outline or decorate various parts of the shaft. The ferrule is handcrafted.

No. 278.
A hand emerges from the toothed edge of a black sleeve, which is the elongated knob handle of the cane, painted with gold dots, now faded. The individual fingers have nails painted gold. Small gold circles line the edge of the opening in the diamond willow wood. Below, a carved black pig with a protruding brown head splits itself around the shaft as if cut and stretched, resulting in two curling tails. Extending down the shaft are gold painted letters in rectangles: *1861/Mike/War/Co A7/Orion*. Below is a black trefoil corps badge (second corps), a rifle with bayonet, and a small black house with a gold roof and large door—perhaps a guardhouse. There are numerous gold dots along the waving lines of the wood. The ferrule is handcrafted.

No. 279.
The elongated knob handle is painted black with brown spots. Gold lettering in the rectangles with punched background reads *Alvin N. Hall/Co. C. 3d/Mich. Inft./1864* (see p. 186). There is a black trefoil badge (second corps). Several large animals are boldly carved along the shaft: a black-painted turtle, lizard, and snake face toward the bottom of the cane. In the middle of the lizard's back is a rectangle inscribed *Mike*. The lizard's belly is formed by

a natural hole in the wood, and the lizard rests its head on a portion of the shaft formed by another natural opening. Below the head is a flag and then *Orion—1861/War.* A rifle with bayonet is opposite the lizard, and a shield rests between two branches. The ferrule is handcrafted.

According to his discharge papers, Alvin N. Hall enlisted in the Third Regiment Michigan Infantry on September 5, 1864, in Pontiac, Michigan, and was discharged on May 25, 1866, in Victoria, Texas.

Alvin N. Hall (first man on left), ca. 1865.

Hall's certificate of discharge from the Union army.

No. 280.
The plain elongated knob handle is decorated with black paint and small silver painted stars. Below are several carved sections, each with a rectangular frame and punch-marked background setting off the raised lettering *Orion/Mike.to/my.friend/1839. W.A. Burch/1317* is handwritten on a section of plain polished wood

that is the largest of the four natural diamond forms. The shaft is also decorated with four carved rectangles with punch-marked backgrounds containing a bass, heron, trout, and anchor, all painted silver. The carved lettering also contains traces of silver paint. The ferrule is handcrafted.

No. 281.
A plain elongated knob handle forms the top of the cane, which is made from a twisted branch. A knothole appears to be an eye, and a protrusion in the branch, a nose. Below this, a carved man hangs upside down. This is followed by three natural divisions in the shaft, one of which is broken. A carved snake winds down the shaft with a lizard beside him. At the bottom is a shallowly carved square with the word *Mike.* The ferrule is handcrafted.

CONTEMPORARY CANES

No. 283.
York has made and sold several similar canes.

No. 284.
The maker of the cane, a musician, reportedly carried the cane over his shoulder and would press a lever at the back of the dog's head to make the tongue stick out at women. The back of the handle, which holds the device, also appears to be a face. The cane was acquired about 1987 from Cathart's estate.

No. 285.
Willis stated that his goal in the 1930s was to put a cane in the hands of every person. He said he became so skilled at cane making that during the depression he was able to earn a living from his carving. Willis also painted pictures. See William Ferris, *Local Color: A Sense of Place in Folk Art* (New York: McGraw-Hill Book Company, 1982), 192–212.

No. 286.
The shaft is a vine, and the handle a piece of wood carved separately and attached with gimp to conceal the juncture. Bark serves as the snake's skin, and the shaft is decorated with punch marks. The handle is incised with cross-hatching and punch marks. Townsend made similar canes.

No. 287.
HW is carved on the handle. "Eve" wears green platform high-heeled shoes. The alligator wraps its tail around an owl at the base of the shaft. There are several known canes by Williams, who during the last few years of his life lived in a van parked beneath an overpass. Williams carved a wood nose and attached it to sunglasses to replace his own nose, which had been shot off in a fight.

No. 288.
Miller made and sold a number of similar canes in the 1970s and 1980s.

No. 290.
McKee has made several similar canes.

No. 291.
Twenty-six black-painted skulls form the shaft, decreasing in size from handle to ferrule. Spencer, a motorcyclist, also carves exotic ax and knife handles. He has made and sold several similar canes.

No. 292.
The tip of the handle is a cork cap with a metal ring. A black snake with a glass ruby embedded between imitation emerald eyes spirals up the lower half of the metal shaft. Possibly Rastafarian (relating to the Jamaican religious cult). A similarly made staff, which is in the Meyer collection (not illustrated), and a few similar canes by this maker are known.

No. 297.
The handle was made separately and attached to the four-sided shaft with nails. The low-relief carved cane has three cages, two containing wood balls and one holding a four-sided star. Each side of the shaft has linear carvings in rectangles separated by squares of cross-hatching. The side pictured has the signature *W.S./Peavley*, a woman, strange animal, man wearing glasses, crayfish, cat, another woman, and a fish. *Lat Larry* is carved at the top of the next side, followed by a man, bald man, mouse, dog, star, and horse. The third side is dated 1980, followed by a star, woman's head, frog, squirrel, dancing man, and another woman's head. Down the last side are two women's heads, an elephant, woman, man, and woman. The people, all different in appearance, could be portraits. There are several known similar canes by Peavley.

No. 298.
The shaft is signed *Ralph Buckwalter*. Buckwalter, who was a prolific carver, made and sold several similar canes along with other carvings.

No. 299.
The shaft is octagonal. The hat was made separately and attached with a nail. The arms are indicated by lightly carved decorations resembling Pennsylvania German "hex" signs. Jeleznik, born in Austria, was a forester and wood-carver. He was sometimes referred to as Anton Zelezek. Jeleznik also made at least two whirligigs.

No. 300.
McKenzie presently carves for a living. This cane is similar to others he has made.

No. 301.
Baker has made similar canes.

No. 302.
Clay is an assistant pastor at a Baptist church. He began having visions of art while working as a coal miner in Virginia, and started making art in the mid 1970s. His canes, which often include a watch or clock, a flashlight, and a cigarette lighter, are intended to be useful. Clay has long been fascinated with cacti and features them not only in his canes but in the other objects that he makes. Also see p. 220.

No. 303.
Massey carved and painted birdhouses, animals, and canes. He made several similar canes. Massey referred to the house keys on his canes as "tricks."

No. 304.
The cane is signed *Tim Lewis 90*. Carved railroad tracks covered with aluminum paint rest on painted ties and run down the center of the shaft. Lewis is a professional carver who has made a number of similar canes. It is interesting to compare the similar themes of this cane and no. 184. Also see p. 244.

No. 305.
The cane is signed *Tim Lewis 90*. The handle on this contemporary cane might be compared to that on no. 121. See no. 304.

Victor "Hickory Stick Vic" Bobb (left), ca. 1970, Vicksburg,
Mississippi. Photo by William R. Ferris, Jr., courtesy of University
of Mississippi.

Lynda Roscoe Hartigan

Tapping at Art's Door

Wood is the most humanly intimate of all materials. Man loves his association with it, likes to feel it under his hand, sympathetic to his touch and to his eyes. Wood is universally beautiful to man.
— Frank Lloyd Wright

In our youth-oriented culture, the word cane—even the phrase walking stick—is most likely to conjure images of the sterile metal variety forced upon the elderly or infirm. Those drawn to today's cult of walking often sport trendy shoes and Spandex as well as headphones or heart monitors, but nary a trusty walking stick. Long gone is the primarily sixteenth- to nineteenth-century production of canes as accessories to fashion, station, and history or as ingenious storage for a vast array of devices, from deadly swords to games of chance.

Canes have hardly been obsolete, however, among collectors, whose lineage can be traced as far back as the Egyptian king Tutankhamen, enamored of his crook scepter. The greatest surge of acquisition has occurred in the twentieth century as the perception of canes has shifted from functional fashion to intriguing collectible. Frequently the urge to collect canes has hinged on the object's purpose, for key modern collections have focused on the concepts of accessory, souvenir, presentation piece, or gadget and have favored the products of professional firms and distributors. While materials, workmanship, and decoration have been influential factors in the formation of such collections, this approach recognizes "fancy" canes as decorative artifacts but often romanticizes them as curiosities.

Another trend has slowly emerged. In the eyes of folk art collectors, handmade canes now tap at the door of art as carvings and sculptures (no. 266, see second view). Their makers are generally characterized as gifted craftsmen or amateur carvers and are for the most part still unidentified, a fact that has not denied them admission into folk art's fraternity.

In certain respects, this interest in hand-carved canes as sculpture is not out of the ordinary. Folk art collec-

tors since the turn of the century have helped shape the belief that three-dimensional objects—gravestones, figureheads, weather vanes, trade signs, whirligigs, furniture, decoys, tools, and toys—are early American sculpture. Only within the past two decades, however, has the folk art world come to appreciate canes as sculpture. The preferences of a new generation of collectors and dealers have run toward the three-dimensional, a marked change from their predecessors' orientation toward paintings and works on paper. Moreover, the new search for the sculptural has tended to embrace not only different kinds of objects, canes included, but objects dynamic and muscular in character as well.

The recent appeal of canes raises the challenge of developing a framework within which they can be discussed as three-dimensional objects. It would be easy to follow the example set by Holger Cahill in 1931 when he stated his criteria for evaluating early folk sculpture: the object's "esthetic quality rather than technical proficiency" and the maker's "instinctive" feeling for the "fundamentals of art—rhythm, design, balance, proportion."[1] Any number of canes meet, indeed surpass, these criteria. One encounter with the unabashed sensuality (no. 11), clean elegance, breathtaking intricacy, or broad boldness (no. 49) of particular walking sticks ensures that those who gravitate toward the sculptural will be excited both visually and viscerally.

However legitimate a viewer's sensory observations are, they are external to the canes and their makers. Virtuoso carving and eye-catching details can obscure the most basic of facts suggested by the objects themselves. Walking sticks are a natural partnership of material, form, and use. Although whoever makes the stick ordinarily would be given credit for this partnership, makers, techniques, and decoration mean nothing without the material—wood. Its role in the creation of canes cannot be overestimated. Wood is readily available, flexible, durable, tactile, and metaphoric. These properties have underwritten its logic and potential as a functional and artistic medium for centuries. From the moment the first sapling or branch was cut for support, walking sticks have been regular beneficiaries of these properties. How ironic then that wood as the staple of handmade canes has seldom been a priority in their study.

Although many cane makers may never be identified, numerous kinds of woods usually can be, whether by physical traits or scientific testing. If their material were accurately named, the objects could not be consigned to complete anonymity. Features such as bark, grain, checks, burls, whorls, roots, thigmotropic growths such as vines, and the degree of seasoning all determine what can be accomplished with a particular kind of wood, from ease of carving and bending to shaping the ornamental motifs and overall design. A stick carver understands that these natural details are not haphazard, often selects a piece of wood for these very features, and works them to his advantage. The viewer or connoisseur benefits from the same understanding, for it provides keys to identification and the means to distinguish feats of nature from those of the carver.

Consider too how attribution of places and makers could benefit from determining woods indigenous to particular communities, states, and regions or favored by particular social units such as families or ethnic groups. Although foreign woods have regularly been imported for woodworking, geographical (and stylistic) exploration also needs to include other countries since many canes currently described as American were made elsewhere, only to arrive here via trader or tourist.

Looking at a cane prompts curiosity about who knew how to work the wood to marry form and use. Numerous men have made canes, yet few have signed their efforts, forgoing the traditional mark of the self-aware craftsperson or artist. The search for identities can be translated into the pragmatic exercise of unearthing names, locations, and life dates. Diligent archaeology is required, but just as makers of works as diverse as early portraits and decoys have slowly been retrieved from anonymity, so too can cane makers. The romance of their objects has so much to do with notions of the intimate relationship between one man and one piece of wood that issues of identity have great relevance.

This applies as well to reconstructing bodies of work by specific makers. Virtually nothing is known about the carver who identified himself as "Mike/Orion" or "Orion/Mike" on his muscular sticks (no. 277). Nevertheless, the uncommon luxury of so many identified examples facilitates evaluating one man's approach, hallmarks, range, and consistency. Moreover, the canes' characteristics can someday shed light on the maker's relationship to a peer group, designated by an appropriate time frame or locale.

Without diminishing the dignity of individual achievement, it is the cumulative archaeology that will reveal more about cane makers. Are there indeed patterns related to age, occupation, economic background, extracurricular interests, ethnicity, locale, period, and history? One must wonder, for example, about the incidence of cane carving among those involved in the numerous trades and crafts related to woodworking, from fine furniture making to basic carpentry.[2] And, ultimately, individual achievement must be measured against the yardstick of relevant patterns.

Sources as diverse as field research, hearsay, and the objects themselves already tell us that the country's cane carvers are a multifaceted brotherhood. Prisoners of war, convicts, veterans, members of fraternal organizations, experienced regional wood-carvers (no. 59), intrepid amateurs, Americans of native, African, or German descent all come to mind. The point of inquisitive archaeology, however, is not inventories but sifting and synthesis. How else to disrupt, for example, hierarchical distinctions made between the "fancy," marketed efforts of "professional" woodworkers and the "primitive" versions given away or presented by craftsmen, amateurs, and spare-timers? Alanson P. Dean, for example, was in the lumber and the tanning businesses. Quite apart from his trades, he carved a number of canes, breathtaking in their union of precision and grace, moral and mythology (no. 212). Do Dean's separate spheres of activity warrant deleting words like "fancy" and "professional" from the vocabulary of praise his efforts so richly deserve?

Actually, these various pools of talent overlap in illuminating and as yet unsorted ways. Both professionals and hobbyists have carved canes for campaigns, causes, heroes, and brotherhoods. Professional woodworkers and a variety of craftsmen have carved in their spare time. As in other arenas, amateurs have undoubtedly rivaled their trained counterparts in the levels of technical proficiency they attained.

Even the perception of a cane carver's technical skill needs readjustment. A mark of talent and esteem for many, proficiency is a more positive and pertinent measure than is usually acknowledged in artistic quarters. Conversely, its absence need not eliminate those whose experience or approach emphasizes other means. Technical ability, for example, is not a criterion when someone chooses to intervene no more than by cutting a length of vine-entwined branch and finishing off its top and bottom for ease of handling. Emphasizing straightforward natural beauty may be the desired effect rather than mere expediency.

Beauty and expediency have the ring of mutually exclusive concerns. So too do the notions of function and art. Consider the observations of Victor "Hickory Stick Vic" Bobb (1892–1978), machine shop foreman and cane maker in Vicksburg, Mississippi:

There's not a week that goes by when somebody I gave a stick to years and years ago comes to needing it just to get along. It's just something that's useful. I don't think it's a work of art. . . . It's just a case of patience and talent to make something that's useful. The fact that you can't buy them makes them valuable. . . . But I just get a kick out of making them for people and getting to see them when I present their stick to them.[3]

Hickory Stick Vic cannot speak for all American cane carvers, but his words drive straight to the blurred boundaries between function and art. To him and others who have not perceived themselves as artists, the boundaries are not blurred. Since a branch simply cut down or scavenged would suffice as a walking stick, what then accounts for the blatant urge to shape, decorate, and illustrate that so many handmade canes reveal?

Ironically, clues lie in variations on the concept of function. The pictographs and vignettes that appear on canes suggest storytellers, observers, or documenters. The abundance of pithy religious and political inscriptions marks their authors as commentators. The acts of presentation and commemoration connote friends and fans. These roles or functions are all informed by the desire to reach out, to connect. So too is the act of making something of value and beauty, whether executed during work time, spare time, or hard time. In the best sense of the word, the ambition to convey purpose, individuality, and beauty that can be recognized by others is the essence of creativity. Those who make walking sticks reveal the urge to embellish the natural with evidence of the human presence, whether in the form of ornamental tool marks or pungent inscriptions.

Ascribing sculptural qualities to canes relates directly to the tradition of wood carving in which works are created in the round or in high or low relief. Those made in the round—viewable from all sides and unattached to a backing—are often described as sculpture. Those projected in high or low relief from a background surface are usually addressed frontally and more often are identified with the decorative or architectural arts. Canes may well be one of the few instances in which these two approaches to carving occur consistently and symbiotically.

This confluence requires working out an overall form that incorporates details, articulated by nature or man, either top to bottom, bottom to top, or laterally. Juggling the round against the flat, the horizontal against the vertical, determines the success with which a carver resolves almost dizzying organizational considerations. Ultimately, however, the walking stick is about verticality. People walk upright; trees grow upright; walking sticks are for the most part used or held upright. Verticality governs the perception of canes as objects in space even though, ironically, many carvers work on their sticks horizontally. When designs and inscriptions can be read only by continuously turning a cane or laying it horizontally, the carver's defiant departures from verticality are not just about accommodating elements of design. In many cases he has deliberately manipulated a cane's spatial logic.

More than any other art form, sculpture implies an understanding of scale, proportion, and space. Our modern sensibility predisposes us toward identifying sculpture with monumentality and bravado. That orientation, however, sheds no light on canes, for the most part dedicated to the intimacy of hands and the demands of miniaturization (no. 241). Questions of value inevitably arise. Can the concept and execution of a small work be as evocative, accomplished, and ambitious as those of a larger work? Which challenge is greater—the distillation and condensation required when working on a small scale or the multiplicity and expansiveness afforded by grand scale? Eighteenth-century British writer Edmund Burke developed an illuminating aesthetic sensibility, for he singled out smallness as the first consideration in defining the nature of the beautiful—that is, beautiful objects are small objects.[4] He also observed that the wonder induced by certain degrees of smallness could rival the awe generated by great dimension or massive proportion.

Even a quick perusal of Kurt Stein's 1974 book, *Canes and Walking Sticks*, reveals that the elegant, at times pretentious, aesthetic of "fancy" canes has favored simplicity of shaft and elaboration of handle. The latter, it appears, is such a cane's best means of achieving the desired effect—attracting attention to the bearer, not the maker. The emphasis of handmade canes is exactly the opposite, for carver and connoisseur alike. The shaft is prominently articulated in an aesthetic that values the integration of the whole, from handle to ferrule.

This is not to say that carvers have shortchanged their handles. Showmanship rather than a comfortable grasp was on the mind of whoever wrested four entwined athletic nudes from a root formation (no. 121). Or conversely, how better to invite use than to provide a well-positioned carved hand (no. 211)? And, in fact, the handle motifs favored by carvers—shoe, leg, hand, bird, human and animal heads—are so similar to those on "fancy" canes that emulation or influence must have occurred. This likelihood may be strongest for canes on which handles are the sole or most prominent embellishment (no. 131).

The prospect of limitless variation looms in the collaboration between nature and the human imagination. Specific recurring compositional devices and designs suggest, however, that American cane carvers discovered, over time, particularly successful or appealing ways of integrating material and form. Trial and error, occupational skills, and familiarity with canes and other decorative objects made by foreign cultures, professional trades, or peer groups all paved the road to discovery.

How then have many carvers approached the design of their sticks? It is tempting to dwell on the organic and spontaneous; nature grows forms, man spots forms and follows them. Certainly our eyes feast on the vines turned curvaceous snakes, the whorls and branch nubs turned acorns (no. 98), faces, and deer heads. Releasing the forms sighted in natural materials such as wood and stone is the essence of the universal tradition of direct carving. On many canes, the integration of overall profile and individual features seems effortless, but this impression belies the deliberate, schematic approach of many carvers.

Cane makers often capitalize on a vine's spiraling intervals or the whorl and branching patterns of specific trees to demarcate latitudinal or longitudinal zones in which to work. From this comes the sense of wrapped or stacked motifs (nos. 72, 133). On sticks without pronounced natural growths, the disposition of designs is governed much less by zones or intervals (no. 265). Carvers favor either intermittent (no. 236) or allover, closely knit articulation (no. 150) of the stick's surface; the cadence of design is subsequently deliberate or dynamic. In their attempts to integrate the whole, most carvers incorporate the ubiquitous snake or a densely fluid accumulation of details and techniques. Until recently, few have seemed to value shaping the stick into one dominant form or image; a hammer cane is an obvious exception (no. 190). Many carvers emphasize contrast as a design principle: high and low relief (no. 95), positive and negative space, fine and broad rendering, smooth and "crunchy" texture, repeated motifs in varied combinations, the lights and darks afforded by stain, paint, and ink. Dexterous and imaginative manipulation of these elements can yield that final grand sense of unity and syncopation.

The building blocks of the compositional patterns are a wealth of motifs used interchangeably as image, symbol, and ornament. Interpreting the iconography of American walking sticks warrants an exhaustive catalogue of these motifs. There is already, however, a clear working taxonomy that includes images (fauna, flora, figures, words, man-made objects, and geometric designs) and references (political, historical, religious, mythological, occupational, fraternal, and biographical). Although elements of the natural world, inevitably entwined by snakes, seem to dominate, the frequency of any motif, frankly, can be a matter of meaning or convenience, experience or habit.

The universe of motifs used on walking sticks points to the larger issue of what people value as symbols for ideas, events, places, and animate and inanimate things. Equally evident is the fair play carvers give to representation and stylization within their vocabulary of forms. Stunningly naturalistic acorns and figures broadly suggested to the point of caricature or pictograph can coexist comfortably on the same stick. A love of the encyclopedic and eclectic, which

some might dismiss as indiscriminate, also leaps out from the selection and combinations of motifs on many sticks. Penetrating a carver's intent or principal frame of reference is difficult if he is prone, as many seem to be, to a freewheeling, mix-and-match sensibility. What is one to make of a compendium of natural, fraternal, military, religious, and occupational motifs on a single cane (no. 267)?

Although the design and decoration of walking sticks evolve primarily within a sculptural attitude, a strong grasp of the pictorial or graphic is also much in evidence. The dual exploration of forms in the round and in relief is partly responsible; a linear, illustrational look often accompanies low-relief carving in particular. Favoring both naturalistic and stylized imagery and incorporating paint, ink, and pyrography, many carvers have transformed their sticks into handy surfaces for making pictures.

In fact, the uncanny resonance between walking sticks and illustrated popular culture suggests that this pictorial facet is not just about individual ability to create images. In Europe and America during the nineteenth century, publications produced for mass distribution fed what has since been described as the Victorian cult of images. A surreal, schematic sense of scale and design characterizes the puzzle pictures and compendium-style layouts featured in many of these publications. All manner of military, fraternal, religious, and international emblems have been carefully illustrated in manuals and catalogues. A print or reproduction of a Renaissance composition was a likely model for the rendering of female graces on one cane (no. 182), while another carver's saucy bathing beauties are sisters to those in magazines and calendars (no. 108). Still another cane maker replaced handwork with images clipped from magazines (no. 217).

These diverse thoughts help to map the cultural archaeology of American walking sticks. Issues of style, in relation to time, place, groups, and individuals, are important because inevitably we will have to determine the salient features of an American style of cane carving. Crucial to this search is understanding the interrelationship of the aesthetic and cultural character of walking sticks, tapping now at art's door as multidimensional objects.

Notes

1. Holger Cahill, *American Folk Sculpture: The Work of Eighteenth and Nineteenth Century Craftsmen* (Newark: The Newark Museum, 1931), 13.

2. One should take note of the exceptional circa 1820 cane that descended through the family of the cabinetmaker Duncan Phyfe and is now in the collection of the Museum of Fine Arts, Boston.

3. William Ferris, *Local Color: A Sense of Place in Folk Art* (New York: McGraw-Hill Book Company, 1982), 27–28.

4. Edmund Burke, *A Philosophical Enquiry into the Origin of Our Ideas of the Sublime and Beautiful* (London: R. and J. Dodsley, 1757).

Kurt Stein

Dating American Canes

Like many antiquarian objects, canes are difficult to date accurately. The late Harold L. Peterson, as chief curator of the United States National Park Service, observed, "Identifying unmarked objects is like reading tea leaves." Still, we are not without helpful clues in trying to place a cane within a definable period of time.

The majority of canes encountered today in the United States—both formal and folk art—are from the sixty or seventy years following the Civil War. Canes from the first half of the nineteenth century are scarce, and those from before 1800 are rare. Little historical documentation is available from before the late seventeenth century.

American portraiture in paintings, prints, and sculpture of the seventeenth through the nineteenth century substantiates canes as a widely carried accessory. Some portrait subjects are shown with waist-high canes, sometimes leaning on them in casual poses—such as George Washington in a full-length portrait by Charles Willson Peale of around 1776 (Brooklyn Museum). Canes of this length were "carriage" canes—their length intended to help in alighting from a coach. Elizabeth McClellan, in *History of American Costume 1607–1870* (New York, 1937) cites a verse from "The Port Folio" (1806):

Hence view the smart beau,
And you soon ascertain
The depth of his purse
From the length of his cane.

Hints to the Bearers of Walking Sticks, from about 1807, has it that rules of conduct forbid one to carry a cane in the king's presence, and that it is poor form to either carry a cane under one's arm or lean on it. Apparently such admonitions were not universally obeyed—witness Washington's pose in the Peale portrait.

One wonders what canes, if any, were carried by those too poor to have themselves portrayed in works of art. Perhaps it is here that the American folk art cane began. I define folk art canes as those that are essentially naive yet show an individualistic and original perception by their generally untrained creators.

One can assign formal canes to a particular time period with a high degree of certainty by referring to specimens with known provenance or identifying inscriptions, and by considering the crucial evidence of certain decorative trim and tell-tale forms of handles, which were usually made separately and attached to the shaft. Materials and construction, too, play their part in identification.

From the earliest period discussed here, formal canes have had vertically mounted grips, usually of ivory or bone, sometimes of precious metal or even porcelain. An occasional exception is a T-shaped crutch handle. After about 1850, for perhaps another twenty-five years, formal canes had L-shaped handles contemporary with the gradually developing hang-over-the-arm crook handle that became the predominant style until the 1930s, when canes virtually disappeared unless required by infirmity. The first crook handles curved in a rather wide arc but gradually tightened to the semicircular form we know today.

Notable exceptions to the crook handle are certain vertically mounted grips in fashion on formal canes from about the 1870s until World War I. Mounted on ebony or rosewood shafts, most of these handles are flaring, highly ornamented knobs of gold or gold plate, made less often of silver or of real or simulated ivory. This style had all but disappeared by 1935 when a formally attired Fred Astaire danced "Puttin' on the Ritz."

Before about 1830, the great majority of walking sticks had shafts of malacca, a woody cane growing in the Malay regions of Southeast Asia. Although malacca was preferred for formal canes into the twentieth century hardwoods or fruitwoods such as walnut, maple, rosewood, and cherry were gradually used as well.

The late nineteenth century, characterized by a dominance of decoration over form, was marked by an extreme proliferation of ornamentation, including fanciful shapes, colors, and materials. Difficult to classify, not unlike

Fig. 1. Man with snake cane, ca. 1900. Courtesy of George H. Meyer.

the gingerbread architecture of that age, canes from this period are sometimes more ostentatious than artistic. With modern life, canes, while still retaining a certain utility, became primarily accessories of dress. Such examples tend to be rather slender and even a bit flexible: they were not expected to provide support but were simply part of proper fashionable attire. Turn-of-the-century photographic portraits often show well-dressed men with canes in hand (fig. 1). Nevertheless, both formal and folk art canes for the most part retained their sturdy quality.

Apart from differences of style and construction, the appearance of a cane's components, such as an eyelet, can assist in attributing a date. A hole drilled completely through the shaft, several inches below the top, accommodates a thong or tasseled cord, which, in the absence of a crook handle, can secure a cane to the bearer's wrist or forearm (nos. 140, 169). These holes are most often fitted with tiny metal eyelets, the material usually matching other metal trim. Although occasionally the hole is present on folk art canes of this period, generally eyelets are not. By the

middle of the nineteenth century, eyelets disappeared entirely from formal canes as the incoming crook handles rendered the wrist cord obsolete. An occasional folk art cane without a crook handle, however, might still have a hole for a thong or cord.

Almost all formal canes have ferrules, or protective tips, on the end. These are usually metal, although occasionally they are made of horn and, in rare examples, of ivory. In most cases the earlier the cane, the longer the ferrule. Those of the eighteenth and early nineteenth centuries are of plain brass, reach seven or eight inches in length, and have an iron tip protruding at the bottom. By the middle of the nineteenth century, ferrules were shortened to less than two inches and made of nickel- or silver-plated brass or plain iron. From then into the present century, ferrules have become even shorter, sometimes barely larger than a thimble, and have an iron or steel tip.

Metal ferrules may or may not appear on folk art canes of this period. Those that do occur seem to date from the later years under consideration, and their length might be greater than on formal canes of the same age. Some folk art canes have a ferrule simulated with paint (no. 198), but many simply rely on the unadorned bottom of the wood staff to serve as a tip.

An appropriate use of a metal trim does not impair the spontaneous quality of primitive work. Occasionally, a folk art cane is enhanced with a metal collar where a separate handle is mounted on the shaft. The collar can be no more than the simplest of iron bands, most likely obtained from a local blacksmith (no. 242).

Presentation canes merit comment. Although earlier examples of gift canes exist, during the nineteenth century it became widely fashionable to present a suitably engraved walking stick of good quality to a loved one, friend, or anyone held in high regard. A great variety of canes bear inscriptions honoring statesmen, generals, and politicians (nos. 255, 260), expressing thanks to a devoted physician, or extending good wishes on a birthday. There are, for example, sticks whose wood was taken from a ship, sometimes with metal of the same origin, and inscribed to the vessel's captain or a victorious naval commander. American public collections, like the Smithsonian Institution, include numerous canes given to presidents and others in greater numbers than any recipient could possibly use.

Important evidence for identification, inscriptions are only occasionally found on canes. On the metal trim or on the stick itself will appear perhaps an owner's name, an address, a date, or, rarely, a maker's name (no. 205).

A complete discussion of this field encompasses the mainly American art of scrimshaw, most of which was done in the second and third quarters of the nineteenth century. Utilizing the by-products of whale hunting, skillful carvers, usually shipbound sailors, fashioned whale and walrus tooth ivory, bone, and baleen into useful and decorative articles, including canes of full lengths of bone from the jaws of sperm whales (see scrimshaw canes on p. 181).

Folk art canes can follow prevailing styles but do not always. For example, the form of the handle is not a hard-and-fast guide in dating folk art canes. With many examples, a major characteristic is the optimum use of natural forms and materials: unusual tree limbs or interesting roots have offered wonderful opportunities for all sorts of shapes to creative carvers. Usually such imaginative handles are an integral part of the stick (no. 79), in which case the traditional period style of straight or angled handles is abandoned in favor of the desired result. Occasionally handles of a different material are mounted on a folk art cane (no. 237). Several reasons for this practice may be guessed: perhaps the wood was judged too brittle, or the grain ran so that its "head" resisted the carving of details, or perhaps a different medium—like an antler—was desired to add interest (no. 249). Finally, even when a folk art cane does have a handle representative of the style of a formal cane, it might well be a carryover of an earlier type. This is particularly true when a cane is made or purchased by someone who, caring little for the general fashion of the day, wishes it to suit his individual taste.

Canes carved during and soon after the Civil War, the pivotal event in American history, are particularly interesting. Subjects vary widely and can reflect the late nineteenth-century inclination to record the more positive aspects of a crisis. Carvings are crowded with images and symbols of the war: corps and division badges (no. 252), emblems of army branches such as signal corps or artillery, Zouaves with mounted bayonets (no. 243), naval themes, cannons (no. 236), and drums. Popular leaders are portrayed, if not always recognizably. Alternatively, a cane might commemorate victory and heroism with eloquent simplicity, featuring no more than a name, place, and date of an engagement (no. 239).

The emblem of the Grand Army of the Republic on a cane indicates a postwar origin (no. 248). Organized in 1866, the G.A.R. grew to be the nation's largest and most politically active Civil War veterans organization. One hesi-tates to contemplate whether all members had G.A.R. canes. Walking sticks of the United Confederate Veterans are not nearly as numerous.

Our appreciation of folk art canes must necessarily broaden somewhat as we consider those of the last third of the nineteenth and early twentieth centuries. The original and individualistic approach continued, but plainly the arrival of new technology, techniques, and materials after the Civil War and the 1876 centennial had some impact. Other noticeable influences were population growth and the proliferation of ideas, events, and personalities that came to dominate public imagination (no. 267).

A turn-of-the-century folk art cane is less apt to reflect rural imagery but likely to feature a politician (no. 256), statesman (no. 265), symbols of a party or organization (no. 197), and, more recently, trends and social movements. Some of these canes, although retaining strong character, were undoubtedly commercially produced to meet the demand of political, military, and civic groups as well as Masonic and other fraternal associations.

The popular arts flowered during the nineteenth century, with patriotic themes strongly represented in all creative forms, including canes. Uncounted depictions have survived portraying the eagle (no. 235), the flag (no. 251), figures of Liberty and Columbia (no. 266), and variations on these themes. Subjects of the day continued to challenge the folk art carver: the 1876 centennial, the Statue of Liberty, dedicated in 1886, the seemingly endless parade of presidents, politicians, patriots, national issues, and events that moved America and humanity.

The war with Spain in 1898 was another period of high national feeling. From it we see canes with likenesses of President McKinley, Admiral Dewey, and Assistant Secretary of the Navy Theodore Roosevelt, later of the U.S. Cavalry Volunteers, known as the Rough Riders (no. 262).

The art of carving canes continues into the present century, commemorating and celebrating the many events and ideas that have an impact on contemporary minds. Indeed, strong original work is being created by skilled and imaginative folk carvers. They too utilize themes and materials of their day to make canes that reflect the life around them.

Fig. 1. Maury "Steam Train" Graham, former "king of the hoboes,"
with a cane carved for him by a friend, 1989. Photo by Duane
Belanger, reprinted by permission of the Detroit News.

Simon J. Bronner

Cane Making as Symbol and Tradition

Who claims the cane as their special folk art, and why? The cane escapes easy categorization by social grouping in folk culture because it is at once global and personal. Staffs, sticks, and canes pronounce publicly recognized status in many societies, and yet their meaning varies and can indeed be unique to an individual. Commercially made canes became widespread during the nineteenth century, but the use and number of traditional handmade canes have gone mostly uncharted. Although many exceptions can be found, the general pattern of this variety of American folk art is its appeal to men in particular, especially in rural regions, and its association with youth and old age. The object is integral to folk traditions as a material way that young and old men find basic values in themselves and in their surroundings.

Even though the cane carries symbolic references—to defense, age, travel, authority, healing, and individuality—its function for the artist and the viewer typically varies. The form of the cane can range from a utilitarian walking stick made from a limb to an artistic showpiece with carved chains (no. 226), caged balls, animals, figures, and other fanciful decorations. An erect vertical form imitating and extending man's body, it is most often made from sturdy wood but also constructed from tightly woven horse hair or even the stretched and dried penis of a bull.

A study of collections suggests that the cane's historic function has changed from the common aid to walking and weapon of defense of preindustrial lore to a nonutilitarian expression of individuality during the nineteenth and twentieth centuries. Observations of cane making and use, however, offer a less simplistic view. Rarely the primary creation of the contemporary crafts worker (perhaps explaining the paucity of scholarly studies of cane making), the cane is commonly part of a larger repertoire of creative expression in the traditionally male medium of wood. An artist is not identified as a cane carver as much as a craftsman or woodcarver. The cane nonetheless carries important meaning for a maker in the context of his community. Unlike other pieces a carver provides, the cane has connotations less of public use than of private association. Its form is traditional, but its elaboration is personal (fig. 1). Held by a single hand, it is a threatening extension of the body; given by one man to another, it must be offered with caution.

Interviews with carvers reveal cane making to be most often a matter of self-discovery—like carving the wood chain, an experience of hand-wrought creativity within tradition. Being able to turn a simple stick into an eye-catching work of art is a sign of artistic mastery and maybe a bit of magic. Unlike other linear art forms, the cane forces artistic elaboration into an unusually narrow range. Hence the artful piece stands out, even jumps out at the viewer, requiring close inspection as a personal statement of the artist.

So while the American cane defies easy cultural categorization, this brief overview suggests ways in which canes carry meaning for their makers and viewers through form and symbol. With inscription and elaboration, makers can use art in the cane, so closely connected to the body, to convey images and relations neither easily nor lastingly expressed in conversation.

Canes for the Ages

Young boys in city and country today, as in the past, seek canes from models they have seen. The carved cane, probably made with a pocket knife from a found tree branch or a discarded piece of lumber, offers the satisfaction of extending oneself through craftsmanship. As with other boyhood props, from bull-roarers to stilts, a cane allows a boy to announce a growing presence, to explore and intrude into the world. He uses the carved stick to walk in the woods, swipe at foes along the way, fence with buddies, declare authority, and imagine the power of manhood. In adulthood, the cane is less apparent and useful, for a man realizes his strength and strikes at his foes in other ways. In old age, the cane can allow rediscovery of a man's creative potential or at least provide support artistically.

In encounters with others, the carver uses a decorated cane to invite conversation. An elaborate cane simultaneously announces the frailty and strength of an elderly maker. Embellishing an instrument of support, the carving encapsulates the wisdom of age and conveys vitality through everyday artistry. Although the old cane carver might rely on his creation to help him walk, and so direct attention to his body's feebleness, the flights of fancy displayed in the decoration can reveal a lively, imaginative gait. Going beyond the bounds of the utilitarian cane with a design all his own, the elderly carver tells himself and others that he is not to be lumped with a stereotypical group of oldsters but is an individual brandishing the power to create. For some, carving stories and symbols on the wooden canvas of the cane might be one way to review an individual life. Others may prefer the plainness of a useful cane, polished to perfection and given to a grandchild, perhaps to ease the transition from one generation to another—to be passed from the man to the boy and to the man again. In boyhood, the stick is thrown away; in old age, the distinguished support is preserved and memorialized. In both, the cane is often a tool of passage.

Canes between Nature and Culture

On a great number of canes the hand cradles a carved bird (no. 69), snake, horse, or other representation of nature. Many walking sticks have heads and bodies at the top and flora and fauna below (no. 150). In canes humans see their complex relationships with nature and culture. As part of nature, humans are mortal animals susceptible to earthly forces and yet self-assuredly dominant over nature. As part of culture, they seek to assuage their loneliness through social connection, to construct meaning through personal and communal identities in complex environments. Canes themselves derive significance from nature, being formations of roots and branches taken from the woods (no. 95). Cane makers commonly declare this significance by leaving winding roots and extending branches unpainted, preserving their natural state and color. They might convert the formations to animal figures (no. 89), underscoring even more the cane as a sign of nature. With carving, the tree limb becomes a human limb, and with recognizable historical or social signs, the limb conveys the cultural side of human existence. Religious signs or stylistic insignias might display ethnic or regional figures, colors, and patterns. More immediate, a family's legacy might be symbolically inscribed on a walking stick (no. 40).

As both an individual and social statement, the cane represents the dynamic of culture between self and society (no. 205). Kept as a concept to grasp, as an item for friends to observe and admire, as a keepsake for grandsons—the cane, with other arts, creates community by a tangible connection of one hand to another.

Fig. 2. Reverend St. Patrick Clay with his carvings (see no. 302), 1990, Columbus, Ohio. Photo courtesy of Kerry Schuss, New York.

Canes as Markers

Canes allow one to proclaim oneself within the constraints of a culturally acceptable form. The surface of this common tool of living can be marked for a distinctive purpose or can frame a particular message. The artistic message, which often presumes narrative translation, might be personal and cryptic, meant to be revealed in conversation with a friend, or it could be intended to reinforce social identity directly through the portrayal of shared signs.

An elderly Indiana carver I documented was stopped during walks by people asking about his cane with hanging chains which gave him the opportunity to explain his carving and his carpentry background. Although he would have hesitated to decorate his own body or clothes to announce himself in public, his stick seemed to him and others an acceptable, conservative way to herald his accomplishment. Knowing his years were numbered, he gave me a cane and commented that it would stand up straight long after he was lying in the ground. Supporting the human form in life, before the final memorial of the grave marker, the erect cane can carry the mark of individual and social human experience with active rather than spiritual force.

The cane's form is displayed in the scepters used for fraternal and ritual ceremonies, and nonceremonial canes often appear decorated with Masonic and Odd Fellows symbols. Today many fraternity and sorority members and graduating seniors mark their special status by making decorated sticks. The cane form appeals partly because it can be passively leaned on in procession as well as held above the shoulders more aggressively after the completion of a ceremony. Ornamented canes commonly bear signs of national celebrations, particularly elections, centennials, and memorials. As a marker of patriotism or loyalty, it can carry, through the work of the carver, profiles of heroes and banners of unity and thus strongly suggests personal conviction.

As form and function, symbol and story, the cane conveys images that speak to matters of living and aging, creativity and conformity, self and society. Its form is repetitive, its detail changeable, its display and context adaptable. The cane's creation and use, its praxis in folk culture, are as both tool and art. As an object of communication, it is a variable personal symbol and a constant social tradition. As both, the cane offers up basic riddles of human experience.

References

Bastin, Marie-Louise. *Sculptures angolaises: Cannes et batons d'apparat spatule-massue de la collection Barbier-Müller*. Geneva: La Collection, 1982.

Bronner, Simon J. *Chain Carvers: Old Men Crafting Meaning*. Lexington: University Press of Kentucky, 1985.

————. *Grasping Things: Folk Material Culture and Mass Society in America*. Lexington, Ky.: University Press of Kentucky, 1986.

————. *American Children's Folklore*. Little Rock, Ark.: August House, 1988.

————. *Piled Higher and Deeper: The Folklore of Campus Life*. Little Rock, Ark.: August House, 1990.

Burtscher, William John. *The Romance behind Walking Canes*. Philadelphia: Dorrance, 1945.

Dike, Catherine. *Cane Curiosa: From Gun to Gadget*. Paris: Les Editions de l'amateur, 1983.

————. *Walking Sticks*. Buckinghamshire, England: Shire Publications, 1990.

Dow, James R. "The Hand Carved Walking Canes of William Baurichter." *Keystone Folklore Quarterly* 15 (fall 1970), 138–47.

Farrington, Frank. "Hand Me Down My Walking Cane!" *Hobbies*, March 1945, 8–9.

Hackley, Larry. *Sticks: Historical and Contemporary Kentucky Canes*. Louisville: Kentucky Art and Craft Foundation, 1988.

Lindblom, Gerhard. *Spears and Staffs with Two or More Points, in Africa*. Stockholm: Ethnographical Museum of Sweden, 1937.

Nelson, Edna. "Walking Out with the Walking Stick." *Antiques* 32 (1937), 128–30.

Real, Antony. *The Story of the Stick in All Ages and Lands*. Trans. François Fernand-Michel. New York: Bouton, 1892.

Snyder, Yolanda. "Butcher's Bull: A Study in Occupational Folklore." *Mid-America Folklore* 15 (1987), 1–13.

Stein, Kurt. *Canes and Walking Sticks*. York, Pa.: Liberty Cap Books, 1974.

Vlach, John Michael. *The Afro-American Tradition in Decorative Arts*. Cleveland: Cleveland Museum of Art, 1978.

Ramona M. Austin

Defining the African-American Cane

The African-American cane has clearly recognizable motifs whose provenance can be located in specific cultural areas of the African continent. Moreover, canes made by black Americans demonstrate conclusively that African motifs and iconography have been adapted by and retained in the corpus of American folk art. This examination of the formal and functional relationships of the African-American cane to the staffs of Kongo chiefs of Bas-Zaire will consider the cane in African-American culture and its contribution to defining the thought, aesthetics, and formal canons of its artistic tradition.[1]

Unlike most decorative walking sticks, African-American canes are not objects that merely enhance the prestige of the person who carries them, nor are they simply idiosyncratic expressions of ebullient individualism. They are mediums of contact to a spirit world that can affect the psychic and physical disposition of people and things in the nonspirit world. They are the signposts of the efficacy of community, of the indissoluble bonds of kinship that embrace the living and the dead. Because the African-American cane can possess supernatural force, it exists in direct contradistinction to the Anglo-American cane.

Charms and ritual practices recorded in the Americas parallel Kongo beliefs concerning the power connected with the dead, magic, and sorcery. Similarly, Kongo cultural and artistic traditions brought by great numbers of Kongo slaves are found throughout the Western hemisphere.[2] The Kongo sculptural tradition in wood continues to influence cane carving in the continental United States and elsewhere in the Americas.[3]

African-American canes are usually classed in two categories, conjuring canes and walking sticks. Conjurer and root or hoodoo doctor are names for a ritual specialist in the oral tradition of African-Americans which includes their folklore and folk beliefs. This specialist manipulates canes to cure, protect, or afflict with appropriate gestures, words, and powerful medicines. His African equivalent among the Kongo and Kongo-related peoples of central Africa, the *nganga* (classed as magician, healer, or priest), also wields a staff.[4] Identifying the *nganga's* staff and its tradition will continue to require much careful research and the insightful comparison of staffs and related objects as well as the study of supernatural agency in Kongo art and culture.

Although the conjurer/*nganga* as prototype exists in African-American folklore and folk belief, known examples of African-American, or possibly African-American, canes most closely resemble the staffs of Kongo chiefs.[5] Chieftain staffs also possess supernatural power, but unlike the conjurer, the chief manipulates his staff primarily to protect his person and charges from malefic forces and intentions.[6]

In looking at the form and function of African-American canes, aspects of staffs of both chiefs and ritual specialists might be discerned, although categories of meaning and use in Kongo culture are not always sharply defined. For example, the social viability of the entire group is threatened when a chief uses the staff's power not to protect but to control people or for material gain. Obtaining control over individuals, and the selfish acquisition of wealth or power by supernatural force, is the domain of the *ndoki* (sorcerer).[7]

Important methodological issues arise in any discussion of African-American canes. The formal and functional differences between an African-American conjuring cane and a walking stick are not defined. The actual number of published canes that are irrefutably identified as African-American is relatively small. But an examination of visual and thematic correlations between African and African-American examples can provide valuable evidence of formal and functional continuities.

Motifs on canes that we know were made by African-Americans show a recurrence of certain images and relationships. Most striking and repetitive is the occurrence of reptilian figures, usually snakes and, almost as frequently, alligators, lizards, frogs, and tortoises or terrapins (fig. 1, no. 41). These creatures share the trait of occupying two environmental realms, earth and water. They therefore can

Fig. 1. *African-American cane, Henry Gudgell, ca. 1867, Livingston County, Missouri, wood. Yale University Art Gallery, New Haven. Photo by Joseph Szaszfai.*

relationship of the living to the dead. In addition, the serpent represents the authority and power of the chief, derived from the ancestors. In this way the subject is specific to the cultural history of African-Americans, although motifs of reptilian forms, primarily the serpent, are found in many cultures.[11] It should be remembered that Africans came with discrete traditions to the cultural heterogeneity of the Americas.

The method by which African-American carvers organize these animal motifs on canes is also specific. Most often the serpent is central; less frequently the alligator/lizard form is the primary element (fig. 1). A motif is "primary" in relation to the size and placement of other, lesser motifs, which cluster around the central one as though it energized or made sensible the entire composition. The reptilian motif can also occur in stark relationship with figures, heads,[12] and heads with torsos (fig. 5, nos. 139, 144). These figures can also appear in hieratic postures without reptilian forms, sometimes with the arms at the side of the body (no. 110) or tight against the belly, the latter pose very reminiscent of sub-Saharan figural sculpture (no. 285).[13]

The most famous cane known to have been carved by an African-American, the Henry Gudgell cane (fig. 1), is a brilliant example of the organization of reptilian motifs by African-American carvers. Gudgell, a mulatto and former slave from Kentucky who settled in Missouri, carved the cane around 1867 for a Civil War veteran who had sustained a leg wound.[14] Visual evidence strongly suggests that a similar cane in a private collection is from Gudgell's hand.[15] The canes are almost identical in figural and geometric motifs.

Robert Farris Thompson in 1969 was the first to link the Gudgell cane to a Woyo chief's staff. In 1973 Elsa Honig Fine tied the Gudgell cane with a Woyo chief's staff in the collection of the Royal Museum for Central Africa, Tervuren, Belgium.[16] Collected in 1953, this Kongo staff with the motif of a double gong, an emblem of chieftainship, is strikingly similar to the Gudgell cane. The presence of a second and forcefully similar cane that strongly suggests Gudgell's hand reinforces the suspicion that a Woyo staff or an earlier prototype was remembered and served as the possible model for the African-American's work.

The Gudgell cane and the Royal Museum Woyo staff organize similar motifs in roughly the same fashion. On the Gudgell cane the snake curves up the shaft and seems to animate the motifs of a man, a leaf, a tortoise, and what appears to be a lizard. On the Woyo staff, the snake's mouth touches the head of an upside down man, above which is the double gong. Thin bands surround a diamond motif on the Gudgell cane (fig. 1, detail). This feature, which has been discussed as having deep significance in African-American folk art,[17] is commonly found on Kongo staffs of authority and other objects of chiefly regalia. The diamond also represents the Kongo cosmological universe, and it resonates

be classed as liminal creatures, for they operate at the threshold between two domains of existence, the land of the living and the land of the dead.[8]

A very provocative cane with reptilian motifs from the Meyer collection was carved in 1932 by Lenard Megarr, a black inmate of a Georgia prison (no. 49). The Megarr cane disposes a frog and a lizard on opposite sides of the shaft. According to Wyatt MacGaffey these mediating reptiles have oppositional qualities in Kongo thought. He cites studies in which the diurnal lizard and nocturnal frog represent the forms that man (lizard) and woman (frog) take after death. The curved posture of the frog also represents the devious nature of witchcraft.[9] Thus, these creatures represent in the natural world Kongo meditations on the awesome supernatural powers of the ancestors, who can affect the lives of the living and, with the proper ritual acts, be called upon for aid.

The constant repetition of reptile forms and their positioning point to African-American canes as medium iotic objects in the purest Kongo sense. This is not the imagery of the Fall, where snakes conjure Eve, the apple, the serpent, and sin; nor do these reptilian figures recall a Boschian hell. Such imagery has not been characteristic of African-American canes.[10] Rather, these forms signal the

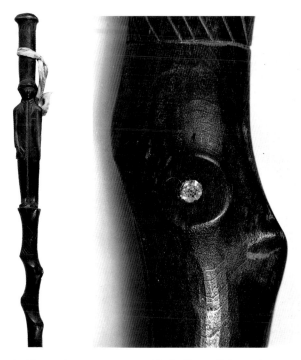

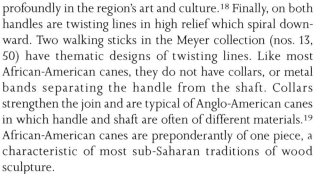

Fig. 2. *African-American cane, ca. 1916, Cherry Valley, Arkansas, wood, imitation gem inlay, cloth. Permanent loan from Dr. Adell Patton, Jr., to Yale University Art Gallery, New Haven. Photo by Joseph Szaszfai.*

Fig. 3. *Woyo chief's staff with cosmogram, 20th century, zone of Muanda, Bas-Zaire, wood, remnants of red cloth, nails. Photo by Ramona Austin.*

profoundly in the region's art and culture.[18] Finally, on both handles are twisting lines in high relief which spiral downward. Two walking sticks in the Meyer collection (nos. 13, 50) have thematic designs of twisting lines. Like most African-American canes, they do not have collars, or metal bands separating the handle from the shaft. Collars strengthen the join and are typical of Anglo-American canes in which handle and shaft are often of different materials.[19] African-American canes are preponderantly of one piece, a characteristic of most sub-Saharan traditions of wood sculpture.

Embedded reflective materials are another characteristic of African-American canes that can be seen in the Meyer collection (nos. 49, 292). A cane dated circa 1916 owned by Dr. Adell Patton of Howard University offers a fruitful comparison (fig. 2). *Rev. G.E. Patton/Haynes Ark* is carved into the back of the shaft. Reputed to have been executed in Cherry Valley, Arkansas, by an unknown carver in the church of Dr. Patton's grandfather, the cane was embedded with rhinestones. A piece of cloth is tied around the handle, which is carved as a frontal figure of a man in a tall top hat and long frock coat.

A Woyo staff photographed in 1986 shows remnants of red cloth that was wrapped around its shaft, under which a now-exposed incised cosmogram in diamond form was once hidden (fig. 3). Wrapping a staff signifies its nature as a

charm, and the swelling form of the mounded cloth indicates occult power (fig. 4). Upholstery nails are placed at each corner of the diamond. A hole bored in its center may have held a charge that invested in the staff the power of the ancestors to protect the chief.[20] The Cherry Valley cane (fig. 2), carved to maintain the integrity of the original limb, has nodules that are still distinct, inlaid in the center with rhinestones. It is significant that the carver inserted flashing material at the point where sap rises through the branch to nourish the life-sustaining leaves (fig. 2, detail). This is analogous to the embedding of life force through the materials of a charm's charge. The rising force is further signified by a snake climbing the shaft, symbolizing the power of the ancestors crossing the watery boundary between the lands of the living and the dead to affect the living. In Kongo figural charms, it is the receptacle of flashing glass and resin that holds the spirit-invested materials.

A cane from the Meyer collection carved in the 1960s by "Stick Dog Bob" of Chicago is a black figure with red, blue, and green glass jewels (no. 292). One large glass ruby is placed in the cavity of a ball-like stomach, and a snake below has a large imitation ruby set in its nose. Highly reflective materials must be carefully analyzed for placement and relationship to figural and geometric motifs before they can be supposed to represent African-American aesthetic canons and systems of meaning.

224

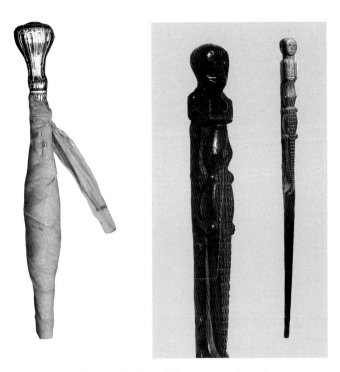

Fig. 4. *Wrapped Woyo chief's staff, late 19th–early 20th century, zone of Muanda, Bas-Zaire, wood, cloth, silver handle with embossed female figure. Photo by Ramona Austin.*

Fig. 5. *African-American canes. Left: William Rogers, 1938, Darien, Georgia, painted cedar, nails. Collection of Mary Granger, Savannah. Right: Attributed to William Rogers, 1939, wood. Lowie Museum of Anthropology, The University of California at Berkeley. Photo courtesy of University of Georgia Press.*

Fig. 6. *Kongo staff, second half 20th century, zone of Seke-Banza, Bas-Zaire, wood. Photo by Ramona Austin.*

There is evidence that swelling motifs on Kongo staffs connote the presence of occult power. The William Rogers walking sticks made in the 1930s (fig. 5) each have a figure with rudimentary head, bead eyes, and half-torso being touched by the mouth of what appears to be an alligator.[21] The figures have deep torsos and appear at attention with chests out. The hands of one image (fig. 5, left) grip its volumetric shortened torso. Significantly, a red imitation gem (red indicates force in Kongo iconography)[22] in the cane by "Stick Dog Bob" is placed in the full, round form of the belly. A startling congruency of this swelling motif can be observed in a modern staff from Bas-Zaire in the zone of Seke-Banza (fig. 6).

Another motif that occurs on Kongo staffs is the hand (fig. 7). Appearing in several forms, it can be completely closed in a fist, closed with only the thumb free, or it can hold a short baton (in exact congruency with no. 177). Informants of the environs of Songololo in Bas-Zaire characterize the hand as a symbol of the corporate relationship between the chief and his charges, of which the clan is the irreducible cell, thus suggesting that the metaphor may predate European influence. Similar data has been collected farther east on the coast,[23] and the theme also appears in West Africa, for example, among the Asante of Ghana.[24]

The appearance of the hand motif on African-American folk canes raises questions about origin which do not exclude the possibility of multiple influences. Other unattributed staffs with hand motifs in the Meyer collection (nos. 173, 179) all carry round objects, possibly following a European model, although they also recall the hand-and-egg device of the Asante—a proverbial comment on the nature of authority. The hand motif may have been introduced among the Kongo by Europeans, who arrived on their shores in 1482, and with whom they had an intense interaction, especially in the trade of decorative prestige items. Whatever the origin, Kongo people apparently came to the Americas with a history of using this motif as an ideograph of power in their art. An African-American cane from Savannah in the collection of the National Museum of American History, Washington, D.C., displays alligator/lizard decorations and a hand as the handle (fig. 8). This may be one case of similar traditions of comple x u lylily reinforcing one another and being adopted by both Anglo- and African-Americans as expressions of their respective cultural traditions.

The African-American cane is definable. Canes from the Meyer collection, other public and private collections, and published sources offer ample illustration of its aesthetic and formal canons. A further discussion would require a complex analysis and catalogue of form, meaning, and function based on fieldwork in Africa and America, and a knowledge of folklore and folk belief in addition to the study of the African staffs and African-American canes in public and private collections. Invaluable to this research

Fig. 7. Kongo staff, late 19th–early 20th century, Bas-Zaire, wood. Institute for the National Museums of Zaire, Kinshasa. Photo by Ramona Austin, assisted by Kiji wa Kiji.

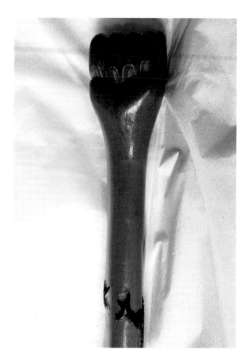

Fig. 8. African-American cane, 20th century, Savannah, painted wood. National Museum of American History, Smithsonian Institution, Washington, D.C. Photo by Ramona Austin.

will be the ongoing scholarship of the demographics of the slave trade as a means of confirming influences from specific areas of the African continent. Instances of a uniquely African-American artistic expression are neither confined to the deep South nor dependent on the slave class; the underground railroad ensured that the community of free blacks in the North was not wholly divorced from that of the slave.[25] African-Americans possess a unique ethos that confirms the vitality and continuity of their culture. The African-American cane defines one plastic idiom in the complex cultural tapestry of the Americas, for which Africa's dispersed artistic traditions are binding threads.

Notes

1. This essay is based on a study of American canes and Kongo staffs in public and private collections in the United States, Belgium, Germany, and Zaire. From 1984 to 1986, while a Fulbright-Hays Fellow working with the collection of Kongo objects at the Institute for the National Museums of Zaire in Kinshasa, the author carried out dissertation research on Kongo chieftain staffs among ethnic groups in Bas-Zaire from the Atlantic coast to Mbanza Ngungu. In the Bandundu region to the west, the Meni Kongo (grand-chief of the Suku) and the Kiamvu (grand-chief of the Yaka) were interviewed.

2. For a succinct discussion of Kongo charms and ritual practices in the United States, Cuba, and Brazil, consult chap. 2 of Robert Farris Thompson, *Flash of the Spirit: African and Afro-American Art and Philosophy* (New York: Vintage, 1984). See also Roger Bastide, *African Civilizations of the New World* (New York: Harper Torchbooks, 1971), 105–12, on bantu religious practices including magicians, healers, and sorcerers. Read

Zora Neale Hurston's firsthand account of the making and application of a charm, the equivalent of a Kongo *nkisi*, by a conjurer known as Dr. Duke, in *Mules and Men* (Bloomington: Indiana University Press, 1963), 230–32.

3. Two examples are the wood staffs of the Obeah men who practiced in Jamaica, Haiti, and the southern United States, and staffs planted around a Santeria altar, photographed in 1980–81 by sociologist Julie Feinsilver in the environs of Havana (personal communication to the author, 1981).

4. See Thompson, *Flash of the Spirit*, 107, for classes of *nganga*. A staff in the collection of the Institute of the National Museums of Zaire is clearly listed as being used to heal sterility in women. I was able to interview two Woyo *ntomasi*, ritual specialists, in the zone of Muanda on the use of staffs. Zora Neale Hurston does not mention staffs in listing the conjuring paraphernalia observed during her research in Louisiana in the late 1930s. She does note, however, that conjurers held the Bible as the greatest conjure book in the world and Moses as the greatest conjurer; see *Mules and Men*, 287. It should be remembered that Moses was given a staff by God as a sign to the Egyptians of the legitimacy of his mission. This staff turned into a serpent (Exod. 4:2–5 and 7:4–13), performed wonders (Exod. 7:14–10:23), parted the sea (Exod. 14:21–28), and in the desert brought water from a rock (Exod. 17:1–7). Balu Balila, Woyo informant/assistant, similarly referred to the Kongo staff as resembling the staff of Moses in that it performed miracles (Muanda Village, Collectivité de la Mer, 1985).

5. That is to say, the motifs of the canes are most like those of staffs of chiefs. Staffs that I have encountered that do not fit this category have figures that resemble *nkisi*.

6. Wyatt MacGaffey, *Religion and Society in Central Africa* (Chicago: University of Chicago Press, 1986), 154. See also John Janzen and Wyatt MacGaffey, *An Anthology of Kongo Religion*, no. 5 (Lawrence, Kans.: University of Kansas Publications in Anthropology, 1974), 42.

7. See MacGaffey, *Religion and Society in Central Africa*, 162–65, on witchcraft and magic.

8. The boundary between the worlds of the living and the dead is a watery one, the Kalunga (land of the dead) line. Thus, creatures who tread on the earth of the living also slip below the water to travel between the two realms. See MacGaffey, *Religion and Society in Central Africa*, 43, for a description of these two worlds. W. H. Councill, in an address delivered in 1900 in Normal, Alabama, recalled being sent as a child in 1862 to a small plantation to live with "Aunt Phillis," a conjure woman. She made him gather, among other things, snake heads, lizard legs, and toad frogs for "voo-doo bags"; see Roger G. Abrahams and John F. Szwed, eds., *After Africa: Excerpts from British Travel Accounts and Journals of the Seventeenth, Eighteenth, and Nineteenth Centuries* (New Haven: Yale University Press, 1983), 372–73. Aunt Phillis's bags can be classed by ingredient and function as the equivalent in the Americas of the Kongo *nkisi*, which are powered by the embedded spirits of the dead. In Haiti they are known as *pacquets-congo*. See Thompson's discussion of *minkisi* in the Americas, *Flash of the Spirit*, 125–30.

9. MacGaffey, *Religion and Society in Central Africa*, 52.

10. The Kongo notions of the serpent and other reptilian forms are codified in oral tradition and figural and geometric ideographs. In contradistinction, the story of the Fall is a story of the Bible, a written tradition. As such, it is shared by "three religions of the book: Judaism, Christianity and Islam"; Beverly Moon, ed., *An Encyclopedia of Archetypal Symbolism* (Boston and London: Shambahla, 1991), 423.

11. We could briefly note some European examples. In the classical world the caduceus is of a different order, with its two serpents entwined on a staff surmounted with wings. The rod represents power; the serpents typify wisdom (as they do in cultures worldwide); and the two wings, diligence and activity. See Willson W. Blake, *The Cross, Ancient and Modern* (New York: Anson D.F., 1888), 17. The snake, rendered representationally and abstracted as a spiral, was a dominant motif in the art of old Europe. The snake represented "the power in the earth that supports life and the transformation of life on its surface. The snake was recognized as the actual force behind creation," writes Marija Gimbutas; *Archetypal Symbolism*, 80. In Europe of the sixteenth and seventeenth centuries, popular emblem books codified the serpent as it was understood by educated men and women of the time. Vestiges of the serpent as representing wisdom are still to be found, but most emblems have the serpent representing negative aspects of social behavior or power in its most aggressive manifestations. See Huston Diehl, *An Index of Icons in English Emblem Books, 1500–1700* (Norman, Okla., and London: University of Oklahoma Press, 1986), 181–82.

12. See the Leon Rucker cane illustrated in John Michael Vlach, *The Afro-American Tradition in Decorative Arts* (Cleveland: Cleveland Museum of Art, 1978), fig. 33.

13. Good examples are two canes by Mississippian Luster Willis of Crystal Springs, illustrated in Vlach, *The Afro-American Tradition in Decorative Arts*, 34, figs. 34 and 35. Also in the Meyer collection is no. 116, holding a banjo. This figure is quite refined and stylistically very much like Kongo figures from the Mayombe area. In another example (no. 119), the human form is extremely reduced. Features rendered with great simplification (often quite dynamically) characterize heads as handles. Examples from the Meyer collection are nos. 139 and 144. Decidedly not African-American is no. 151. This head is a caricature, and its grotesque grimace is more reminiscent of derisive depictions of blacks from the second half of the nineteenth century.

14. Elsa Honig Fine, *The African-American Artist* (New York: Holt Rinehart and Winston, 1973), 59–60.

15. This cane is illustrated in Eugenia A. Perry, "African Art and African-American Art: A Stylistic and Spiritual Kinship," in Robert V. Rozelle, Alvia Wardlaw, and Maureen A. McKenna, eds., *Black Art: Ancestral Legacy, The African Impulse in African-American Art* (Dallas: Dallas Museum of Art, 1989), 40–41.

16. Robert Farris Thompson, "African Influence on the Art of the United States," in Armstead L. Robinson et al., *Black Studies in the University* (New Haven: Yale University Press, 1969), 127–30. Fine, *The African-American Artist*, 59–60, fig. 88. Both figs. 87 and 88 are from the Woyo subgroup of the Kongo people according to the archives of the Royal Museum for Central Africa.

17. Judy McWillie builds on Robert Farris Thompson's work on the Kongo cosmogram as diamond shape, discussing its American context in "Another Face of the Diamond," *The Clarion: America's Folk Art Magazine* 12, no. 4 (fall 1987), 52–53.

18. Thompson, *Flash of the Spirit*, 108–16. Thompson also discusses in depth the ideographs for the Kongo cosmogram in his work co-authored with Frère Joseph Cornet, *Four Moments of the Sun: Kongo Art in Two Worlds* (Washington, D.C.: National Gallery of Art, 1981), 43–48.

19. Kurt Stein, *Canes and Walking Sticks* (York, Pa.: Liberty Cap Books, 1974), 13.

20. In 1985, in the zone of Tchela in Bas-Zaire, a Yombe chief pointed his staff and shot it like a gun when I asked him to show me its function. Informants consistently responded that the staff was to protect the chief from the malevolent intentions of others. MacGaffey speaks of the chief burying his staff in the nkisi nsi, the medicated earth, at times of great danger, in *Religion and Society in Central Africa*, 154.

21. Vlach, *The Afro-American Tradition in Decorative Arts*, 28.

22. Anita Jacobson-Widding, *Red, White, Black as a Mode of Thought*, Uppsala Studies in Cultural Anthropology, no. 1 (Uppsala, Sweden, 1979), 179–80.

23. Data was gathered from field research conducted in 1985 in the zone of Songololo in Bas-Zaire with chief Lubenzo, and in 1986 in the zone of Moanda with Balu Balila.

24. The hand holding an egg, which refers to Asante proverbs dealing with the nature of power, is a popular motif on linguist staffs and umbrella finials; see Timothy F. Garrard's catalogue for the exhibition *Gold of Africa: Jewellery and Ornaments from Ghana, Côte d'Ivoire, Mali and Senegal* (Munich: Prestel Verlag, 1989), 194, pl. 49.

25. Bastide, *African Civilizations in the New World*, 92.

Fig. 1. Sioux chiefs and families, ca. 1900, Crawford, Nebraska.
Photo by C. C. McBride, courtesy of James Rutkowski, Birmingham,
Michigan.

David W. Penney

American Indian Canes: Iroquois and Sioux Traditions

As a source for American folk art canes and their syncretic admixture of cultural content, personal whimsy, and penchant for whittling, American Indian sculptors entered the tradition within fairly recent history. Elaborately carved canes represent yet another cultural concept and technology that American Indian people observed, borrowed, and transformed into tradition, like glass-bead ornament, tailoring of cotton cloth, metalsmithing, and horsemanship. This process involved evaluating the phenomenon observed, comparing it with things more familiar, then classifying it within a larger framework of personal and cultural understanding. In order to distinguish elaborately carved American Indian canes from those made by whites and African-Americans, it is necessary to trace this progression through the ways that American Indians made and used canes.

The greatest difficulty facing such a project is the paucity of well-documented examples. Undoubtedly, canes produced by American Indian carvers exist, but few have been preserved with the history of their manufacture and use. Canes in many collections have been represented as American Indian made, but the authority for such statements is found to be based on vague generalizations, often some sense of or "feeling" for an Indian aesthetic. This is presuming an Indian sensibility of the visual arts that is somehow distinguishable from those of other cultures. However tempting as a method, cultural or national characterizations of style have invariably proved to be politically motivated, serving either to promote the art of one group or denigrate by condescension the art of another; it leads nowhere. We can safely assume that canes have been produced by artists of American Indian ancestry that are absolutely indistinguishable from those made by non-Indians.

What basis is there, then, to attribute canes to American Indian carvers? The key lies in understanding the means by which canes were absorbed into discrete Indian societies, or more specifically, into their traditions of crafting and using wood products. The sculptural practices of different tribal peoples produced separate categories of objects with widely ranging sculptural treatment. If individual canes without definite historical provenance can be situated within these tribal traditions, then their attribution as "Indian" indeed carries far greater weight. But such an attribution is meaningless without some understanding of the Indian community in which the cane originated and the heritage that the artist drew on. This notion can be illustrated by examining two such carving traditions in some detail, the Iroquois and Sioux (fig. 1), in an effort to determine the tribal identity of some of the canes in the Meyer collection.

Iroquois Canes

According to Iroquois belief, as related by anthropologist William Fenton, the ancient spirit, or "Great World Rim Dweller," walked with a staff made from a giant hickory tree.[1] When the world was born, the Creator had encountered the Great World Rim Dweller skulking at its edge. After a contest of power, the spirit agreed to help men against disease if they would organize the Society of False Faces. Members of the False Faces wear masks and carry wooden staves in imitation of this seminal spirit and lesser forest spirits. The gray hair, wrinkled and distorted faces of the masks, and the stooped posture of the impersonators supported by staves emphasize their identity as ancient spirits. Through such associations, as Fenton explained, the cane has become a symbol of age and wisdom among the Iroquois. When mature men forgo the weapons of their warrior youth, they take up the staff or cane as a symbol of their status as respected elders. Iroquois elder Harry Isaacs, for example, held a cane when he was photographed on his way to a condolence ceremony in 1917 (fig. 2). Resident of the Onondaga Reservation in New York State, maker of "rustic chairs," and advocate for preserving traditional ways, Isaacs was not a "chief" but a senior male of a venerable family and a highly respected elder.[2]

Fig. 1, detail

Fig. 2. Onondaga elder Harry Isaacs holding a bentwood cane. Since Isaacs made bentwood furniture, he probably made this cane. September 8, 1917. Photo by Fred R. Wolcott, Syracuse, N.Y., courtesy of Onondaga Historical Association, Syracuse.

In the photograph, Isaacs holds a simple bentwood cane with a crook grip. Although the Iroquois evidently used canes instead of traditional staffs for a considerable period of time, canes and walking sticks as a form ultimately stem from European sources. Here I distinguish between a staff that is held along its shaft and a cane that is provided with a grip at the top. The marketability of bentwood canes to non-Indians may have contributed to Iroquois adoption of the cane over the staff. The production of bentwood canes, along with bentwood furniture and lacrosse sticks, generated income on several Iroquois reserves and reservations.[3]

In his study of the famous condolence cane (actually a converted pictographic record stick) collected from Andrew Sprague of the Six Nations Reserve and now at the Cranbrook Institute of Science, William Fenton discussed a number of additional canes that had belonged to prominent Iroquois men. In keeping with the association between canes and respected elders, they are sometimes called chief's canes, and several are decorated with carvings. A bentwood cane with the handle carved as a bird head had belonged to the grandfather of David Jack, whom Fenton identified as a chief of the Six Nations Reserve.[4] Another cane; which belonged to David Springer of Brantford, Ontario, has fine chip carving and hatching along its shaft and a Janus-head grip, with both rudimentary faces contained within the bulbous form of the handle.[5] A third cane, collected by Samuel Barrett for the Milwaukee Public Museum, is carved with the image of a wolf above the grip and engraved with the Onondaga chief's title, S'agogen'he.[6] A False Face appears on the grip of another cane collected by Barrett from the Senecas of the Cattaraugus Reservation in New York State. Reportedly, it was carried by the man elected to lead the False Faces from one council house to another at the annual midwinter ceremonies.[7]

All of these canes, in addition to a few others discussed by Fenton, are carved with effigies on the grip—either animals, animal heads, human faces, or False Faces. Although it is tempting to interpret the sculptural images as clan effigies or other such insignia tied to social identity, this reading does not stand under close scrutiny. Instead, the carvings seem to relate to a more personal symbolism associated with unique individuals. The only overarching symbolism visible among the set is the False Face, with its links to that society's rituals and practices.

Fig. 3. Iroquois wood spoon, date unknown, Six Nations Reserve, Ontario. The finial on the handle is carved with a head resembling the masks of the False Face Society. Photo by Dirk Bakker, courtesy of the Cranbrook Institute of Science, Bloomfield Hills, Michigan.

In these visual and conceptual factors, canes are comparable to Iroquois spoons or ladles, also carved of wood. Like canes, some ladles have animal or human effigies at the end of the handle, corresponding in position to the grip of a cane. They may also be decorated with chip carving and hatching along the length of the handle, as on the shaft of the Springer cane. Effigies on ladle handles and cane grips stand or sit on small platforms or stages; in other instances the heads of effigies, either animal or human, rise directly out of the cane shaft or spoon handle.

Ladles, like canes, are personal possessions for the Iroquois. Their carved embellishment responds to the personal symbolism of power spirits or individual identity. It is not surprising, therefore, to find similar imagery carved on ladle handles and cane grips; both are occasionally carved with False Face images as well. In centuries past, among the Algonkian and Siouan neighbors of the Iroquois, special bowls and ladles were distributed to initiated members of religious societies. A spoon collected by Milford Chandler from around Grand River, Ontario, with a False Face carved on the handle (fig. 3), like the one on the Barrett cane, also may have played some role in False Face rituals.

Several canes in the Meyer collection with less definite collection histories correspond to the general stylistic tendencies visible in better documented Iroquois canes and spoons. Several are carved with diminutive human heads (no. 161). In an older style wherein the bark is not stripped from the wood,[8] the head on one cane is contained within a bulbous grip (no. 162), like that of the Springer cane. Other carved faces display a kind of reductive expressiveness and individuality in keeping with styles seen on Iroquois ladles. One cane in the Meyer collection (no. 156), with a twisted grip that mimics the crook of a bentwood cane, is carved with a long, thick-lipped visage resembling one of the False Faces. An understanding of Iroquois woodworking traditions and the significance of these personal objects to their owners contributes to the attribution of these canes as "Indian," or more properly Iroquois.

Sioux Canes

Photographs made by John Anderson illustrating life on the Rosebud Reservation in South Dakota at the turn of the century reveal a relationship between elderly Sioux and staves or canes similar to that of the Iroquois. Older women, the "grand mothers," invariably held a heavy staff or a crook-handle cane in portraits, or a cane was always visible close by when people were photographed engaged in work or other activities.[9] "Old Harney," who had scouted for the U.S. military during the plains campaigns of the 1850s, was photographed at the age of one hundred with his sturdy cane resting against his knee.[10]

In his book on Plains Indian sculpture, John Ewers mentions effigy canes among the Sioux but illustrates only a few examples. Among the best documented is a cane with a catlinite (pipestone) grip carved as a dog's head, purchased around 1875 from a Santee Sioux resident named Good Thunder of Flandreau, South Dakota.[11] A similar cane, with a catlinite grip carved as a closed hand, which also came from the Sioux of Flandreau, is in the Meyer collection (no. 176). The settlement of Flandreau, located in southeast South Dakota, was established in 1868 by a group of Santee Sioux who had been forced to leave Minnesota after the Sioux uprising of 1862. They chose a site close to the catlinite quarry at Pipestone, and several generations of Sioux from Flandreau quarried the stone, which they carved into pipes and other curios to sell to non-Indians. These objects apparently included handles fitted onto canes. The images of the dog and the closed hand were selected, no doubt, in anticipation of their success in the marketplace.

Other carved canes from the Sioux were not so market oriented, however. One illustrated by Ewers was carved with an inverted foot as a grip, while plaited porcupine quills wrap around the length of the shaft.[12] The porcupine quill wrapping resembles the treatment of pipestems,

Several canes in the Meyer collection judged to be from the Sioux illustrate a sculptural relationship with pipestems. One delicate and elegantly carved cane is divided into cylindrical and twisted sections, the transitions punctuated by balls and collars (no. 232). A second cane is also composed of alternating segments arranged in a regular pattern, emphasized by yellow, red, and blue paint (no. 229). A buffalo horn functions as the grip. Another cane (no. 3), made from a twisted root, includes a long section carved as a ball-and-cage, a common whittler's theme often emulated by later Sioux carvers. Additional puzzle configurations found in Sioux pipestems include detached rings on the shaft and chain links. Such formal relationships to Sioux pipestem carvings fortify the attribution of these canes.

Although adopted by Indian communities from sources exterior to their culture, canes and cane carving were easily absorbed into more familiar ways of thinking about objects and methods of making them. The Iroquois carver crafted a cane the way he would shape a spoon, with a personalized effigy of a human head or an animal located at the grip. Similarly, Sioux carvers made canes that resemble the configuration of pipestems by dividing the shafts into variant, alternating segments. The practice of carving canes was folded into the sculptural traditions already present. Merging the concept of the elder's staff with traditional wood sculpture produced an indigenous identity for canes as they were adopted and re-created by both the Iroquois and Sioux.

Fig. 4. Sioux holding a pipe and pipe bag, ca. 1870. The stem is made of ash with the upper section carved as plaited porcupine quills. Photo probably by William Henry Jackson, courtesy of James Rutkowski, Birmingham, Michigan.

carved of wood by the Sioux. Here the traditions of carving pipestems may have contributed to the production of carved canes (see no. 30 for an Algonkian example), just as ladles influenced the design of canes among the Iroquois.

Pipestems were most often made of ash. The earliest known were not elaborately carved but instead decorated with wrapped porcupine quills and pendant fans of eagle feathers. William H. Keating, who accompanied Major Stephen H. Long on his expedition to Minnesota in 1823, wrote of Dakota pipestems (see fig. 4 for an example):

Its length was about three feet. It is flattened, being about two inches wide and three eighths of an inch thick. It tapers a little toward the upper extremity. . . . The upper extremity, about one third its length, is ornamented with porcupine quills variously dyed so as to present beautiful designs. It is also adorned with small feathers of birds, pigeons and etc., and with the hair of the deer stained red.[13]

Later Dakota pipestems retain the concept of dividing the length into segments. Flattened sections alternate with round or spiral shapes, the latter pattern causing the pipestem to appear twisted.

Notes

1. William N. Fenton, *The False Faces of the Iroquois* (Norman, Okla.: University of Oklahoma Press, 1987), 204.

2. Dennis J. Connors et al., *Onondaga: Portrait of a Native People* (Syracuse, N.Y.: Syracuse University Press and Everson Museum of Art, 1986), pl. 21.

3. William N. Fenton, *The Roll Call of the Iroquois Chiefs: A Study of a Mnemonic Cane from the Six Nations Reserve*, Smithsonian Miscellaneous Collections, vol. 3, no. 15 (Washington, D.C., 1950), 1–73.

4. Ibid., pl. 3b.

5. Ibid., pls. 4a–b.

6. Ibid., pl. 4d.

7. Ibid., 34, pl. 4c.

8. Ibid., 31.

9. Paul Dyck, *Brule: The Sioux People of Rosebud* (Flagstaff, Ariz.: Northland Press, 1971), 104–9, 251.

10. Ibid., 153; see also 157.

11. John C. Ewers, *Plains Indian Sculpture: A Traditional Art from America's Heartland* (Washington, D.C.: Smithsonian Institution Press, 1986), 200–201.

12. Ibid., fig. 199, left.

13. William H. Keating, *Narrative of an Expedition to the Source of St. Peter's River*. . . (London: G. B. Whittaker, 1825; Minneapolis: Ross and Haines, 1959), 261.

John D. Hamilton

Fraternal Motifs in Canes

At the beginning of the twentieth century, over three hundred secret societies, fraternities, and sisterhoods were active in the United States. According to Albert Stevens's *Cyclopaedia of Fraternities* (New York, 1907), their ranks totaled more than ten million members—a remarkably large proportion of the U.S. population, which in 1900 was around seventy-six million. (The count, however, probably includes many individuals who belonged to several fraternal orders.) Reasons for the existence of these fraternal organizations seemed infinite, promoting almost every viewpoint within American society, be it military, patriotic, political, socialistic, recreative, benevolent, mystical, philosophical, theosophical, cooperative, or educational.

Both the initiation rites and routine meetings of fraternal groups involved the ceremonial use of a variety of staffs, wands, and batons ornamented with the insignia of the organization. Canes decorated with a society's emblems, although not used in ceremonies, were owned by members as personal articles expressing their allegiance. Distinguished members of fraternal societies, such as a state governor or other high official, customarily received mementos from admiring brethren. Such tokens of admiration and appreciation took many forms, including canes carved to commemorate the recipient's ties to an organization. The majority of canes, however, appear to have been hand-carved by their owners. The Meyer collection includes several examples of canes bearing the arcane symbols of American fraternal groups (nos. 122, 201, 203, 206).

Freemasons established America's earliest fraternal organization in Boston in 1733, initiating candidates for membership by secret ritual. That process, acquired from their English brethren, later provided other fraternal groups with a model on which to pattern their own distinctive ceremonies. In essence, the rituals enacted parables drawn from various sources, including biblical or historic events having significance in the lore of the organization. Each parable represented yet another level or "degree" of enlightenment within the total philosophy. Exemplification by

theatrical performance provided the most impressive and memorable method of conveying the parables to initiates.

The establishment of American Freemasonry preceded the founding of the Independent Order of Odd Fellows, Ancient Order of Druids, Improved Order of Red Men (fig. 1), Knights of Pythias, Woodmen of the World, and a host of other fraternal societies that arose to offer alternative paths to brotherhood, social fellowship, and mutual assistance. By mid nineteenth century many brotherhoods had established adoptive or associated degrees for female relatives and friends. Sisterhoods such as the Order of the Eastern Star, Daughters of Rebekah, Daughters of Pocahontas, and the Pythian Sisters observed their own appropriately conceived rituals.

Each organization adopted specific iconography to visually allude to the tenets of its particular philosophy (figs. 2–3). Key symbols were incorporated into logos by which the groups were generally recognized, and the presence of these symbols in lodge rooms and on ritual paraphernalia and regalia became commonplace. Proud of their fraternal affiliation, members often applied the symbols to household furnishings and more personal possessions.

Logos not only identified a specific society but distinguished various bodies within an organization. The cane of Fred P. Cone, governor of Florida from 1937 to 1941, reflects his membership in a number of Masonic bodies that included the Ancient Arabic Order of Nobles of the Mystic Shrine, Royal Arch Chapter, and Knights Templar Commandary as well as his symbolic Blue Lodge, where he received the first three basic degrees of Freemasonry (no. 195).

Many fraternal societies were mutually compatible in philosophy and purpose. Often Freemasons and Odd Fellows jointly owned and shared buildings in which they held their meetings. In such instances, members experienced no moral dilemma in belonging to more than one fraternity at a time. Dual, even plural affiliations account for a curious admixture of fraternal logos on members' personal possessions. One cane (no. 183) is a bewildering tour

233

Fig. 1. TOTE (mystic anagram of the Improved Order of Red Men), Helen M. Lane, 1889, oil on canvas. Collection of George Meyer.

Fig. 2. Masonic chart, Currier & Ives, 1876, lithograph. Museum of Our National Heritage, Lexington, Massachusetts.

de force of emblems representing the Knights of the Golden Eagle, Junior Order of United American Mechanics, Independent Order of Odd Fellows, Independent Order of Mechanics, Knights of Pythias, Modern Woodmen of America, Christian Endeavor, Daughters of America, and various Masonic bodies.

The normal order of conducting lodge meetings called for an assortment of staffs adorned with various symbols of office. Members forming "degree teams" found themselves cast as costumed characters in exemplification plays (no. 207), equipped with a wide array of pole arms, shepherd's crooks, and assorted scepters. Of these various props, the pilgrim or wayfarer's staff most closely resembled a walking stick. As described in the *Odd Fellows Monitor and Guide* (Indianapolis, 1878), the pilgrim's staff "was used as a help in walking, and especially so when tired and wearied of travel and yet compelled by circumstances to go on." By specific allusion, the cane thus became a symbol of overcoming the vicissitudes of fortune.

Many who joined secret societies remained steadfast members throughout their adult lives. As is often experienced in the twilight of life, the dictates of youthful fashion, expressed by an elegant walking stick purchased in a stylish shop, gave way to a utilitarian support demanded by the infirmity of old age. It was then that a stout unadorned cane offered an almost irresistible surface on which to carve the symbols of a revered fraternal organization.

Fig. 3. Odd Fellows chart, Currier & Ives, 1877, lithograph. Museum of Our National Heritage, Lexington, Massachusetts.

Guide to Common Fraternal Initials

Freemasons

G.	Geometry, alludes to supreme diety
J. B.	Jachin and Boaz, names of the two bronze pillars of King Solomon's temple
W. S. B.	Wisdom, Strength, Beauty, attributes assigned to the three principal officers of the lodge
F. H. C.	Faith, Hope, Charity, principal rungs of Jacob's ladder to heaven

Improved Order of Red Men

T. O. T. E.	Totem of the Eagle, clan badge of the order
F. F. C.	Freedom, Friendship, Charity, tenets of the order

Independent Order of Odd Fellows

F. L. T.	Friendship, Love, Truth, tenets of the order

Knights of Columbus

C. U. F.	Charity, Unity, Fraternity, tenets of the order

Knights of Pythias

F. C. B.	Friendship, Charity, Benevolence, tenets of the order

Modern Woodmen of America

B. S. F.	Benevolence, Secrecy, Fraternity, tenets of the order

Royal Arcanum

V. M. C.	Virtue, Mercy, Charity, tenets of the order
1105	with mystical number

Woodmen of the World

D. T. C.	*Dum Tacet Clamot*, motto of the order

Fig. 1. G.A.R. reunion, ca. 1900, location unknown. Pasting figures on group photos was not an unusual practice during this period. Courtesy of William Spencer, Portland, Michigan.

Fig. 2. G.A.R. encampment, probably St. Louis, 1887. Courtesy of James Rutkowski, Birmingham, Michigan.

Fig. 3. Union veteran with 1892 "Grant" souvenir G.A.R. cane, ca. 1910, Columbus, Ohio. Courtesy of Roger Heiple, South Lyon, Michigan.

George H. Meyer

Civil War Veterans Canes

A substantial number of folk art canes were made by veterans of the Civil War, which involved approximately 2,200,000 Union and 1,000,000 Confederate military personnel. Soldiers on both sides of the conflict made canes, usually while prisoners of war or convalescents,[1] with little more than a jackknife. Although most of these canes are simple with perhaps a lettered or carved reference to a battle or veterans organization, others are handsomely decorated (no. 243).

After the Civil War hundreds of Union veterans organizations were formed, the most important of which was the Grand Army of the Republic (G.A.R.), founded in 1866 (fig. 1). Over the years more than 1,000,000 men belonged to the organization, which reached its peak membership of 427,000 in 1890. With local posts in almost every state (over three hundred in Michigan), the G.A.R. was organized in departments of one or more states which held annual and biannual encampments. The national organization held annual encampments (fig. 2) each year until 1949, when six of the Grand Army's sixteen surviving members heard taps played in Indianapolis at the last encampment.

Many G.A.R. members carried canes, some by necessity, some for ceremonial purposes or to communicate their affiliation with the G.A.R. and like organizations (fig. 3), and others simply because canes were fashionable. Veterans who required the help of a cane after losing a leg in the war were not an unusual sight in any town; in 1866 Mississippi spent one-fifth of its revenue on artificial limbs.[2] Those infirm from age also relied on canes; photographs of groups of older veterans frequently show men with walking sticks. Many post halls had racks at the first-floor door with a dozen or so plain communal canes available to members. Both federal and state homes for disabled and aged veterans established later in the century were a source of hand-crafted canes and other remembrance carvings (figs. 4–5, no. 150).

For many veterans the Civil War was the most important event in their lives. Veterans organizations, by providing opportunities to socialize and reminisce (at weekly "bean suppers," for instance) and by supporting pensions and state homes for the disabled and orphans, reflected the qualities of the G.A.R. motto—Fraternity, Loyalty, and Charity. In this period of enthusiasm for secret societies, men who belonged to veterans organizations often were also members of fraternal groups such as the Masons or Odd Fellows. The symbols of these fraternal groups were sometimes added to canes along with personal symbols.

In the North the G.A.R., although sometimes purporting to be nonpartisan, wielded great political power for the balance of the nineteenth century, particularly on the Republican side. Veterans often were the deciding vote in elections—their influence was exercised, according to the terminology of the time, by "waving the bloody shirt." Service in the Civil War, affiliation with the G.A.R., and political issues are frequently symbolized together on canes.

Walking sticks were offered for sale or presented as gifts at veterans reunions, at battlefields, and at state and national encampments. A number of canes were made of wood from battlegrounds and structures that had played a part in the war (fig. 7, no. 241). These were sold or given as souvenirs, reminders of the conflict, or testimonials for service as an officer in a veterans group. Although occasionally made by professional carvers, most of these commemorative canes were probably crafted by veterans for themselves or a friend (no. 251).

Numerous post–Civil War canes were carved with corps badges and other references to the war (no. 250) and the G.A.R. (no. 243), such as the organization's badge or interlocking initials. Corps badges were strictly Union the Confederate army had none. Most nineteenth- and early twentieth-century post–Civil War canes available today seem to relate to the North and the G.A.R. This may be partly due to the sectionalism and hostility of the North which discouraged Confederate veterans from organizing nationally until 1889, when the United Confederate Veterans

Fig. 4. Stereopticon picture of Civil War veterans with carving of a miniature boat, ca. 1900. National Military Home Series, Ohio, courtesy of James Rutkowski, Birmingham, Michigan.

Fig. 5. Postcard of a veteran at a veterans home with carvings apparently done by him, ca. 1890. National Military Home, Grand County, Indiana, courtesy of James Rutkowski, Birmingham, Michigan.

Fig. 6. Reunion of Company E, 157th New York Volunteers, ca. 1890, Devil's Den, Gettysburg battlefield. Courtesy of Gettysburg National Military Park, Gettysburg, Pennsylvania.

Fig. 7. 1907 advertisement for canes made from historic bridge. Courtesy of Gettysburg National Military Park, Gettysburg, Pennsylvania.

(U.C.V.) was formed at New Orleans. The active membership of the U.C.V. reached about 47,000 in 1903, with 35,000 additional inactive members. These two categories were approximately one-third of all living Confederate veterans. The last reunion of the U.C.V., held in 1951 in Norfolk, Virginia, was attended by three of the approximately twelve veterans still living.[3] There are, of course, Confederate Civil War and post–Civil War canes. Interestingly, several of the carved canes in the excellent collection of the Museum of the Confederacy in Richmond, Virginia, appear to be almost identical to northern post–Civil War canes in concept, carving, and much of the symbolism (fig. 8).

Post–Civil War canes were frequently made by professional or at least highly trained carvers, some of whom seem to have crafted canes for specific individuals (see nos. 270–81), while others apparently carved canes for inventory. These "speculative canes" often had generic themes, such as corps badges, that would be common to many veterans (no. 252). The name of the purchaser could then be added and the handle perhaps changed to suit the new owner's taste or pocketbook.

Without some specific symbolism, wording, or provenance, it is almost impossible to determine whether a cane was made during or after the war, or whether it was made in a prisoner-of-war camp or in a hospital. Moreover, without a blue or gray motif or other specific detail of uniform, identifying a soldier or scene as Union or Confederate is difficult (no. 242).

Cane carrying reached its height in the late nineteenth century, and walking sticks continued to be adorned with Civil War imagery, sometimes coupled with the symbolism of the Spanish-American War (1898), a conflict strongly supported by both Union and Confederate veterans in the ensuing wave of nationalism that swept the country. The walking sticks of Civil War veterans were evident at the fiftieth reunion of Gettysburg in 1913 (fig. 9). Carved canes have appeared in American wars of this century, but with less frequency as the fashion of the walking stick faded.

Fig. 8. Confederate veteran holding a carved cane at the 1932 Confederate reunion, Richmond, Virginia. Courtesy of Demente-Foster Studios, Richmond.

Fig. 9. A Union and a Confederate veteran at the fiftieth anniversary reunion at Gettysburg, 1913. Photo by American Press Association, courtesy of Roger Heiple, South Lyon, Michigan.

Notes

1. It is unlikely that many canes were made during military campaigns because of the difficulty in carrying them from place to place. Also see E. Norman Flayderman, *Scrimshaw and Scrimshanders: Whales and Whalemen* (New Milford, Conn.: N. Flayderman, 1972), 261, for a description of Civil War prison conditions as related to carvings made in prison.

2. Geoffrey C. Ward with Ric Burns and Ken Burns, *The Civil War: An Illustrated History* (New York: Alfred A. Knopf, 1990), 404.

3. Virginius Dabney, *The Last Review: The Confederate Reunion, Richmond 1932* (Chapel Hill, N.C.: Algonquin Books, 1984), 27, 47.

Fig. 1. Denzil Goodpaster, 1991. Photo by Larry Hackley, courtesy of
Larry Hackley, North Middletown, Kentucky.

Fig. 2. Golmon Crabtree, 1991. Photo by Larry Hackley, courtesy of
Larry Hackley, North Middletown, Kentucky.

Larry Hackley

Themes in Contemporary Folk Canes

Contemporary cane makers have adapted their craft to the forces and materials of present-day society. Although cane making over time remains unchanged in many fundamental ways, contemporary cane carvers have found startling new means to make their canes look and feel different from those of the past. Most cane makers today work as their grandfathers did, without artistic pretensions or aspirations. But for some of the better-known craftsmen, a heightened awareness of the cane as a work of art (an object of value?) has altered their approach and expanded the range of themes that is expressed in the basic form of the carved stick.

Nature has long been a theme in cane making. The organic material of cedar, cherry, poplar, or pine lends itself to myriad enhancements that echo nature, from bird handles to decorative vine patterns. Natural forms, both found and cultivated—such as burls, thigmotropic growths, and roots—often result in canes which spontaneously suggest that man is both in harmony with and in control of nature itself. As in times past, a great many canes are made today from natural forms.

But canes that draw on the rich material of popular culture and erotic imagination express distinctly contemporary ideas. Political figures, celebrities, and personality types peculiar to our society have become modern-day icons on canes. While heroic figures such as Abraham Lincoln or Daniel Boone have long been accepted motifs among cane makers and Jesus remains a favorite, Denzil Goodpaster's Dolly Parton cane and Elisha Baker's Elvis (no. 301) point the art form in a new direction. The marriage of the seemingly superficial imagery of American popular culture with the permanence of the cane as an object and a keepsake creates a tension that can only bring about new creative possibilities.

Similarly, canes enlivened with erotic imagery lead cane makers and collectors into surprising territory. Goodpaster's women in bikinis (no. 282) carved on the phallic form of the staff are as repellent as they are fascinating. In some of Goodpaster's works, women are devoured by wild animals (fig. 1). As in film and literature, exoticism and violence add yet another charge to sexual imagery. As eroticism invades daily life through advertising, videos, and changing social and sexual mores, so has it entered the repertoire of today's cane makers.

How the awareness of art as a commodity may or may not affect contemporary cane making is difficult to gauge. At the very least, it is fair to say that canes are increasingly perceived as an art form. Tim Lewis, who combines painting and sculpture with the cane's unusual vertical format, has created on shafts unique landscapes that enhance the handle motifs (nos. 304–5). This blend of painting and carving clearly emerges from an awareness of the cane as an art object, and an understanding of art as inherently worthwhile.

Symbolic canes, such as those decorated with Masonic or other fraternal symbols, may take on new expressive power in the hands of the contemporary cane maker, but the prevalent tendency to embellish is most striking in purely decorative walking sticks. These seem increasingly extravagant with an endless variety of color, glitter, found objects, and discarded man-made elements: the cast-off material of a wasteful culture becomes a creative resource (no. 303).

By approaching contemporary canes from a thematic perspective, one is instantly impressed with the array of meaning that is effectively *held* in the essential simplicity of the form. Perhaps nature is the purest theme, as it permits the cane to remain closest to its source and least altered by the artist. But the presence of popular culture, eroticism, and aesthetic concerns in many of today's examples suggests important changes have occurred. A closer examination of these themes will enhance our understanding of how the contemporary cane maker has evolved and adapted to a changing world.

Nature

Most walking sticks are rather mundane. A basic piece of wood is stripped of bark, and a bent handle may or may not be provided by boiling or steaming the wood and tying it to dry into the desired shape. The stick may be left natural or given a simple finish. Easy variations on this theme include branch nubs on a pine stick, splotchy varnish designs, or smoke patterns. Thigmotropic forms, which occur when vines and saplings grow together, often result in canes that remain amazingly close to nature.

Among the many ways in which the natural world asserts itself in cane making, the frequent presence of the snake is perhaps the most common. Snakes and sticks have been coupled in man's imagination since the serpent slithered up the tree of life and since Moses threw down his rod. And yet, contemporary cane makers are remarkably vague about the popularity of the snake as a motif. They usually maintain that snakes are "easy made" or "seen" in the piece of wood, as if the power of the image were beyond their control. For many carvers, the first canes result from happening upon a thigmotropic stick and realizing its potential as a snake cane. Similarly, bird handles (fig. 2) often suggest themselves because the top of a stick is an obvious perch for a bird, becoming both handle and finial. For cane makers today, as in the past, the satisfaction of discovering such fluid connections between the natural universe and the world of utilitarian objects is immensely satisfying. Nature is a primary theme in cane making because canes are, essentially, natural objects.

Popular Culture

The increasing removal of the contemporary cane from a strictly natural environment is one of its distinguishing features. The rich abundance of popular culture has contributed to this trend in some surprising ways. From an Oldenburgian change in proportion, as in a cowboy cane made by Kentuckian Denzil Goodpaster, to the creation of a contemporary mythology of celebrities, carvers have been inspired by mass culture.

The use of collective symbols, heroes, and public personalities as subjects for folk artists has a long history in this country. But contemporary cane makers have gone beyond the customary likeness of Abraham Lincoln. Golmon Crabtree, for example, has depicted Daniel Boone, John Wayne, Big Foot, and Crystal Gayle on his canes. Carl McKenzie (no. 300) and Denzil Goodpaster have immortalized Dolly Parton. And Elisha Baker has rendered several Elvis canes (no. 301), complete with attributes such as hound dogs and guitars. From university mascots to cultural stereotypes, contemporary canes are rapidly evolving into a portrait gallery of our times.

How and why this shift in imagery has occurred bears consideration. Technology is certainly a contributing factor; through recent advances artists and craftsmen have gained access to culture in the broadest sense. Through satellite dishes, video stores, and grocery-store tabloids, cane makers have at their disposal remarkable visual resources, regardless of their remote location. Just as canes have come out of the forest, so have cane makers come out of their restricted environments into the full panoply of American culture.

Eroticism

While modern technology has expanded the flow of information and imagery, social forces in modern society have expanded the boundaries of acceptable subject matter. Women in bikinis, sometimes devoured by animals, and deep cleavages carved in wood are not as shocking as they would have been a century ago, although today their misogynistic connotations might offend those with an enlightened perspective of the changing role of women in society. As canes increasingly become vehicles for self-expression, it is not surprising to find carvers, who tend to be male, expressing their views on sexual politics along with their erotic imaginings.

But erotic canes are not restricted to the straightforward depiction of the female form. In addition to suggestive—even seductive—imagery, contemporary canes can explicitly explore sexual activities, including gay and lesbian sex. "Daddy Boy" Williams is known for canes featuring graphic homosexual encounters as well as heterosexual coupling. Others, like Henry York (no. 283), often incorporate exotic Africanesque figures into their imagery, believing it to heighten the erotic charge. Clearly, the subject is open to many interpretations and personal expressions.

The expressive freedom of today's cane makers on the subject of eroticism is noteworthy. Like fine artists of almost a century ago who claimed world culture, including that of the Far East and Africa, as appropriate to their art, contemporary cane makers seem to have an instinct for what can be erotically effective. They delight in non-Western faces, jungle animals, and dark bodies unhampered by clothing. The universal nature of the theme of eroticism seems to unleash the imagination of the carver.

Aesthetic Concerns

It is commonly assumed that contemporary canes are often more aesthetic than their predecessors and that contemporary cane makers approach their craft with a heightened awareness of the cane as an objet d'art. In fact, there exist numerous historical examples of highly decorative canes made by people whose primary purpose was the act of self-expression. Contemporary cane makers are often criticized for producing objects that are so sculptural as to be nearly nonfunctional. The stick, however, has found surprising sculptural form for many years. If there is a difference, it lies in the often less polished, more experimental and inventive approach of the latest cane makers. The trend in recent walking sticks toward bright color and incorporation of more found materials significantly separates them from older specimens. Not the aesthetic approach, but the constantly evolving definition of "aesthetic" sets contemporary canes apart from the past.

For example, the carving style of Elisha Baker (fig. 3) has gone through many changes as he responds to his evolving market. Initially, Baker decorated his walking sticks with bright dabs of paint. When it became apparent that his local audience preferred subdued color and natural wood, he shifted his style. In recent years, he has returned to his personal preference for intense color as the taste for bright, lively color among contemporary folk art collectors has begun to influence his work. Unlike fine artists who feel protective about their rights of self-expression, cane makers often see themselves as craftspeople, ready and willing to respond to the requests of their patrons. Current definitions of taste and style, combined with the recent momentum of the contemporary art market, have certainly influenced the art of cane making.

Among the increasingly popular found materials, snake skins are often used to cover carved serpents or simply to create a pattern. In addition to this material, leather, feathers, bones, beads, and deer hooves and antlers are commonly used by those carvers interested in back-to-the-land life-styles, historical and pioneer reenactments, and American Indian lore. Others might choose rhinestones or chains for decorative purposes. Whether the embellishment is with natural forms or man-made objects, the approach, significantly, is usually purely decorative, not based on historical models or ethnographic symbols.

This is not to say that contemporary cane makers do not employ traditional decorative approaches. Notching, incising, and carved improvisational patterns and designs are evident in the work of Elisha Baker, among others. But contemporary cane makers do not restrict their decorative efforts. In fact, they are quite comfortable appropriating another's cane to embellish by drawing, painting, or carving their own motifs. Collaboration also is not uncommon.

Perhaps the maker most comfortable with these methods is Denzil Goodpaster. He often returns from visits to flea markets with walking sticks carved by others which he adorns with his characteristic carving and painting. Goodpaster has been known, for example, to take an ordinary stick with a crook handle and carve a snake head, complete with plastic teeth, at the top (no. 293). He might then paint and carve the bottom of the shaft with a rattle motif. Ready-made canes with animal subjects, such as an African "airport art" example with three monkeys, are another natural choice for his collaborative instincts.

Collaborative canes are more common than many people realize. Goodpaster has been known to carve canes that he then turns over to others to paint. Some makers, such as Kentucky carver Baker Riddle, leave the decoration to others as a matter of course—Riddle's wife draws on the carved sticks. It is not unusual to encounter friends who pass a cane back and forth for a dialogue of carving and painting, as if the cane were the primary substance of their communication. For example, Kentucky cane makers William Miller and Rick Bryant subsist on jointly produced walking sticks. "Miller and Bryant" sticks are becoming common examples of the trend toward collaboration.

Ball-in-cage whimsies carved from a single piece of wood continue to be a measure by which carvers judge each other's skill. Only snakes are more common images on walking sticks than cages and the many objects they may contain. The most impressive demonstration of this form of carving is to produce a ball within a cage. Some carvers, however, prefer the colorful appeal of marbles over wooden balls. The marbles are inserted in the chamber while the wood is green, or after soaking or boiling the wood. Other contemporary variations include placing small bottles of oil, plastic figures, or hickory nuts in the cage. As with other motifs and traditions, results from the hands of contemporary cane makers are often more elaborate, innovative, or object oriented.

Contemporary Carvers

Does the emergence of a new, contemporary style in cane making mean that the maker himself is different from his forefathers? To a remarkable degree, the answer is no. Today, as in the past, the typical cane maker is a man in his seventies who was born in a rural community and, most likely, continues to live there. His one-room schoolhouse education was probably limited to the fifth or sixth grade, and his working life may have involved a craft or trade in which he worked with his hands. Carving is probably a family tradition: the cane maker's childhood memories often include watching his father or grandfather whittling or carving toys and simple objects.

If his youthful activity included the Civilian Conservation Corps or the armed forces, the experience probably figures prominently in his skill. Wooden chain carving and ball-in-cage carving in particular seem to have been promoted by the exchange of techniques, ideas, and cultural experience that the C.C.C. permitted. Although these techniques were first introduced by European immigrants, it cannot be overlooked that young men from all over the country were brought together in camps and communities where whittling was a popular pastime. The Civilian Conservation Corps, primarily designed for young men to work on public projects and learn a trade, played a significant role

Fig. 3. Elisha Baker, 1991. Photo by Larry Hackley, courtesy of Larry Hackley, North Middletown, Kentucky.

Fig. 4. Tim Lewis, 1991. Photo by Larry Hackley, courtesy of Larry Hackley, North Middletown, Kentucky.

in disseminating and perpetuating the craft of cane making.

Although the typical cane maker has whittled or carved sporadically since childhood, his concentrated work as a maker of walking sticks often begins late in life with a crisis or disabling injury. He returns to carving, an absorbing, inexpensive pastime for which he is likely to earn praise and recognition despite his infirmity. Depending on his innate creativity and the response of friends, family, and patrons, the cane maker's talent may evolve into an important phase of his life.

Elisha Baker is a perfect example of someone who began carving after a disabling accident over thirty years ago. He made his first canes of natural walnut and cherry wood with bright color accents for his own use. As he adjusted his style to suit his audience, Baker's work developed into highly creative, experimental works of art, among the most decorative and colorful available.

Ironically, what often begins as a personal pastime becomes a connection with the community. Canes are gifts

appreciated by friends and family; they are also valuable barter at flea markets, auctions, and stockyards. Canes can be reassuring weapons for older people, such as the one by Kentuckian Joseph Smith, with a heavy brass hame knob for a handle and a knife fitted in the shaft.

More often a cane is a commemorative keepsake, a fraternal symbol of respect or shared experience, much as quilts have become among rural women. Like quilts, canes mark life's passages and special events. And, as with quilts, the very material of which the object is made can be symbolic, as cane makers carefully select wood from cemetery fences or old houses where the honored person may have lived. The content too can be commemorative, as in Tim Lewis's space shuttle cane, which marks an important collective moment in American history (fig. 4).

No matter how complex modern life becomes, contemporary cane makers find ways to incorporate that complexity into their essentially simple craft. While recent canes have marked out new thematic territory, their carvers remain centered in a world where a useful object, made with skill and human attention, continues to act as a carrier of cultural meaning.

Regardless of how a cane maker approaches his craft, the purpose of his cane is always to communicate beyond the limits of the object: contemporary canes reflect the world we know. Part of the delight of these sticks is that they are so easily shared, stored, and used in daily life. Like old friends, they walk with us through life's mysteries.

SELECTED BIBLIOGRAPHY

Bishop, Robert C. *American Folk Sculpture.* New York: E. P. Dutton, 1974.

Bishop, Robert, Judith Reiter Weissman, Michael McManus, and Henry Nieman. *The Knopf Collectors' Guide to American Antiques: Folk Art.* New York: Alfred A. Knopf, 1983.

Blake, Joyce E. *Glasshouse Whimsies.* East Aurora, N.Y.: Joyce E. Blake, 1984.

Boothroyd, Albert E. *Fascinating Walking Sticks.* London: Salix Books, 1970.

Bronner, Simon J. *Chain Carvers: Old Men Crafting Meaning.* Lexington: University Press of Kentucky, 1985.

Buck, Paul H. *The Road to Reunion.* Boston and Toronto: Little, Brown and Company, 1937.

Burtscher, William J. *The Romance behind Walking Canes.* Philadelphia: Dorrance and Company, 1945.

"A Cane for Every Occasion." *Fine Woodworking,* September/October 1989, 118.

Carpenter, Charles H., Jr., and Mary Grace Carpenter. *The Decorative Arts and Crafts of Nantucket.* New York: Dodd, Mead and Company, 1987.

Chase, Judith Wragg. *Afro-American Art and Craft.* New York: Van Nostrand Reinhold Co., 1971.

Cochran, Robert. "Sticks." *Country Journal,* January 1981, 50–59.

Cooke, B. W. "Canes from Many Countries." *Hobbies,* May 1935, 10–11.

Cosner, Shaaron. "Antique Walking Sticks and Canes." *Early American Life,* December 1976, 50–51, 74.

Curtis, Cecil. *On Walking-Sticks.* Pensacola, Fla.: Placebo Press, 1976

———. *More on Walking-Sticks.* Pensacola, Fla.: Placebo Press, 1977.

———. *Walking-Sticks: A Handbook.* Pensacola, Fla.: Placebo Press, 1980.

Dike, Catherine. *Cane Curiosa: From Gun to Gadget.* Paris: Les Editions de l'Amateur, 1983.

———. *La Canne—Objet d'art.* Paris: Les Editions de l'Amateur, 1988.

———. *Walking Sticks.* Princes Risborough, England: Shire Publications, Ltd., 1990.

Douglas, John Murchie. *Blackthorn and the Art of Making Walking Sticks.* Ayr, Scotland: Alloway Publishing, 1984.

Ewers, John C. *Plains Indian Sculpture: A Traditional Art from America's Heartland.* Washington, D.C.: Smithsonian Institution Press, 1986.

Farrington, Frank. "Hand Me Down My Walking Cane!" *Hobbies,* March 1945, 8–9.

Fenton, William N. *The Roll Call of the Iroquois Chiefs: A Study of a Mnemonic Cane from the Six Nations Reserve.* Smithsonian Miscellaneous Collections, vol. 3, no. 15. Washington, D.C., 1950.

———. *The False Faces of the Iroquois.* Norman: University of Oklahoma Press, 1987.

Ferris, William R. *Local Color: A Sense of Place in Folk Art.* New York: McGraw-Hill Book Company, 1982.

Field, Richard Henning. *Spirit of Nova Scotia.* Toronto and London: Dundurn Press, 1985, 180–82.

Flayderman, E. Norman. *Scrimshaw and Scrimshanders: Whales and Whalemen.* New Milford, Conn.: N. Flayderman, 1972.

Fossel, Theodore. *Walking and Walking Sticks.* Beaconsfield, Montreal: Apostle Press, 1986.

Franco, Barbara. *Masonic Symbols in American Decorative Arts.* Lexington, Mass.: Museum of Our National Heritage, 1976.

———. *Fraternally Yours: A Decade of Collecting.* Lexington, Mass.: Museum of Our National Heritage, 1986.

George, Phyllis. *Kentucky Crafts: Handmade and Heartfelt.* New York: Crown Publishers, 1989.

Georgia Council for the Arts and Humanities. *Missing Pieces: Georgia Folk Art, 1770–1976.* Exh. cat. Atlanta, 1976.

Gong, Xie. "Walking Sticks—Useful, Ornamental and Legendary." *China Reconstructs,* August 1983, 50–51.

Hackley, Larry. *Sticks: Historical and Contemporary Kentucky Canes.* Exh. cat. Louisville: Kentucky Art and Craft Foundation, 1988.

Hart, Edward. *Walking Sticks.* Wiltshire, England: Crowood Press, 1986.

Hartigan, Lynda Roscoe. *Made with Passion: The Hemphill Folk Art Collection.* Exh. cat. Washington, D.C.: National Museum of American Art, Smithsonian Institution, 1990.

Hawthorn, Audrey. *Art of the Kwakiutl Indians and Other Northwest Coast Tribes.* Seattle and London: University of Washington Press, 1967.

Haythornwaite, Philip. *Uniforms of the Civil War: In Color.* New York: Sterling Publishing Co., 1990.

Kaufman, Barbara Wahl, and Didi Barrett. *A Time to Reap.* Exh. cat. South Orange, N.J.: Seaton Hall University; New York: Museum of American Folk Art, 1985.

Klamkin, Marian, and Charles Klamkin. *Wood Carvings: North American Folk Sculptures.* New York: Hawthorne Books, 1974, 81–82.

Lambert, Margaret, and Enid Marx. *English Popular Art.* London: Batsford, 1951.

Lavitt, Wendy. *Animals in American Folk Art.* New York: Alfred A. Knopf, 1990.

Lindblom, Gerhard. *Spears and Staffs with Two or More Points in Africa*. Stockholm: Ethnographical Museum of Sweden, 1937.

Lipman, Jean. *Provocative Parallels*. New York: E. P. Dutton, 1975, 39–41.

Livingston, Jane, and John Beardsley. *Black Folk Art in America, 1930–1980*. Jackson: University Press of Mississippi, 1982.

McClellan, Elizabeth. *History of American Costume 1607–1870*. New York: Tudor Publishing Company, 1937.

Machmer, Richard S., and Rosemarie B. Machmer. *Just for Nice*. Exh. cat. Reading, Pa.: Historical Society of Berks County, 1991.

Margetts, Martina, ed. *Classic Crafts: A Practical Compendium of Traditional Skills*. New York: Simon and Schuster, 1989.

Meyer, George H., ed. *Folk Artists Biographical Index*. Detroit: Gale Research Company, 1987.

Mississippi State Historical Museum. *Made by Hand: Mississippi Folk Art*. Exh. cat. Jackson, 1980.

Monek, Francis H. "Canes: Staffs of Many Lives." In *Buttons to Chess Sets*. Vol. 3, *The Encyclopedia of Collectibles*. Alexandria, Va.: Time-Life Books, 1978, 42–53.

Nelson, Edna. "Walking Out with the Walking Stick." *The Magazine Antiques* 32 (September 1937), 128–30.

"Ornamental Canes." In *American Country: Folk Art*, ed. Marya Dalrymple. Alexandria, Va.: Time-Life Books, 1990.

Phillips, Stanley S. *Civil War Corps Badges and Other Related Awards, Badges, Medals of the Period*. Lanham, Md.: S. S. Phillips and Assoc., 1982.

Real, Antony. *The Story of the Stick in All Ages and Lands*. Trans. Francois Fernand-Michel. New York: J. W. Bouton, 1875.

Ricco, Roger, and Frank Maresca. *American Primitive: Discoveries in Folk Sculpture*. New York: Alfred A. Knopf, 1988.

Richardson, E. P. "Walking Sticks of the Eighteenth Century." *Bulletin of the Detroit Institute of Arts* 23 (1943), 6–8.

Rosenak, Chuck, and Jan Rosenak. *The Museum of American Folk Art Encyclopedia of Twentieth-Century American Folk Art and Artists*. New York: Abbeville Press, 1990.

Rozelle, Robert V., Alvia Wardlaw, and Maureen A. McKenna, eds. *Black Art: Ancestral Legacy: The African Impulse in African-American Art*. Exh. cat. Dallas: Dallas Museum of Art, 1989.

Rubin, Cynthia Elyce, ed. *Southern Folk Art*. Birmingham, Ala.: Oxmoor House, 1985.

Selfridge, Oliver G. *Sticks*. Boston: Houghton Mifflin, 1967.

Spencer, William B. "The Curiosity of Canes." In Heart of Country Antique Show (Nashville) brochure. St. Louis: Richard E. Kramer and Assoc., 1990.

Stein, Kurt. *Canes and Walking Sticks*. York, Pa.: Liberty Cap Books, 1974.

———. "Carved Canes." *Spinning Wheel*, July/August 1975, 19–21.

Stevens, Albert C., ed. *Cyclopaedia of Fraternities*. New York: E. B. Treat and Company, 1907. Reprint. Detroit: Gale Research Company, 1966.

Terry, George D., and Lynn Robertson Myers. *Carolina Folk: The Cradle of a Southern Tradition*. Columbia, S.C.: McKissick Museum, 1985.

Thompson, Robert Farris. "African Influence on the Art of the United States." In *Afro-American Folk Art and Crafts*. Jackson: University Press of Mississippi, 1983.

Tibodeau, Michelle. "A Cane Scrutiny." *Better Homes and Gardens, Traditional Homes*, Spring 1989, 70–73.

Vance, Joel. "Something to Lean On." *Audubon*, November 1986, 69–72.

Vlach, John Michael. "Arrival and Survival: The Maintenance of an Afro-American Tradition in Folk Art and Craft." In *Prospectives on American Folk Art*, ed. Ian M. G. Quimby and Scott T. Swank. New York: W. W. Norton and Company, 1980.

"Walking Sticks." In *Country Collections*, ed. Marya Dalrymple. Alexandria, Va.: Time-Life Books, 1989.

INDEX